Mastering Apache Velocity

Joseph D. Gradecki
Jim Cole

Wiley Publishing, Inc.

Publisher: Joe Wikert
Executive Editor: Robert Elliott
Editorial Manager: Kathryn Malm
Managing Editor: Vincent Kunkemueller
Book Producer: Ryan Publishing Group, Inc.
Copyeditor: Elizabeth Welch
Compositors: Gina Rexrode and Amy Hassos

Published by Wiley Publishing, Inc., Indianapolis, Indiana

Published simultaneously in Canada

ISBN: 0-471-45794-9

Printed in the United States of America

10 9 8 7 6 5 4 3 2 1

CONTENTS

Part II Velocity Basics

ABOUT THE AUTHORS

Joseph D. Gradecki is a software engineer at Comprehensive Software Solutions, where he works on their SABIL product, a enterprise-level securities processing system used by traders. He has built numerous dynamic, enterprise applications using Java, Velocity, AspectJ, servlets, JSPs, MySQL, XML, and more. He has also built P2P distributed computing systems in a variety of languages including Java/JXTA, C/C++, and Linda.

Joe is also an associate professor of computer science at Colorado Technical University, where he teaches Java, C++, and Software Engineering. He is also an accomplished writer with John Wiley & Sons, Inc. where he has published several programming books on Java and MySQL, AspectJ, and JXTA.

Jim Cole is a senior software engineer specializing in Internet and knowledge management systems. He is an active J2EE developer who regularly uses open source tools such as Struts and Velocity, and also has experience with Perl and PHP. Jim serves as a system administrator for several Web-based projects, where his duties include custom software development, database management, and security maintenance.

Introduction

In the beginning, a Web page was a static entity that provided the same information to all visitors. Developers soon wanted the ability to provide unique data for their users. A large assortment of technologies came along to address this desire--technologies like PHP, ASP, and JSP. While these languages do solve the problem, they all lead to a much bigger issue.

Adding personalization to a Web site used to entail using one of those languages and embedding it directly into the HTML tags for the site presentation. Although this intermixing of code worked, it resulted in maintainability issues. If developers wanted to alter the look and feel of a site, they had to reapply all of the personalization code to the new HTML templates, or designers had to be given access to the code to make changes directly.

Fortunately, the Model-View-Controller (MVC) paradigm completely separates the personalization from the presentation and the data. With MVC, Web designers create the presentation and Web developers handle the code. Velocity is a technology that allows the separation of Java Web code from the presentation code using MVC. Through the use of Java-based templates, Web designers reference personalization code written in Java.

With the help of extensive examples, this book provides a comprehensive approach for using Velocity 1.3.x to create maintainable sites.

What's in This Book

Because Velocity is designed to be used by both Web designers and developers, this book contains a comprehensive overview of the Velocity Templating Language. We show you how to apply the language to your data in the form of Velocity templates, and how to develop applications that use those templates.

We don't assume you know Velocity and therefore provide examples so that you can understand how the system works before coding your first application. For instance, we show you how to build a CD collection application that utilizes the MySQL database for storing information. Through this application, you learn how to write code that follows the MVC paradigm. You also learn to use Velocity templates for Web output as well as text reporting and XML generation.

A second example in this book, a hotel reservation system, demonstrates how to build a complete Web application that uses both Maverick and Velocity templates. The application enables users to search for a room using certain criteria, book the desired room, and then display the confirmed reservation. A dozen or so Velocity templates and three controller classes are used for the complete application, and a Velocity template provides a common look and feel.

Who Should Read This Book

This book has been written for the Web developers and designers who are responsible for maintaining or developing Web sites and applications. Many organizations separate these two roles and hire graphics designers for the Web designer role and software developers for the Web developer role. Both roles are critical; the Web developer is responsible for providing back-end support for Velocity in the servlets, and the Web designer takes advantage of that support.

We assume that Web developers have a good knowledge of and working experience with Java. They should be comfortable using servlets and have a basic understanding of how they interact with EJBs. We assume that Web designers have a good knowledge of and working experience with HTML. If they have exposure to JSP, ASP, or other server-side languages, Velocity will be an easy transition (although we don't assume knowledge of these languages).

Book Organization

This book consists of three parts. The first is an introduction to MVC and Velocity. Once you have this introductory information under your belt, we move into a discussion on the Velocity language and its features. Finally, the third part provides many examples and a comprehensive sample application that illustrates how to use Velocity.

Part I: Introduction to Velocity and MVC

Chapter 1: Web Development Basics

The development of the Internet was just a small part of a revolution that continues today. The interconnectivity produced by the Internet has allowed individuals and companies alike to present information to millions of customers and friends around the world. Initially, the development process for Web pages involved using HTML to produce a static page.

As the sophistication of Internet languages evolved and the needs of sites increased, development moved to the use of dynamic pages, utilizing databases for data management and applications for complex processing. The new complexity, however, often resulted in view and processing code mixed into the same files. Velocity utilized under the Model-View-Controller (MVC) paradigm presents a solution for both designers and developers. This chapter provides a comprehensive overview of the development history of the Internet and what Velocity brings to the table.

Chapter 2: MVC Fundamentals

When Smalltalk-80 was designed, an architecture called Model-View-Controller was created to allow the separation of the view from the data and controlling logic. Over the years, MVC has been molded into a paradigm that can be used in all modern languages. MVC has been brought into the Web arena and can be fully utilized with Velocity.

This chapter gives you a comprehensive overview of MVC and explains its role in the Internet development process. We present code examples and describe how each of the MVC components works to resolve the problems created with combined code.

Chapter 3: Introduction to Velocity

In this chapter, we introduce Velocity. We show you how Velocity works and examine code we'll use throughout the rest of the book. You should have a good understanding of the system as you move to the remaining chapters in this book.

Part II: Velocity Basics

Chapter 4: Installing Velocity

Before you start looking at the specifics of Velocity, you have to install it. This chapter provides a comprehensive guide to installing Velocity. All of the necessary development tools and prerequisite packages are covered, for both Windows and Unix. We discuss the full Velocity test suite and provide a guide to executing the example applications and servlets supplied with the package. Some of the support packages include a Java SDK and an application server (such as Tomcat or Resin).

Chapter 5: Building a Hello World Example

As you might expect, a new development paradigm has to start with the Hello World application. In this chapter, you write your first Velocity application--but with a twist. You write the application in both stand-alone and Web formats, thus demonstrating how Velocity can be used for just about any type of application that has to generate output.

Of course, writing the code is only part of the battle--you must be able to deploy and execute your applications. This chapter also details the steps involved.

Chapter 6: Understanding Templates and Context

The two primary components of Velocity are *templates* and the *context*. The template provides an area for the Web designer to build the look and feel of the application. The look and feel can be a Web page or a report produced by a stand-alone application. The context provides an area for the Web developer to place all of the information needed by the designer and the Velocity template. This chapter introduces both of these components. We examine a complete example to show how the components work together, and we discuss general usage patterns.

Chapter 7: Exploring References

Within Velocity, a reference provides an interface between the template and context as well as a place to hold data. In this chapter, we describe the three types of references: syntax, formal, and informal. We also discuss escaping and quiet and property notation, and provide examples to illustrate those concepts.

Chapter 8: Using Directives

Velocity is like many other Internet languages in that it provides control and decision structures called *directives*. These directives--like #foreach and #if--provide the Web designer with powerful tools for manipulating the data provided in the context. This chapter covers the directives and includes examples. It also contains a reference section for quick lookups.

Chapter 9: Introducing Velocimacros

When you find yourself repeating the same Velocity code over and over, it's time to lean on the *velocimacros*. These macros allow you to build modularity into your templates in order to produce clean-looking code, and they help with maintenance down the road. This chapter covers velocimacros and offers extensive examples.

Chapter 10: Taking Control of Velocity

The developers of Velocity have included several constructs--such as events, resource loads, and other system properties--designed to help you customize Velocity's behavior. This chapter uses examples to illustrate how to change Velocity in a manner that suits your application.

Part III: Developing with Velocity

Chapter 11: Velocity, XML, and Anakia

XML is one of the most-hyped technologies to be introduced in quite some time. Building on the ease of use of HTML, XML allows user-defined tags to be used for the identification of data within a text file. To help facilitate the use of XML, XSLT was designed to allow for the easy manipulation and transformation of the XML data.

The designers of Anakia use the power found within XSLT and XML to build outputs using Ant tasks. This chapter explains how to set up the necessary files and begin using Anakia with Velocity.

Chapter 12: Using Velocity with Servlets

When you're developing applications with Velocity, the Model-View-Controller paradigm should always be the guiding force behind your application. One of the first controllers developed was the *servlet*. In this chapter, we show you how to write a CD collection application using servlets and Velocity. Numerous templates are illustrated, and we discuss using Velocity to output text in the form of downloadable files. The application also uses EJBs for the model component of the MVC paradigm. From the EJBs, data is passed to the template through the context in the form of a Collection object. VTL directives are used to pull the database row data from the Collection for display to the user.

Chapter 13: Velocity and Internationalization

When you're designing a Web application, it's far too easy to just consider writing all of the text in your native language and forget that users in other countries might want to use its functionality. Although Velocity doesn't change the way internationalization is performed on a Java-based Web application, it does provide a framework for building a comprehensive site that can be understood in many languages. This chapter shows how to add the German language text to your CD collection Velocity application built in Chapter 12. Using the techniques shown in this chapter, you can easily add languages to your Velocity application.

Chapter 14: Using Velocity and Turbine

Under the Jakarta umbrella, Turbine is an application framework designed to give developers the tools they need to build enterprise-level applications. The goal is to provide a comprehensive framework that has all of the components developers would typically build themselves either before starting an application or during its development.

In this chapter, we discuss how to obtain, install, and develop an application using Turbine and Velocity. Using Velocity lets you take advantage of Turbine's support of the MVC paradigm.

Chapter 15: Using Velocity and Maverick

If you are building applications using J2EE and MVC, consider using the Maverick framework. This framework combines Velocity along with DVSL to enable you to build enterprise-level XML applications. You can incorporate JDBC or EJBs for a complete application.

Chapter 16: Velocity IDEs

Although many developers and designers use text editors to manipulate their Web pages, some prefer integrated development environments (IDEs). This chapter provides an overview of the various third-party add-ons and plug-ins available for a host of IDE and text editors. We cover plug-ins for such tools as IntelliJ's IDEA, UltraEdit, JEdit, TextPad, and Emacs.

Chapter 17: Using Struts and Velocity

Struts is probably the most popular MVC framework available today. The Velocity team anticipated developers' desire to use Velocity as the view component within the framework and made available an interface package that handles the integration. This chapter provides complete instructions for building an application using Struts and Velocity.

Chapter 18: The Hotel Reservation Velocity Application System

In this chapter, we document the building of a full-blown Web application using Velocity and the Maverick MVC framework. We use many templates to provide input and display pages for the Web user. The controllers work with a MySQL database to keep track of the rooms in the hotel as well as all pending reservations.

Chapter 19: Using JSP and Velocity

Many Web designers and developers are comfortable with JSP and either don't want to make a complete switch to Velocity or don't have the ability to abandon JSP pages and thus need to mix JSP and Velocity. This chapter shows how to use the Velocity tag library to allow Velocity commands to be embedded within JSP pages.

Chapter 20: DVSL and Velocity

The Declarative Velocity Style Language (DVSL) is designed to be a stylesheet with many of the features found in XSLT. What makes DVSL so powerful is that you can transform XML using many of the same methods found in XSLT but with access to Java objects. This chapter provides extensive examples using DVSL.

Appendix A: The Velocity Specification

The Velocity system consists of many classes and interfaces. This appendix provides an overview of them.

Appendix B: Velocity Sites

This appendix provides both the new Velocity and the experienced user with a comprehensive list of Internet sites containing information on Velocity or tools available for the Velocity developer.

CHAPTER 1

Web Development Basics

If you remember back almost 10 years ago, you might be able to visualize how the World Wide Web got its start. Telnet and FTP were among the first examples of this profound way of communicating. These technologies weren't directly associated with the Web, but they were certainly a precursor. Gopher, on the other hand, was a technology that demonstrated how machines connected on the Internet could be used to share information with people all across the world.

Soon after gopher was being used to pull information from various places and sites, the World Wide Web was developed—and the rest is history. This book explores a part of Web development that has flourished in recent years: the presentation of dynamic data to the client. Our focus is on a new technology called *Velocity*. In this chapter, we provide an overview of the history of Web development and bring us into the present.

Static Web Pages

It all started with static Web pages; individuals posted photographs of their family and students posted their lasted research findings. As you would expect, this was in the early '90s. Amazon was still a concept in budding entrepreneurs' heads, and the trading of pictures was basically nonexistent. A page was written in HTML and had no content produced from a database or other application. The closest thing to a WYSIWYG GUI for HTML was a yellow legal pad.

The information provided on a static Web page consisted of the content the page creator wanted to put on it—and nothing more. If users didn't need that particular information, they had no way to interact with the Web page in order to bring forward the desired content. The page creator could provide links that led the user to other pages of information, but the content was still that of the page creator.

Introducing CGI

CGI (Common Gateway Interface) was one of the more profound technologies to invade the development of Web pages. Developed in 1993, CGI is a way of interfacing the Web page with the back-end server responsible for serving pages to the user. You can see an example of the interface in a search site. If you go to Yahoo! or Google, you type a topic that you want to learn about into an edit line typically positioned next to a Submit button. This edit line and button are part of an HTML form. When you click the Submit button, an action takes place that is typically a call to another Web page or possibly an application.

When you're using CGI, the action is an application written in a variety of languages, such as C, Perl, or C++. CGI is not the application itself but serves as the interface between the form action and the application. When a user clicks the Submit button, the CGI is responsible for transferring any information from the HTML form to the server and activating the application on the HTTP server. The application on the server executes a set of instructions and returns to the interface a Web page that is displayed to the client browser. Listing 1.1 shows an example of a simple C CGI application.

```
int main(int argc, char* argv[]) {
  printf("content-type: text/html\r\n");
  printf("\r\n");
  printf("<html><body>");
  printf("<h1>Hello World!</h1>");
  printf("</body></html>\n");

  return(0);
}
```

Listing 1.1 A simple CGI application in C.

Because CGI applications execute on the Web server, the issue of security is important. Most servers require that the CGI applications be placed in a directory called /cgi-bin. The server typically won't allow a CGI application to execute anywhere than on the server. It is important to note that CGI applications are built using high-level languages, and were in the beginning quite frustrating to write until proper libraries came along. At first, these languages weren't typically used by graphic designers or those who just wanted to put up an interactive page. As the Web industry started to grow, another option was needed.

Scripting: JSP/ASP/PHP

As you might expect, using CGI and Perl, C, or C++ wasn't something the new crop of Web designers were going to be able to do. This meant that Web development companies had to hire both Web designer and software development talent in order to produce the results the new demanding clients expected. In addition to this fact, the major players in the software development community, like Sun and Microsoft, wanted in on the dynamic Web development world. So they each created a server-side language that could handle getting information from a back-end system to the client.

Unlike high-level languages that typically have to be compiled into a binary that will execute on a specific machine, scripting languages are designed to make it easy to write applications and execute them within an interpreter. The interpreter is written in a high-level language and executes on the machine where the HTTP server is located, thus eliminating the need for the Common Gateway Interface.

To use the scripting languages, you create a Web page in which the statements and keywords of the scripting language are embedded in the same file as the HTML that will be displayed to the user. Listing 1.2 shows an example of such a page.

```
<HTML>
<HEAD>
  <TITLE>Time Example</TITLE>
</HEAD>
<BODY>
  The time is  <?php time() ?>
</BODY>
</HTML>
```

Listing 1.2 A scripting language page.

In Listing 1.2, we added some scripting code that displays the current time. When users browse to this page, they see the current time as supplied by the HTTP server. So, how does this all occur?

The scripted Web page is placed on the Web server just like any other HTML page. However, the extension applied to the scripted file is not .html or .htm; it has an extension like .asp, .jsp, .php, or something else. These extensions are important because they tell the Web server how the file should be handled when accessed by a client. If the requested file has an extension other than .htm, the server sends the file to an interpreter. The system administrator will have already told the Web server about all possible extensions it might have to handle and the associated interpreter for the file type.

The interpreter then processes the scripted file and interprets only the scripted code, leaving all of the HTML intact. During the processing of the file, the scripted code might place additional HTML into the file as needed. The additional HTML probably relates to information requested by the user.

At this point, the interpreter returns the final HTMl file to the HTTP server, which in turn provides the page to the client's browser. By using a scripting language, the Web designer doesn't have to be familiar with high-level programming languages. Unfortunately, the scripting languages can become complex and using them may be no more efficient than using CGI and a C++ program.

Future Development

While we are on the subject of scripting languages, it should be noted that there are some available—like JavaScript, Java, and ActiveX—which can be used and subsequently compiled by the server for better performance compared to the interpreted languages. Listing 1.3 shows an example of using Java in an HTML page.

```
<%@ page language='java' import='java.sql.*' %>
<HTML>
<HEAD>
  <TITLE>Test</TITLE>
</HEAD>
<%
  ResultSet rs;
  try {
    Class.forName("com.mysql.jdbc.Driver");

    connection = DriverManager.getConnection(
      "jdbc:mysql://localhost/products");
    statement = connection.createStatement();
%>
```

Listing 1.3 Using Java in an HTML page. (continues)

```
<BODY>
</BODY
</HTML>
```

Listing 1.3 Using Java in an HTML page. (continued)

Embedding Java into an HTML page is probably the ultimate in adding dynamic capabilities to a Web site. Not only do you have to know Java, but an additional piece of server software is needed to execute the embedded code. An application server like Resin or Tomcat compiles the Java into a servlet, which is then executed by the application server when a user browses the HTML page.

In all of the different types of dynamic pages we've discussed so far, the code for the view and the business logic is intermixed. As you learn in the next chapter, this intermixing can produce headaches for an organization.

What's Next

In this chapter, we examined the history of Web page development. While many readers will already be aware of this history, this material is a good background for those just getting into the Web arena. In the next chapter, we dive into the methodologies commonly used in the development of Web applications and focus specifically on the MVC (Model-View-Controller) paradigm.

MVC Fundamentals

If you had the privilege to be part of the early Internet revolution, you might have been like me, coming from a traditional software development role. As a leader tasked with guiding a newly formed team toward the release of an innovative site, the most common thought running through my head was doing what I could to move my team toward the technologies and methodologies that would provide success for the individuals, team, and clients.

Unfortunately, several forces came into play that caused this lofty goal to evaporate. The client, "time-to-market," and "underdeveloped skill sets" are just three of the forces that caused our team to revert from using all the ideal methodologies to just trying to meet our client's deadlines. This doesn't mean we had to let everything go; in fact, we delivered three successful iterations of the site using three different teams. However, the one area that clearly caused us the most grief was separating the code from the presentation.

In this chapter, we take a fairly in-depth look at the initial problem of mixing presentation and logic presents, introduce the MVC (Model-View-Controller) methodology, and explain how MVC attempts to solve the mixing problem.

Mixing Presentation and Logic

So what's the big deal? We've all created Web pages or applications in which we embed calls to the database directly into the (typically) HTML tags. For example, consider the code in Listing 2.1.

```
<%@ page language='java' import='java.sql.*' %>
<HTML>
<HEAD>
  <TITLE>Test</TITLE>
</HEAD>
<%
  ResultSet rs;
  try {
    Class.forName("com.mysql.jdbc.Driver");

    connection = DriverManager.getConnection(
      "jdbc:mysql://localhost/products");
    statement = connection.createStatement();
%>

<BODY>
<%
    if (request.getParameter("submit") = "submit") {
      rs = statement.executeQuery("SELECT username, password,
        city, state FROM product where username = " +
        request.getParameter("username"));
      if (rs.next()) {
%>
        <form action="test.jsp" method="post">
        <input type="text" name="username"
          value="<%= rs.getString("username") %>">
        <input type="text" name="password"
          value="<%= rs.getString("password") %>">
        <input type="text" name="city"
          value="<%= rs.getString("city") %>">
        <input type="text" name="state"
          value="<%= rs.getString("state") %>">
        <input type="submit" name="submit" value="Update">
        </form>
<%    } else { %>
        No Information
<%    }
    }
%>
    else if (request.getParameter("submit") = "update") {
      statement.executeUpdate("UPDATE product set password= '"
        + request.getParameter("password") + "'" +
        ", city = '" + request.getParameter("city") + "'" +
        ", state = '" + request.getParameter("state") + "'" +
        "where username = '" +
        request.getParameter("username"));
    }
  } catch(ClassNotFoundException e) {
      out.println("Driver Error");
```

Listing 2.1 A mixed presentation logic page. (continues)

```
   } catch(SQLException e) {
      out.println("SQLException: " + e.getMessage());
   }
%>
<form action="test.jsp" method="post">
<input type="text" name="username">
<input type="text" name="password">
<input type="text" name="city">
<input type="text" name="state">
<input type="submit" name="submit" value="Submit">
</form>
</BODY>
</HTML>
```

Listing 2.1 A mixed presentation logic page. (continued)

The code in Listing 2.1 is a good example of a JavaServer Pages (JSP) page that mixes both the logic of the application and the HTML. Let's consider several problems an organization would face when using just this simple page.

As a developer in your company, suppose you are asked to create a simple HTML form that will allow information for a particular username to be displayed and updated as needed. The requirements of the page include its use only within the organization, so there isn't much need for security (right or wrong, but for illustration purposes we don't want our example to be too complex). The result of your efforts is the code in Listing 2.1. Using a combination of JSP and HTML, you bang out the code in 15 minutes and push it to the person who made the request.

Of course, nothing is this simple, and some sort of graphics have to be added so that the new page will blend into the corporate intranet site. "I'm a developer, not a graphics designer," says the original developer, pushing the assignment to the "other side of the company." The graphics designer pulls up the page's code and begins working her graphics magic on the page. After several hours of work, the designer sends the page to the IT department to be placed on a server. The person who requested the work attempts to use the page, only to see a browser filled with error information instead of the date for "jsmith". The user calls the developer, who calls the designer, and an unpleasant exchange occurs. The developer wants to know what the designer did to break the code, and the designer wants to know if the code even worked in the first place. The "client" just wants some code that works so he can do his job.

After several minutes, the developer gets the code working and posted to the intranet. Some days or weeks later, a decision is made to move the primary database off the Web server to its own server. Somebody has to go through all of the pages and be sure they don't try to access the database on the old machine. Of course, your code will attempt the connection and has to be changed. Who does the work? The developer will get into the page code and make the change.

Six months have passed, and the marketing department wants to change the look and feel of the intranet to match the company's Internet site. Who makes that change to the code? The graphics or Web designer is responsible for opening the same file the developer had accessed previously to make the needed modifications.

I hope this story isn't too familiar to you, but it is reality in many software shops. Maybe things didn't start out this way, but with time-to-market issues and a client's ever-changing requirements list, it is bound to happen without the proper tools and time investment. What makes this story all the more interesting is that even though it occurs in the late '90s or early 2000s, a solution was formulated back in the '80s way before the Web was popular.

Smalltalk-80 MVC Triad

When Smalltalk-80 was being formulated, there was a need to develop a methodology in which the presentation of information for the user could be separated from the logic required to both obtain and format the data. Once the data was obtained and formatted based on some business rules, it could be presented to the user. That was the easy part of the entire process. Figure 2.1 shows an example of the original MVC triad developed for Smalltalk-80.

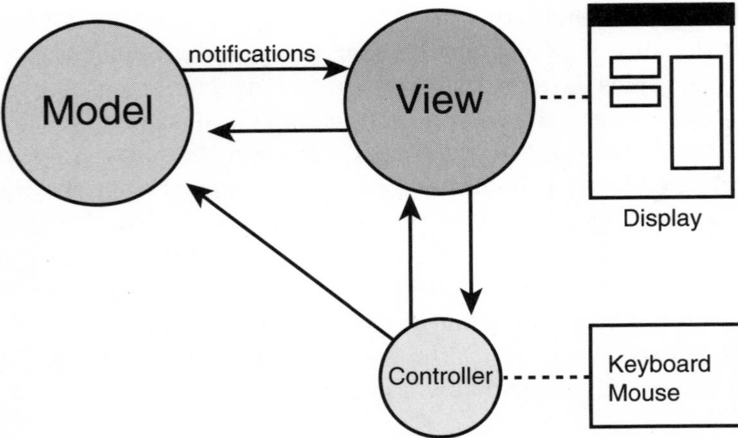

Figure 2.1 The Smalltalk-80 MVC triad.

In Figure 2.1, we find three primary components: the model, the view, and the controller. Let's explore each of these components, their functionality, and their relationship to each other, the client, and the system.

The Model

The model part of the MVC methodology usually consists of two parts:

- Classes or other data structures that represent the state of the system or application
- Actions/methods that can be executed to change the state of the system

In most cases, the model represents the data contained in a database or other data storage system. If you are using MVC in Java, the model will typically be created using JavaBeans with appropriate methods for accessing or updating the system data.

One of the core ideas behind the model concept is complete separation of the data from the user presentation. This means the model is independent of all input or output. Access to the model comes from both the view and the controller. The controller receives input from the user in the form of information that needs to be processed. When information must be processed, the controller updates the model with the appropriate data.

In order to display the information from the model, view components register themselves with the model. When information has been changed, the model informs all registered views about the change and allows them to present the new information to the user. The model isn't restricted to a single view, but instead allows any number of views to be registered and works to keep them informed of the current state of the system.

Figure 2.2 shows an example of the inputs and outputs associated with the model.

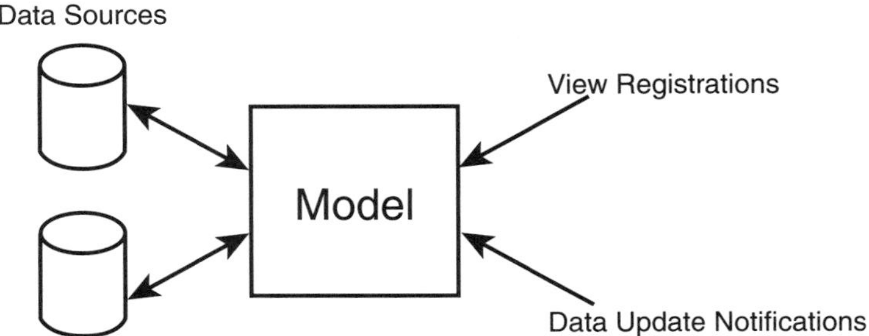

Figure 2.2 Model inputs and outputs.

As you can see in Figure 2.2, the model's primary connection is to the data sources, which can be databases, flat files, or some external interface. The model is responsible for maintaining the integrity and potentially the availability of the data. Other inputs to the model include view components registering for updates and the actual update notifications coming from the model and going to the registered views.

The View

We've touched on the view in our discussion of the model. The view component is a visual component that the user employs to analyze the information found in the model. In many cases, the view is designed in several formats, such as a chart, a simple listing, or a combination of many styles.

When a user needs to use information from the model, the application instantiates a new view component, which shows the data in some specific format. The view automatically registers itself with the model so it can be notified when the state of the model changes. How the view actually gets the data is an implementation issue. The view might call a specific method of the model, or it might expect to receive serialized objects with the data. In other implementations, the data could come from the controller, which we discuss next.

The Controller

The controller component is responsible for handling all interactions between the application and the user. All inputs from the keyboard, mouse, and other external interfaces are routed to the controller component. Using predefined logic, the controller determines if the data needs to be updated in the model or whether new view components should to be created based on the desire of the user.

As you might expect, some level of business logic is probably contained in the controller as well as in the model. There shouldn't be any business logic in the view components.

The MVC Architecture

The MVC architecture is so powerful that it is mentioned in the Gang of Four book, *Design Patterns: Elements of Reusable Object-Oriented Software*. The design pattern, Observer, describes the subscribe/notify process that occurs between the view components and the model. There has been quite a bit of work to incorporate the concepts found in MVC into modern languages. For example, Java includes two utility interfaces, called java.util.Observable and java.util.Observer, which allow classes to be created that can be observed and informed of state changes. In the remainder of this chapter, we look at the progression the MVC paradigm has gone through to make it relevant to Web development.

Sun Models 1 and 2

We have just described the typical MVC architecture as defined for Smalltalk-80 and further refined into an architectural paradigm. During the initial days of Web development, new technologies were created to handle the rapid development needs and creativity of Web developers. JSP, one such technology, allows Web pages to move from static content using just HTML to dynamic pages using the statements from within JSP. Using JSP is considered to be Model 1 of the MVC paradigm. Unfortunately, unless you are very careful, a dynamic Web page will look like the one in Listing 2.1 and have so much view and controller code mixed in it that it isn't productive.

With the development of the servlet, developers are allowed to remove the controller code found in the dynamic page and put it in its own components. This is considered Model 2 because two components of the MVC paradigm are used. Many will consider the possible association between Model 2 and MVC to be very distinct and thus they won't allow the connection. The most typical reason for this is the inability of Web applications to take advantage of the Observer pattern.

Extending MVC to Web Applications

The HTTP protocol used for Web sites is designed as a pull protocol. When a user accesses a Web site, a click on a button or link results in a GET or POST HTTP protocol request being sent to a Web server. The Web server then processes the request and returns an HTML page to the user's browser. Figure 2.3 shows an example of the process a Web page goes through.

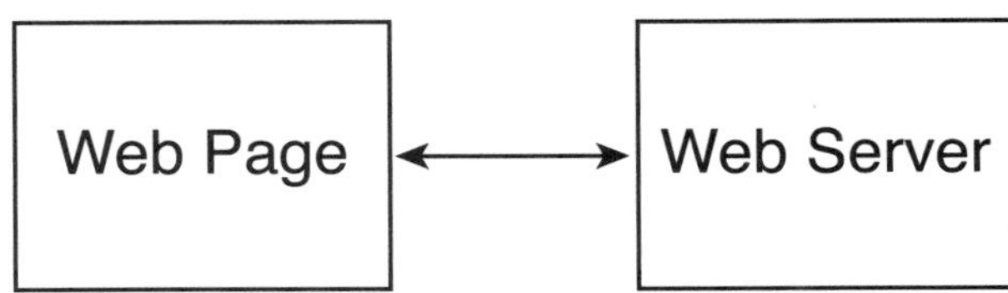

Figure 2.3 Web page processing.

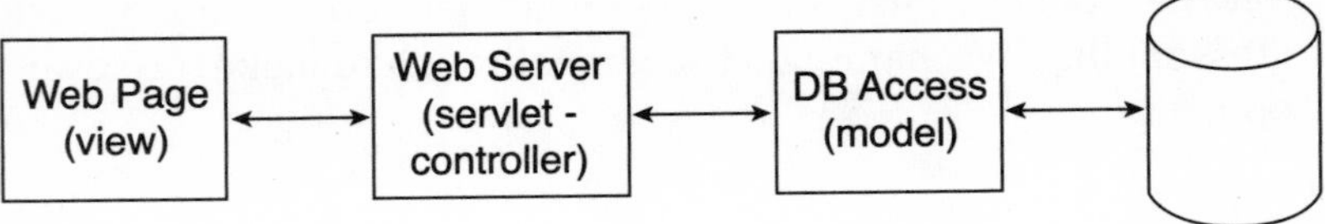

Figure 2.4 Three-tier Web page processing.

As Figure 2.3 shows, the processing of a Web page is fairly linear, with all information transferred to the user upon request. In fact, the process in Figure 2.3 shows the Web page directly accessing data; thus a query is being made from the view to the data without any intermediary process or layer. As you might expect, this isn't a good process. To solve this dilemma, other layers are added to the process and functionality is separated appropriately. Figure 2.4 shows how a three-tier Web application might appear.

In Figure 2.4, we've attempted to bring the Model-View-Controller paradigm into the Web development process by separating the functionality each layer or tier of the process is responsible for handling. Even though the HTTP protocol isn't push based, we can still take advantage of the underlying spirit of the paradigm.

A Practical MVC

With all of your newly gained knowledge, let's look at how the code in Listing 2.1 could be changed to support MVC and make the jobs of the Web designer and developer a little easier. First, we need to build the view containing all of the information we want to display to the user. Listing 2.2 shows a possible solution.

```
<HTML>
<HEAD>
  <TITLE>Test</TITLE>
</HEAD>
<BODY>
 <form action="ControllerServlet.jsp" method="post">
   <input type="text" name="username"
      value="$$username">
   <input type="text" name="password"
      value="$$password">
   <input type="text" name="city"
      value="$$city">
   <input type="text" name="state"
```

Listing 2.2 Example view code. (continues)

```
      value="$$state">
   $if ($$first) {
     <input type="submit" name="submit" value="Submit">
   $else
     <input type="submit" name="submit" value="Update">



  </form>
 </BODY>
 </HTML>
```

Listing 2.2 Example view code. (continued)

As you can see in Listing 2.2, we still require the Web designer to have some ability to manipulate the information provided from the model through the controller. Based on personal experience, giving the Web designer knowledge of loops and conditionals at the view layer relieves the Web application developer of quite a bit of work. The code won't be directly accessed by the user but instead is a template processed by the Web server before being displayed to the user.

To handle the requests from the view, let's build a servlet (using Java) as shown in Listing 2.3.

```
public class ControllerServet extends HttpServlet {
  private AccountLocalHome home = null;

  public void init() throws ServletException {
    try {
      Context cmp = (Context) new
InitialContext().lookup("java:comp/env/cmp");
      home = (AccountLocalHome) cmp.lookup("AccountBean");
    } catch (NamingException e) {
      e.printStackTrace();
    }
  }

  public void doGet(HttpServletRequest req, HttpServletResponse res)
    throws IOException, ServletException {
             if (home == null) {
                out.println("home is null");
             } else {
               AccountLocal account = home.create();
```

Listing 2.3 Example servlet code. (continues)

```
            ServletContext app = getServletContext();
            app.setAttribute("username", account.username);
            app.setAttribute("passowrd", account.password);
            app.setAttribute("city", account.city);
            app.setAttribute("state", account.state);

            RequestDispatcher disp;

            disp = app.getRequestDispatcher("/ViewAccount.tmp");
            disp.forward(request, response);
          }
        }
      }

      public void doPost(HttpServletRequest req, HttpServletResponse res)
        throws IOException, ServletException {
        doGet(req, res);
      }
    }
```

Listing 2.3 Example servlet code. (continued)

The servlet will possibly use Enterprise JavaBeans as the model component to access the data for the application. In many cases, the controller servlet will delegate processing to other servlets or objects for specific business functionality. Our servlet will obtain an Account object and associate parts of the object with the current context of the Web application. The process is passed to the template code in Listing 2.2, where the information saved to the context is used to display information to the user.

What's Next

In this chapter, we explored the Model-View-Controller paradigm, which goes a long way in separating functionality between system components as well as business roles. One of the outstanding questions is what language should be used for the view component. Our solution is to use Velocity—a language designed specifically for Web designers to handle the presentation of information to the user. In the next chapter, we introduce Velocity, examine its architecture, and explain how it integrates into the MVC paradigm.

CHAPTER 3

Introduction to Velocity

In Chapter 2, you saw how a Web developer and a designer can work together on the presentation and logic of an application. You've seen how languages like ASP, JSP, and PHP can be used to manipulate the information provided by the back end. In this chapter, we begin our exploration of Velocity, describe how it works, and explain the underlying architecture of the system.

What Is Velocity?

Velocity is a template language designed to give Web designers an easy way to present dynamic information to users of a Web site or application. To support the language, a collection of Java-based classes is used to create a bridge between the model and view components of the Model-View-Controller (MVC) model. One of the profound features of Velocity is the clear separation between the view and the rest of the paradigm by providing only a simple syntax set, which the Web designer uses to display content. At the same time, the Java programmers concentrate on the logic behind the application.

Velocity isn't a language to be used only by developers of Web pages, but also by those who create standalone applications. The output generated from Velocity templates can yield HTML as well as other content, such as source code, SQL, or XML. Some of the major components of Velocity are:

- A complete language for manipulating content including loops and conditionals

- Access to Java object methods
- Direct support for the Turbine Web application framework
- Transformation from XML to other content using Anakia
- Texan
- Direct support for servlets

How It Works

To get a feel for how Velocity works, let's consider an organization that needs to create a Web application that will allow users to view their account information. Let's assume for this example that the user has already logged into the system. The page we need to create displays information about the user's account.

Designing the Page

Because we are working in an organization where the MVC paradigm is used extensively, a designer and a developer share responsibility for the new page. The designer builds the look and feel of the page, and the developer makes sure the information is available to display. One of the first steps is to lay out the visual design. The designer uses HTML tags to create the new page, including all of the graphics and text needed. For the dynamic information, such as the user's account number and address, the designer includes placeholders like <**user account name**>. Listing 3.1 shows how this might look.

```
<HTML>
<HEAD>
  <img src="header.jpg">
</HEAD>
<BODY>
Hello, <**user account name**>
</BODY>
</HTML>
```

Listing 3.1 The designer page example.

Once the page has been completed visually and the appropriate signoff obtained, the designer sets up a meeting with the developer to discuss the dynamic context that must be available so that the page can be accurately displayed to the user.

Requesting the Right Information

The meeting between the designer and developer will probably be fairly short because the designer has already indicated the information needed for the new page. The most important result of the meeting will be the variables that will store the information for the page. This is a good time to stop and look at how Velocity gets information to be displayed on the Web page.

Because we are using the MVC paradigm, we know that putting Java code into the new Web page isn't the right way to get content for the page. Velocity works by giving the Web designer scripting elements that can be placed in the HTML code to produce a template. The scripting elements consist of logic statements, like loops and conditionals, but also a syntax for accessing Java objects. We wouldn't want the view component to directly access the model component, so Velocity has a collection called the *Context*, which is passed between the MVC layers. The Context object is filled by either the controller or model components and provided to the Web page template.

Code that implements Velocity parses the template and replaces all of the Velocity scripting elements with text obtained from the objects in the context. Since the Web designer is using objects from the context, there has to be an understanding between the designer and developer as to the names of the objects in the context. This agreement is just as strong as the agreement formed between developers when they create an application programming interface (API). Any changes to the API result in an error when the Velocity parser comes across an object reference in the Web page template that cannot be resolved against an object in the context.

Coding the Information

After the meeting takes place between the designer and developer, both parties return to work on the final pieces of the Web page. The true power of MVC is evident at this step because the designer adds in the scripting elements and the developer focuses on coding the information needed in the context.

For the developer, there is a little work to do, such as integrating the new page into the current framework, making sure all of the information about the current user (such as the account number) is available, and pulling the data needed by the designer and placing it in the context. We won't look at the first two tasks but instead jump to the third one.

In many Java-based MVC applications, the user browses to a Web page based on a servlet. The servlet (or multiple ones for that matter) acts as the controller in the MVC paradigm. The servlets will have already created, or will create on their first instantiation, Enterprise JavaBeans representing sessions and entities. The entities make up the model part of the paradigm, and the session might also be considered part of the controller. The controller or the servlet will be responsible for adding information from the model to the context.

Once the context is populated with the necessary dynamic information for the current user, the developer needs to determine the template to use for the current request by the user, and then merge or apply the template to the context and produce HTML output. Listing 3.2 shows a short example of what the developer must create.

```
Velocity.init();

VelocityContext context = new VelocityContext();

context.put( "name", new String("Jane Doe") );

Template template = Velocity.getTemplate("account.vm");

StringWriter sw = new StringWriter();

template.merge( context, sw );
```

Listing 3.2 Developer code for Velocity.

In Listing 3.2, the developer begins by initializing the Velocity engine and creating a new context. With the put() method, a String object is assigned to the key "name" and attached to the context. (It would have been previously agreed upon that the key "name" would relate to the name of an account.) Next, the template created by the designer is obtained using the getTemplate() method, as well as a StringWriter that handles the HTML output. Finally, the template and the context are merged together with the merge() method.

A few details are missing from this example, which we cover in the next chapter, but it serves to illustrate what the developer must do in order to provide the dynamic information needed by the designer's template. In this example, we assigned a simple String object to the context, but we could have also introduced more complex objects and used Velocity to access both the attributes and methods of the objects.

Displaying the Information

The designer might have the easiest part of the process once the API for the page and context has been set. Using the Velocity Templating Language (discussed extensively starting in Chapter 6), all of the dynamic information placeholders are replaced with code like that shown in Listing 3.3.

```
<HTML>
<HEAD>
  <img src="header.jpg">
</HEAD>
<BODY>
Hello, $name
</BODY>
</HTML>
```

Listing 3.3 Example Velocity Web page.

Here the username placeholder is replaced with the $name Velocity statement. When the template is merged with the context, $name is used as a call to the $name object found in the context.

Velocity Features

In the short example we've presented, you saw how to use a simple scripting element defined in Velocity along with the context to produce a dynamic Web page, all defined within the MVC paradigm. Velocity includes many other features that we have outlined here so you can become familiar with the terms before we start looking at them in detail:

References—Velocity includes three different types of references: variables, properties, and methods: *Variables* start with the $ character and are followed by an identifier. The value for the variable comes from the Java code via the context or the Set directive. *Properties* start with the $ character, followed by an identifier, then a dot, and finally another identifier. The property reference is used either to obtain the attribute of a Java object in the context or to call a method of the object and use its return value. The method must have the format of get<identifier>. *Methods* start with the $ character, followed by an identifier, then a dot, followed by an identifier and method body, such as (<parameter>). A call is made to the exact method identifier specified.

Directives—Velocity directives allow the Web designer to have control over the references. Scripting elements include set (assigning a variable and value), looping constructs, conditionals, and includes, among others.

Velocimacros—A Velocimacro allows the designer to build macros of commonly used HTML and Velocity scripting elements that are to be repeated when the macro is used.

Logging—Velocity makes use of the log4J system for easy logging.

Resource loaders—The resource loaders give you control over the templates used in the production of Web pages.

Anakia—This is an example application that allows XML to be processed using Velocity instead of Extensible Stylesheet Language (XSL).

Application servers—Velocity supports all major application servers and servlets like Resin, Tomcat, and BEA WebLogic.

What's Next

In this chapter, we provided a quick overview of the Velocity system and explained how it is used by both the Web designer and developer. In the next chapter, we begin the process of using Velocity by learning to install it as well as any ancillary software needed for execution.

CHAPTER 4

Installing Velocity

After reading the previous introductory chapters, you are no doubt anxious to get started using Velocity in your Web pages and applications. Before you can dive into the language and example applications, you must have properly set up and configured a development environment. In this chapter, we cover the prerequisites for Velocity, and we describe how you can obtain, install, and test Velocity. We also cover the installation of an application server for those examples in the book that rely on servlets. If you aren't a developer, don't worry—we plan to go slowly through the installation to make sure you have everything installed correctly. And if you are a developer, it's good practice.

Prerequisites

Velocity requires that you install the following packages:

- A Java Virtual Machine (JVM) is required to execute Velocity. At a minimum, you should install a Java Runtime Environment (JRE) package. If you want to compile Velocity itself, you need the Java 2 SDK, Standard Edition (J2SDK); if you are using servlets or want to work through the servlet examples in this book, install J2SDK. You can find both packages at http://sun.java.com. We created and executed the examples in this book using the 1.4.1 version of Java.

- Velocity relies on the build utility called Ant, which is part of the Jakarta project. Ant can be downloaded from http://jakarta.apache.org/ant; use version 1.3 or greater. Once it's installed, be sure to set up your environment so that the Ant application can be accessed from any path.

Obtaining Velocity

You can download the most current version of Velocity at http://jakarta.apache.org/velocity, as shown in Figure 4.1. Under the release directory, there are numerous versions, as Figure 4.2 shows. For this book, we used version 1.3.1. Click on the v1.3.1 directory to see the files displayed in Figure 4.3.

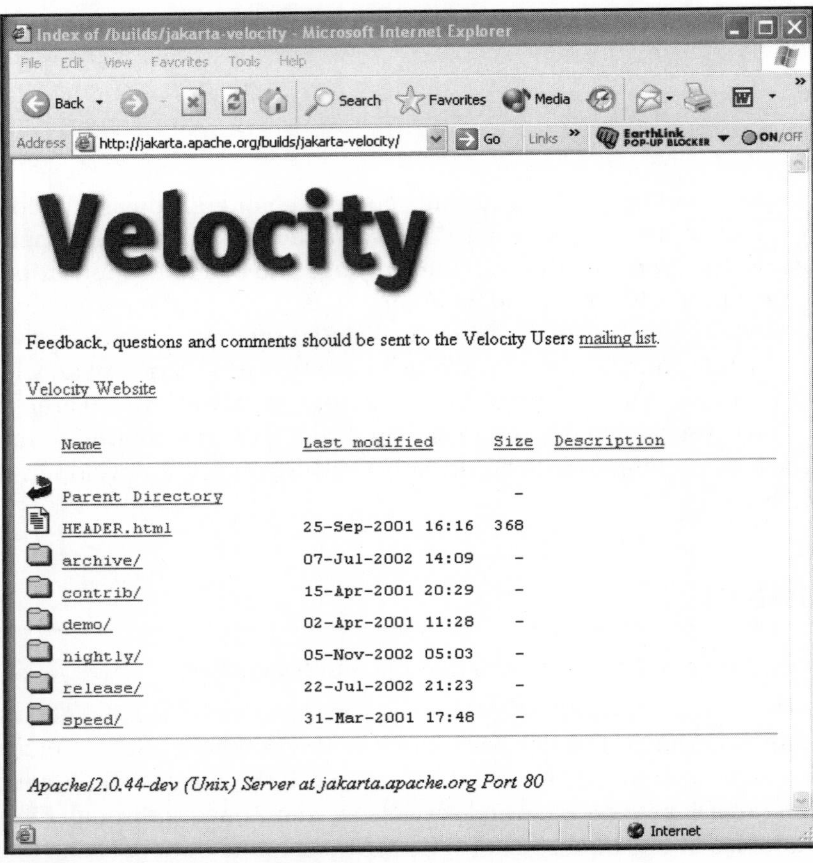

Figure 4.1 The primary download page for Velocity.

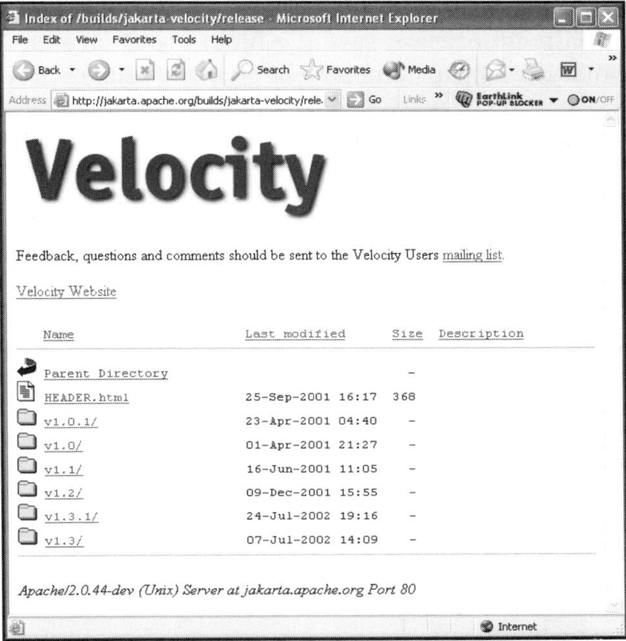

Figure 4.2 Available Velocity versions.

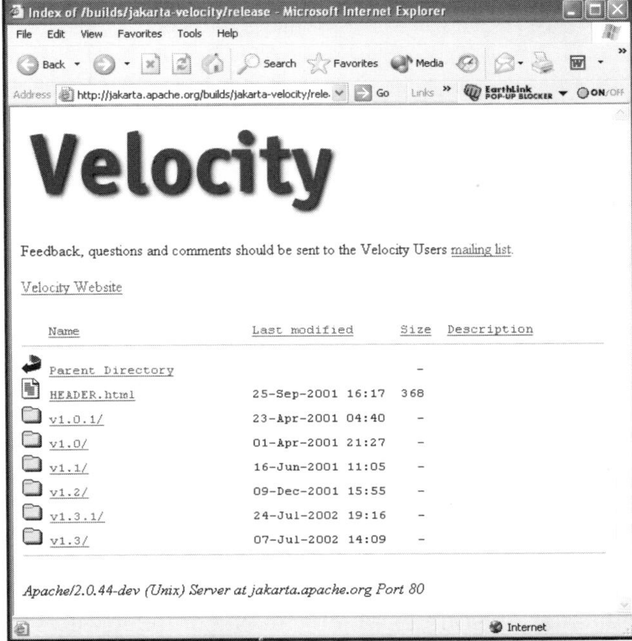

Figure 4.3 Velocity v1.3.1 files.

If you are on a Unix/Linux system, the GZ file is the best choice; Windows users should pull the zip file. In either case, save the file on your local system and uncompress using either the gunzip command or an unzip utility.

For UNIX/Linux, the gunzip command is:

```
gunzip -xvf velocity-1.3.1.tar.gz
```

In both cases, a directory structure is produced under a root directory (like /velocity-1.3.1) The full directory structure as shown in a Windows system appears in Figure 4.4.

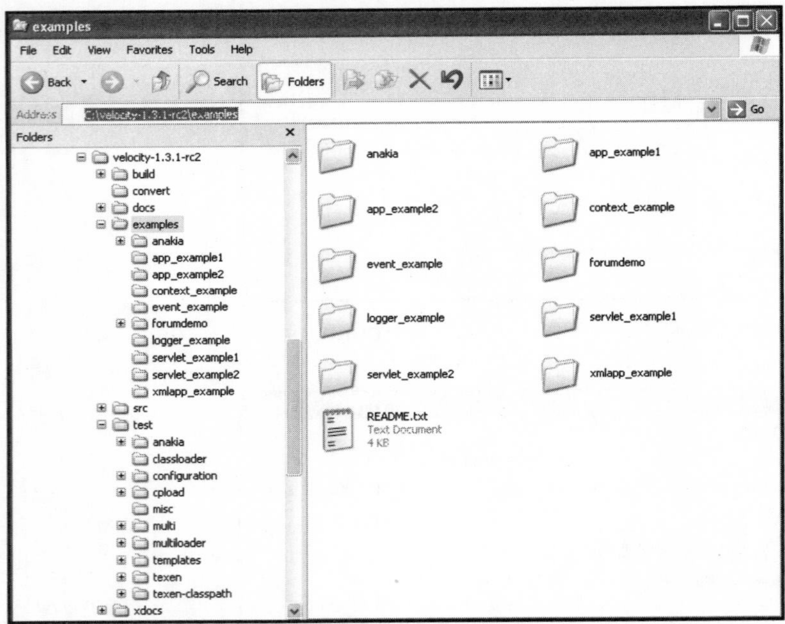

Figure 4.4 The Velocity directory structure.

As Figure 4.4 shows, the Velocity distribution includes several directories:

/build—All of the Ant build scripts

/convert—WebMacro conversion templates

/docs—Documentation for Velocity in HTML format

/examples—Demonstration source code

/src—Source code for Velocity, Anakia, and Texen

/test—All smoke test applications and templates

/xdocs—The documentation source, which can be compiled into various output formats

When you use any of the build targets explained in the next section to create a Velocity JAR, a /bin directory will appear.

Velocity Versions

If you've pulled Velocity out of a version directory from the release download area, Velocity will be provided in three different flavors:

- Precompiled with all dependencies
- Precompiled with no dependencies included
- Source code

With the first and second flavors, the issue of dependencies arises. In the root Velocity directory, you find two JAR files, like the following:

- velocity-1.3.1.jar
- velocity-dep-1.3.1.jar

Obviously, the filename velocity-dep has the dependencies compiled into it. The dependencies are:

Jakarta Commons Collections—A collection solution is required by Velocity.

Jakarta Avalon Logkit—If your solution will be logging to a file, this JAR dependency is required; otherwise, it is not.

Jakarta ORO—This is required for the WebMacro template conversion utility. If you aren't going to be converting any WebMacro templates (or don't even know what WebMacro is!), these dependencies aren't needed.

The developers of Velocity have included the dependencies as separate JARs in order to allow the end developer the option of using the Jakarta solutions or some other third-party components. All of the dependencies are included in the /build/lib directory and will be added to a compile of the system shortly. If you are going to use one of the precompiled JARs, simply copy the appropriate one into your classpath and skip the rest of this section.

Compiling Velocity

With the third flavor of the Velocity download, the system is supplied as source files that need to be compiled. As we mentioned earlier, Velocity is designed to use the build tool called Ant, which allows for the organization, compiling, and deploying of Java applications. Ant will build all of the source code for Velocity based on a *build target*. Build targets tell Ant to perform some specific task and are currently defined as:

jar-dep—This builds a full Velocity JAR, including all of the dependencies listed earlier. The command line is:

```
ant jar-dep
```

The result of the build is a file in the path:

```
C:\velocity-1.3.1\bin\velocity-dep-1.3.1.jar
```

jar—This build target also builds a full Velocity JAR but without the dependencies. However, since the Jakarta Commons Collection is required, you need to have the path to this JAR in your classpath. If you have to use the WebMacro utility or require logging, the JARs for handling that specific functionality also must be in your classpath. If you are including all of the supplied dependencies, just use the jar-def build target listed first. The command line is:

```
ant jar
```

The result of the build is a single JAR in the path:

```
C:\velocity-1.3.1\bin\velocity-1.3.1.jar
```

jar-core—This build target compiles Velocity in the same manner as the jar build target but does not include any examples, utilities, or servlet support. The command line is:

```
ant jar-core
```

The result of the build is a single JAR in the path:

```
C:\velocity-1.3.1\bin\velocity-core-1.3.1.jar
```

jar-util—This builds only the Velocity utilities, Anakia, Texan, and WebMacro. The command line is:

```
ant jar-util
```

The result of the build is a single JAR in the path:

```
C:\velocity-1.3.1\bin\velocity-util-1.3.1.jar
```

jar-servlet—This build target compiles the VelocityServlet class to provide servlet support with Velocity. The command line is:

```
ant jar-servlet
```

The result of the build is a single JAR in the path:

```
C:\velocity-1.3.1\bin\velocity-servlet-1.3.1.jar
```

jar-J2EE—This build target compiles a complete Velocity JAR just as in the case of the jar build target, but it also includes the J2EE JAR file. The build target requires a copy of j2ee.jar in the /build/lib directory or a link. The command line is:

```
ant jar-J2EE
```

The result of the build is a file called

```
C:\velocity-1.3.1\bin\velocity-J2EEdep-1.3.1.jar
```

jar-J2EE-dep—This build target compiles a complete Velocity JAR with J2EE support, including all dependencies listed earlier. The command line is:

```
ant jar-J2EE-dep
```

The result of the build is a single JAR file:

```
C:\velocity-1.3.1\bin\velocity-J2EE-1.3.1.jar
```

examples—This build target compiles all of the examples included with Velocity that are located in the /examples directory. Use this target if you used one of the other targets that didn't include the examples. The command line is:

```
ant examples
```

The result of the build is a series of examples:

```
C:\velocity-1.3.1\bin\forumdemo.war
C:\velocity-1.3.1\examples/appexample1
C:\velocity-1.3.1\examples/appexample2
C:\velocity-1.3.\examples/servletexample1
C:\velocity-1.3.\examples/servletexample2
C:\velocity-1.3.\examples/context_example
C:\velocity-1.3.\examples/logger_example
C:\velocity-1.3.\examples/xmlapp_example
C:\velocity-1.3.\examples/event_example
```

forumdemo—This build target only builds the Forum Demo located in the examples/forumdemo directory. The command line is:

```
ant forumdemo
```

The result of the build is a single Web archive (WAR) file:

```
C:\velocity-1.3.1\bin\forumdemo.war
```

docs—This builds the Velocity docs using the Anakia tool. There are additional dependencies for this build target. The Jarkata Site2 project must be installed on the build machine. The Site2 project's installation directory must be at the same hierarchy level as the Velocity installation directory. You can find information about the Site2 module at http://jakarta.apache.org/site/jakarta-site2.html. Either pull the jakarta-site2 project from apache.org CVS or create a directory called /jakarta-site on the same directory hierarchy as the Velocity distribution directory. Then, copy the entire directory called /examples/anakia/xdocs to the jakarta-site2 directory. The command line is:

```
ant docs
```

The result of the build consists of HTML files in the /docs directory under the Velocity distribution directory.

docs_print—This build target produced the documents for Velocity in HTML format appropriate for printing. The command line is:

```
ant docs_print
```

The result of the build consists of HTML files in the docs directory that you can print.

jar-src—This build target bundles all of the source code and places it into a single JAR. The command line is:

```
ant jar-src
```

The result of the build is a single JAR file in the path:

```
C:\velocity-1.3.1\bin\velocity-1.3.1.src.jar
```

javadocs—This build target builds the Velocity JavaDoc. The command line is:

```
ant javadocs
```

The result of the build consists of appropriate JavaDoc files in the /examples/api directory.

test—This build target tests a subsequent JAR build to be sure it was created successfully. The JAR will be used with a number of smoke tests. The command line is:

```
ant test
```

For the examples in this book, the Velocity JAR used is velocity-dep-1.3.1.jar (as found precompiled in the distribution). This JAR is equivalent to executing Ant with a build target of jar-dep with all of the dependencies combined. Add the appropriate Velocity JAR to your classpath.

Testing the Velocity Installation

After compiling a particular version of Velocity using Ant and the appropriate build target, you should test the compile to be certain it was successful. The developers of Velocity included a test suite in the distribution that you can execute using Ant and the test build target. The Ant task associated with the test suite uses the Velocity JARs found in the /bin directory of the installation when compiling the examples. When you execute the command ant test, the system utilizes JUnit to run through a couple dozen tests.

Running the Examples

After you have built the Velocity JAR (with or without the dependencies included), tested the JAR, and built the examples, you should execute the examples to see some of the power behind Velocity. We have a total of eight example applications.

examples/appexample1

This example demonstrates using Velocity in a Java application. You run the example by executing the file ./example.bat (on a Windows machine) or ./example.sh (on Unix). The result of the example should be:

```
Velocity is great!

    ArrayList element 1 is great!
    ArrayList element 2 is great!
    ArrayList element 3 is great!
    ArrayList element 4 is great!


    The condition is true!
```

examples/appexample2

This example uses Velocity convenience utilities to output text. You run the example by executing the file ./example2.bat (on a Windows machine) or ./example2.sh (on Unix). The result of the example should be:

```
template : Hello from Velocity in the Jakarta project.

 string : We are using Jakarta Velocity to render this.
```

examples/servletexample1

This example shows how to use a servlet with Velocity. You must have a servlet engine installed on your system in order to execute this example, as well as the next one. Let's run through the steps that you must perform to execute this example:

```
Install a servlet engine like Resin (www.caucho.com) or Tomcat
   (http://jakarta.apache.org/tomcat/).
```

1. Add the following directory structure to the /docs (Resin) or /webapps (Tomcat) directory:

```
/velocity1/
/velocity1/WEB-INF
```

```
/velocity1/WEB-INF/classes
/velocity1/WEB-INF/lib
```

2. Under Resin add a <web-app> tag, such as <web-app id='velocity1'/>.
3. Copy the Velocity JAR built earlier to the /lib directory.
4. Copy the SampleServlet.class file to the /classes directory.
5. Copy the sample.vm file to the /velocity1 directory.
6. Create an appropriate web.xml file for your server. Here's an example using Resin:

```
<web-app>
  <servlet-mapping>
    <url-pattern id="/servlet/*"/>
    <servlet-name id="invoker"/>
  </servlet-mapping>
</web-app>
```

7. Restart Tomcat—Resin will detect the new application.
8. Browse to the server using this URL:

```
http://localhost:8080/velocity1/servlet/SampleServlet
```

Figure 4.5 shows an example of the expected output from the servlet example.

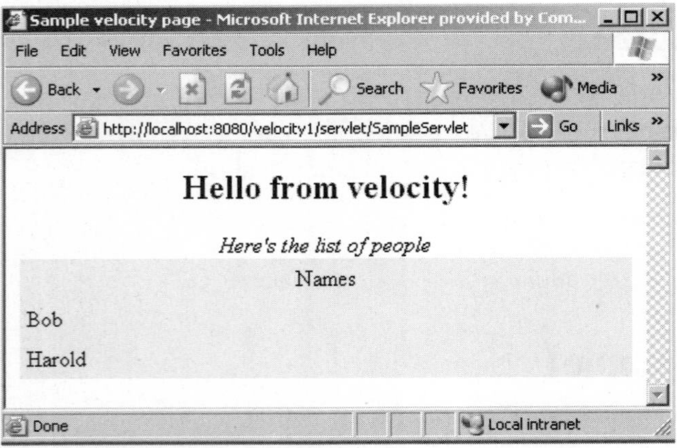

Figure 4.5 Servlet Example1 output.

examples/servletexample2

This second servlet example is more complex than the previous one because it uses a properties file and shows how to load a template from an external file. The steps are similar but more detailed since there are two ways to load the template. You can check out the readme.txt file found in the /examples/servlet_example2 directory of the distribution.

examples/context_example

This example shows how to use the context in a couple of implementations. The example uses a file in a database to store serialized information. The application assumes a MySQL database driver is in the classpath, a database called test, and a table defined as:

```
create table contextstore(id int not null auto_increment primary key, k
varchar(128), val blob);
```

To execute the example, use this command:

```
C:\velocity-1.3.1\examples\context_example>java -cp
 "./;../../bin/velocity-dep-1.3.1.jar;"
DBContextTest dbtest.vm
```

The output will look something like that shown in Figure 4.6. depending on the data in your database table.

```
Command Prompt
C:\velocity-1.3.1-rc2\examples\logger_example>logger_example
Using classpath:  .;..\..\bin\velocity-dep-1.3.1-rc2.jar;..\..\build\lib\werken.
xpath.jar
level : 1 msg : ***************************************************************
level : 1 msg : Starting Jakarta Velocity v1.3.1-rc2
level : 1 msg : RuntimeInstance initializing.
level : 1 msg : Default Properties File: org\apache\velocity\runtime\defaults\ve
locity.properties
level : 1 msg : Default ResourceManager initializing. (class org.apache.velocity
.runtime.resource.ResourceManagerImpl)
level : 1 msg : Resource Loader Instantiated: org.apache.velocity.runtime.resour
ce.loader.FileResourceLoader
level : 1 msg : FileResourceLoader : initialization starting.
level : 1 msg : FileResourceLoader : adding path '.'
level : 1 msg : FileResourceLoader : initialization complete.
level : 1 msg : ResourceCache : initialized. (class org.apache.velocity.runtime.
resource.ResourceCacheImpl)
level : 1 msg : Default ResourceManager initialization complete.
level : 1 msg : Loaded System Directive: org.apache.velocity.runtime.directive.L
iteral
level : 1 msg : Loaded System Directive: org.apache.velocity.runtime.directive.M
acro
level : 1 msg : Loaded System Directive: org.apache.velocity.runtime.directive.P
arse
level : 1 msg : Loaded System Directive: org.apache.velocity.runtime.directive.I
nclude
level : 1 msg : Loaded System Directive: org.apache.velocity.runtime.directive.F
oreach
level : 1 msg : Created: 20 parsers.
level : 1 msg : Velocimacro : initialization starting.
level : 1 msg : Velocimacro : adding VMs from VM library template : VM_global_li
brary.vm
level : 3 msg : ResourceManager : unable to find resource 'VM_global_library.vm'
 in any resource loader.
level : 1 msg : Velocimacro : error using  VM library template VM_global_library
.vm : org.apache.velocity.exception.ResourceNotFoundException: Unable to find re
source 'VM_global_library.vm'
level : 1 msg : Velocimacro :  VM library template macro registration complete.
level : 1 msg : Velocimacro : allowInline = true : VMs can be defined inline in
templates
level : 1 msg : Velocimacro : allowInlineToOverride = false : VMs defined inline
 may NOT replace previous VM definitions
level : 1 msg : Velocimacro : allowInlineLocal = false : VMs defined inline will
 be  global in scope if allowed.
level : 1 msg : Velocimacro : messages on  : VM system will output logging messa
ges
level : 1 msg : Velocimacro : autoload off  : VM system will not automatically r
eload global library macros
level : 1 msg : Velocimacro : initialization complete.
level : 1 msg : Velocity successfully started.
C:\velocity-1.3.1-rc2\examples\logger_example>
```

Figure 4.6 Context example output.

examples/logger_example

This example looks at using the logging ability of Velocity. The example can be executed using logger_example.bat (on Windows) or logger_example.sh (on Unix). The output generated from the example is shown in Figure 4.7.

```
Command Prompt
C:\velocity-1.3.1-rc2\examples\logger_example>logger_example
Using classpath:  .;..\..\bin\velocity-dep-1.3.1-rc2.jar;..\..\build\lib\werken.
xpath.jar
level : 1 msg : ************************************************************
level : 1 msg : Starting Jakarta Velocity v1.3.1-rc2
level : 1 msg : RuntimeInstance initializing.
level : 1 msg : Default Properties File: org\apache\velocity\runtime\defaults\ve
locity.properties
level : 1 msg : Default ResourceManager initializing. (class org.apache.velocity
.runtime.resource.ResourceManagerImpl)
level : 1 msg : Resource Loader Instantiated: org.apache.velocity.runtime.resour
ce.loader.FileResourceLoader
level : 1 msg : FileResourceLoader : initialization starting.
level : 1 msg : FileResourceLoader : adding path '.'
level : 1 msg : FileResourceLoader : initialization complete.
level : 1 msg : ResourceCache : initialized. (class org.apache.velocity.runtime.
resource.ResourceCacheImpl)
level : 1 msg : Default ResourceManager initialization complete.
level : 1 msg : Loaded System Directive: org.apache.velocity.runtime.directive.L
iteral
level : 1 msg : Loaded System Directive: org.apache.velocity.runtime.directive.M
acro
level : 1 msg : Loaded System Directive: org.apache.velocity.runtime.directive.P
arse
level : 1 msg : Loaded System Directive: org.apache.velocity.runtime.directive.I
nclude
level : 1 msg : Loaded System Directive: org.apache.velocity.runtime.directive.F
oreach
level : 1 msg : Created: 20 parsers.
level : 1 msg : Velocimacro : initialization starting.
level : 1 msg : Velocimacro : adding VMs from VM library template : VM_global_li
brary.vm
level : 3 msg : ResourceManager : unable to find resource 'VM_global_library.vm'
 in any resource loader.
level : 1 msg : Velocimacro : error using  VM library template VM_global_library
.vm : org.apache.velocity.exception.ResourceNotFoundException: Unable to find re
source 'VM_global_library.vm'
level : 1 msg : Velocimacro :  VM library template macro registration complete.
level : 1 msg : Velocimacro : allowInline = true : VMs can be defined inline in
templates
level : 1 msg : Velocimacro : allowInlineToOverride = false : VMs defined inline
 may NOT replace previous VM definitions
level : 1 msg : Velocimacro : allowInlineLocal = false : VMs defined inline will
 be  global in scope if allowed.
level : 1 msg : Velocimacro : messages on  : VM system will output logging messa
ges
level : 1 msg : Velocimacro : autoload off  : VM system will not automatically r
eload global library macros
level : 1 msg : Velocimacro : initialization complete.
level : 1 msg : Velocity successfully started.
C:\velocity-1.3.1-rc2\examples\logger_example>
```

Figure 4.7 Logger example output.

examples/xmlapp_example

This example shows how to import XML data from a file format using Velocity and a template. The example requires that the JDom JAR be in your classpath as well as Apache's Xerces package. Execute the example using xmlapp_example.bat (on Windows) or xmlapp_example.sh (on Unix).

examples/event_example

This example shows how to use the event-handling features of Velocity. To execute the example, use this command:

```
java -cp "./;../../bin/velocity-dep-1.3.1.jar;" EventExample
```

Figure 4.8 shows the result.

```
Command Prompt
C:\velocity-1.3.1-rc2\examples\logger_example>logger_example
Using classpath:  .;..\..\bin\velocity-dep-1.3.1-rc2.jar;..\..\build\lib\werken.
xpath.jar
level : 1 msg : ****************************************************************
level : 1 msg : Starting Jakarta Velocity v1.3.1-rc2
level : 1 msg : RuntimeInstance initializing.
level : 1 msg : Default Properties File: org\apache\velocity\runtime\defaults\ve
locity.properties
level : 1 msg : Default ResourceManager initializing. (class org.apache.velocity
.runtime.resource.ResourceManagerImpl)
level : 1 msg : Resource Loader Instantiated: org.apache.velocity.runtime.resour
ce.loader.FileResourceLoader
level : 1 msg : FileResourceLoader : initialization starting.
level : 1 msg : FileResourceLoader : adding path '.'
level : 1 msg : FileResourceLoader : initialization complete.
level : 1 msg : ResourceCache : initialized. (class org.apache.velocity.runtime.
resource.ResourceCacheImpl)
level : 1 msg : Default ResourceManager initialization complete.
level : 1 msg : Loaded System Directive: org.apache.velocity.runtime.directive.L
iteral
level : 1 msg : Loaded System Directive: org.apache.velocity.runtime.directive.M
acro
level : 1 msg : Loaded System Directive: org.apache.velocity.runtime.directive.P
arse
level : 1 msg : Loaded System Directive: org.apache.velocity.runtime.directive.I
nclude
level : 1 msg : Loaded System Directive: org.apache.velocity.runtime.directive.F
oreach
level : 1 msg : Created: 20 parsers.
level : 1 msg : Velocimacro : initialization starting.
level : 1 msg : Velocimacro : adding VMs from VM library template : VM_global_li
brary.vm
level : 3 msg : ResourceManager : unable to find resource 'VM_global_library.vm'
 in any resource loader.
level : 1 msg : Velocimacro : error using  VM library template VM_global_library
.vm : org.apache.velocity.exception.ResourceNotFoundException: Unable to find re
source 'VM_global_library.vm'
level : 1 msg : Velocimacro :  VM library template macro registration complete.
level : 1 msg : Velocimacro : allowInline = true : VMs can be defined inline in
templates
level : 1 msg : Velocimacro : allowInlineToOverride = false : VMs defined inline
 may NOT replace previous VM definitions
level : 1 msg : Velocimacro : allowInlineLocal = false : VMs defined inline will
 be  global in scope if allowed.
level : 1 msg : Velocimacro : messages on  : VM system will output logging messa
ges
level : 1 msg : Velocimacro : autoload off  : VM system will not automatically r
eload global library macros
level : 1 msg : Velocimacro : initialization complete.
level : 1 msg : Velocity successfully started.
C:\velocity-1.3.1-rc2\examples\logger_example>
```

Figure 4.8 Event example output.

What's Next

In this chapter, we offered a comprehensive look at obtaining and installing the Velocity distribution. We also explained how to test the compile. In addition, we looked at the examples included with Velocity that you can use along with this book as a teaching aid.

In the next chapter, we look at building our first Velocity application.

CHAPTER 5

Building a Hello World Example

Now that you have a good understanding of Velocity and how it works in the arena of the Model-View-Controller paradigm, and you've created a working installation, it's time to begin learning how to use Velocity. As you might expect, the first application we build is a version of the Hello World example.

Hello World!

One of the first issues you must tackle is determining the type of information that you want to appear on the HTML page returned to the browser from the Hello World template. Since we are only talking about a Hello World example, we could simply output "Hello World"--but this wouldn't illustrate how to use Velocity references. Instead, let's produce a template that will output the text "Hello World, Sam is Here", where "Sam" is a reference.

Now that you know the information that will be produced from the template, you have to discuss with your Java developer the object name you want to use for your reference. I would suspect that "name" could be agreed upon without too much trouble. As you build your Hello World example, you are actually going to produce three versions:

- A Velocity template without the context from an application
- A Velocity template with the context from an application
- A Velocity template from the Web

If you are familiar with server-side languages such as PHP, you're probably wondering why we have not discussed the interpreter a Web server launches when a Velocity template is browsed. This is because no such piece of software is available in Velocity. All of the substitutions between the template and the context are performed within the scope of some Java code. This Java code could exist in the middle of a servlet, embedded within a JSP or as part of an application. In situations where you are using Velocity in the Web arena, you will most often use a servlet to handle the transformation of the template into a response for the user.

A Velocity Template without Context

Our first Hello World example, shown in Listing 5.1, uses a Velocity directive statement called #set that can be used in a template to assign a value to a reference. What makes the listing a Velocity template is the use of #set and the $name reference embedded in the Hello World text line.

This example isn't hard to understand. When the template is supplied to the Velocity parser, it encounters the normal text, ignores it, and sends it directly to the output. When the parser hits the #set directive, it creates a variable internal to the parser that handles the new variable called $name. The value "Sam" is assigned to the new variable. Next, the "Hello World" text is found and directed straight to the output stream. When the $name reference is located in the code, the system attempts to find an object called $name in the context. If a match isn't found in the context, previously created references are matched and their content used as appropriate.

```
#set( $name = "Sam" )
Hello World, $name is Here
```

Listing 5.1 The Velocity Hello World template.

Of course, just having the template itself doesn't do you much good--you need a way to merge the template with a context to produce output for your client. Listing 5.2 shows the code you can use for a stand-alone Velocity application.

```
import org.apache.velocity.app.Velocity;
import org.apache.velocity.VelocityContext;
import org.apache.velocity.Template;
import org.apache.velocity.exception.ParseErrorException;
import org.apache.velocity.exception.ResourceNotFoundException;
```

Listing 5.2 The Velocity application without context. (continues)

```
import java.io.*;
import java.util.ArrayList;

public class Example {
  public Example(String templateFile) {
    try {
      Velocity.init();
       VelocityContext context = new VelocityContext();


      Template template = null;
      try {
        template = Velocity.getTemplate(templateFile);
      } catch(ResourceNotFoundException e2 ) {
          System.out.println(
            "cannot find template " + templateFile );
      } catch(ParseErrorException e ) {
          System.out.println(
            "Syntax error in template : " + e);
      }

      BufferedWriter writer = new BufferedWriter(
        new OutputStreamWriter(System.out));

      if ( template != null)
        template.merge(context, writer);

      writer.flush();
      writer.close();
    } catch( Exception e ) {
        System.out.println(e);
    }
  }

  public static void main(String[] args) {
    Example t = new Example(args[0]);
  }
}
```

Listing 5.2 The Velocity application without context. (continued)

As with most Java applications, this example needs a few imports to do its job effectively. The first five imports in the example code pull in the various Velocity specific classes referenced in the code. When the example code is first executed, the name of the template is given as the first command-line parameter. For example:

```
java Example example.vm
```

Refer back to Listing 5.1 for the template example. The name of the template placed on the command line is passed to the newly created Example object. The first operation performed in the example code is to initialize the Velocity engine. This example uses a Singleton pattern for the relationship between your application and the Velocity engine. This means only one static engine is available for all the application objects. It is important to remember this fact because you won't see any code in this example to instantiate the engine.

Once the engine has been initialized, it's time to load the template from the local hard drive. The template is loaded using the getTemplate(String) method of the Velocity engine object. The result of the method call is a Template object; otherwise, an exception is thrown. One of the important exceptions that can be thrown is ResourceNotFoundException (when either the template file specified on the command line cannot be found or an error occurs when the template file is parsed from its flat-file representation into the Template object). A parse error during the reading of the template throws a ParseErrorException exception.

After the template has been read into the system, you can begin the process of producing the intended output. Because you are using a Java application, you output the text from the Velocity template to the console. Note the output could be generated to a file, a socket, or other output mechanism as long as a Writer object can be created for it.

At this point, you have several different objects active in your application:

- **Velocity**—a static object representing the Velocity engine
- **Context**—a Context object
- **Template**—a Template object created when the Velocity template is read from the local drive
- **Writer**—a BufferedWriter object that will be used to direct output to the console through the System.out stream

Back in your application code, the BufferedWriter object is checked against null to be sure the object was instantiated successfully. The actual work of the Velocity engine is accomplished using the merge() method of the Template object. The merge() method takes two parameters: a Context object and a BufferedWriter object. When the merge() method is executed against a template, the context is merged with the associated template and its scripting elements to create the desired output.

Finally, the output stream is flushed and closed. Figure 5.1 shows the output generated by the template.

Figure 5.1 Output from the Hello World example.

For this example, we saved the template in Listing 5.1 into a file called helloworld.vm. The extension applied to the template file isn't limited to VM; it could be anything that will distinguish the file from others, like HTML or JSP. For instance, we saved the code in Listing 5.2 in a file called Example.java and compiled the application with the command

```
javac Example.java
```

We executed the example with the command

```
java Example helloworld.vm
```

If the Velocity engine is unable to locate the template file specified or an error occurs in the template, an error is produced.

The Velocity Template with Context

In the previous example, you relied on the #set directive to assign a value to the $name reference. While this might be a good illustration tool, it doesn't provide you with much in the way of dynamic behavior. To give your template the ability to change the name of the user, you need to take advantage of the Context object that is merged with the template. For our second example, let's use the same template shown in Listing 5.1 but delete the #set directive line, leaving just the

```
Hello World, $name is Here
```

line. After the line of code

```
VelocityContext context = new VelocityContext();
```

place the following line:

```
        context.put("name", "New Sam");
```

Save the files, and then compile and execute. You should see the output "Hello World, New Sam is Here." Now let's try something else. Open up the application code and change the context.put line to read

```
context.put("names", "New Sam");
```

Now compile and execute the code again. The result is the text "Hello World, $name is here". Why did you get this output? Well, let's consider what the context.put() statement did.

As you learned in the previous chapters, the Velocity engine does its magic by merging a template with the context. All references in the template, such as $name, are matched against object key value pairs in the Context object. Thus, Velocity attempts to match the $name reference with a key in the context of "name". If it locates the key, the value associated with it is returned--"New Sam" in our case. If the key isn't found in the context, the engine assumes that the "$name" string is literal and just copies it to the output without any type of substitution.

When you changed the context.put() statement to place a "names" key in the context, the Velocity engine wasn't able to find $name and simply passed the $names reference to the output stream without any substitution.

Velocity and the Web

In both of the examples thus far, we have used Velocity in a stand-alone Java application. However, since Velocity is billed as a possible replacement for JSP, you'd expect that you could use it with a Web application as well. In this section, we provide a small glimpse at using Velocity with a servlet. For more information on this topic, see Chapter 12, "Using Velocity with Servlets." Listing 5.3 shows a new template that you can use to display an XML document in a user's browser. As you can see, the template has a little more functionality to it.

In future chapters, we examine the statements in the template more closely. For now, the first statement you should notice is the #foreach directive paired with #next. These directives allow a loop to be created based on some supplied reference. In this case, the reference is called $list and is actually a Java vector object supplied in the context. The code loops through the vector and displays the associated $value.

```
<?xml version="1.0" encoding="ISO-8859-1" ?>

<list>
#foreach( $value in $list )
  <number>$value</number>
#end
</list>
```

Listing 5.3 The servlet example template.

Listing 5.4 shows the servlet code you can use on the server to produce the XML. As we mentioned, we discuss the functionality of servlets in Chapter 12; however, for now notice that a Vector object is created in the code and three values are added to it. The entire Vector object is attached to the context with the context.put("list", v); statement.

```
import java.util.Vector;
import javax.servlet.http.HttpServletRequest;
import javax.servlet.http.HttpServletResponse;
import org.apache.velocity.Template;
import org.apache.velocity.context.Context;
import org.apache.velocity.servlet.VelocityServlet;
import org.apache.velocity.exception.ResourceNotFoundException;
import org.apache.velocity.exception.ParseErrorException;

public class VelocityServletExample extends VelocityServlet {
  public Template handleRequest( HttpServletRequest request,
                                 HttpServletResponse response,
                                 Context context ) {

    Vector v = new Vector();
    v.add("one");
    v.add("two");
    v.add("three");

    context.put("list", v);

    Template template = null;
    try {
      template = getTemplate("displaylist.vm");
    } catch( Exception e ) {
      System.out.println("Error " + e);
    }
    return template;
  }
}
```

Listing 5.4 The servlet code for our example.

Once the vector is placed in the Context object, the template used to display the context information is obtained from the local server hard drive. Now instead of using the merge() method of the Template object, you simply return the template. The template doesn't actually get returned directly to the user; instead, there is a process in the background that merges the "returned" template and the context. In Figure 5.2, you can see the XML output created from the servlet and the template. You could have used Velocity to output HTML to the user's browser if you wanted.

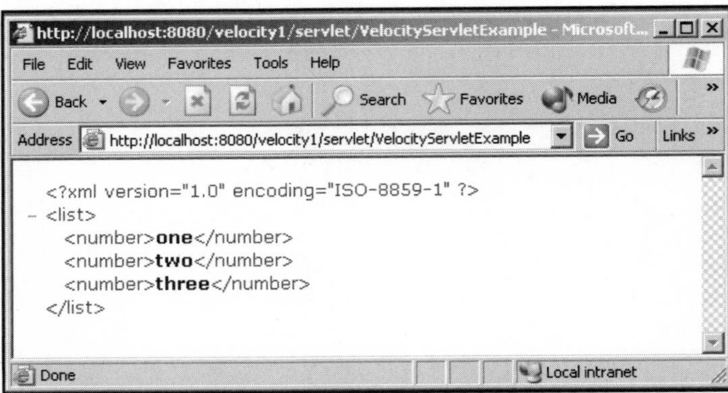

Figure 5.2 The servlet and template example output.

What's Next

In this chapter, we showed you how to write Hello World applications using Velocity. You used Velocity in a stand-alone Java application as well as with a Web application. In the next chapter, we begin exploring the details of Velocity and learn about its various language features.

CHAPTER 6

Understanding Templates and Context

In the previous chapter, we introduced Velocity with the requisite Hello World example (or examples in this case). Now that you have seen some simple cases of Velocity in action, it's time to take a step back and examine the core components responsible for powering Velocity. This chapter begins with a discussion of templates and the context. Subsequent chapters build on this introduction, discussing in detail Velocity's references, directives, and macros.

Using Templates

Given that Velocity is a template engine, it is not surprising that templates play a critical role in any use of Velocity. But what constitutes a Velocity template? As it turns out, Velocity's definition of a template is quite similar to that used in a number of other areas. Many word processor packages provide predefined starting points for common documents, such as office memos and fax cover sheets; these are good examples of electronic templates that correspond closely to the notion of a Velocity template. The Club Velocity application form shown in Figure 6.1 is another example of a general template.

```
                    CLUB VELOCITY APPLICATION


First Name: ____________________________________________
Last Name: _____________________________________________
Address: _______________________________________________
City: ____________________ State: ______ Zip: __________
Phone Number: __________________________________________
Email Address: _________________________________________
Occupation: ____________________________________________
Other Interests: _______________________________________


Is this a new memebership request or a renewal?_____
How long have you been using Velocity? _____
Do you use Velocity for work or play? _____
Do you want to receive our newsletter? _____
```

Figure 6.1 An example of a general template.

The content of the Club Velocity application includes two general content types: static and dynamic. The static content consists of the title, the labels (e.g., First Name:, Last Name:, etc.), the questions, and the overall layout. This is the portion of the document that is to be reused as-is for any application for membership. The dynamic content loosely corresponds to the blanks (underlined sections), which are to be filled in on a case-by-case basis, with each applicant providing his or her own personal information.

The primary difference between the general template defined by the Club Velocity application and a true Velocity template is the manner in which the dynamic content is specified. While the application form relies on blank sections to specify where the dynamic content should be inserted, Velocity uses the concept of references. For now, you can think of a Velocity reference simply as some sort of entity that refers to a value stored elsewhere. As an example, using the basic syntax for Velocity references, a template might include an entity named $name to refer to the string "John Doe", where the string itself is stored somewhere outside the template (e.g., in a database). We discuss references in detail in the next chapter, so don't be concerned if you are somewhat confused by this rather vague definition. The important thing to keep in mind for now is that a Velocity reference is essentially a placeholder for some piece of dynamic data.

If you want to transform the club application form into a true Velocity template, all that you have to do is replace the blank sections with appropriate Velocity references. What constitutes an appropriate reference is specified by Velocity reference syntax and the contract negotiated between the designer and the programmer. One possible template implementation is shown in Listing 6.1.

```
                CLUB VELOCITY APPLICATION


        First Name: $firstName
        Last Name: $lastName
        Address: $streetAddress
        City: $city              State: $state Zip: $zip
        Phone Number: $phoneNumber
        Email Address: $emailAddress
        Occupation: $occupation
        Other Interests: $otherInterests


        Is this a new membership request or a renewal? $appType
        How long have you been using Velocity? $useTime
        Do you use Velocity for work or play? $useType
        Do you want to receive our newsletter? $wantNewsletter
```

Listing 6.1 The club application form after conversion to a Velocity template.

As you can see, the Velocity template is essentially identical to the original application form, except that the blanks have been replaced by Velocity references. Assuming the following mapping for the references, the processed template would result in the output shown in Listing 6.2:

```
$firstName       =>   "John"
$lastName        =>   "Doe"
$streetAddress   =>   "123 Jane Ave. "
$city            =>   "Azusa"
$state           =>   "CA"
$zip             =>   "91702"
$phoneNumber     =>   "626-555-1234"
$emailAddress    =>   "john@nodom.com"
$occupation      =>   "Web Developer"
$otherInterests  =>   "Hiking,Biking"
$appType         =>   "New"
$useTime         =>   "6 months"
$useType         =>   "Work"
$wantNewsletter  =>   "Yes"
```

```
                    CLUB VELOCITY APPLICATION


        First Name: John
        Last Name: Doe
        Address: 123 Jane Ave.
        City: Azusa                  State: CA Zip: 91702
        Phone Number: 626-555-1234
        Email Address: john@nodom.com
        Occupation: Web Developer
        Other Interests: Hiking,Biking


        Is this a new membership request or a renewal? New
        How long have you been using Velocity? 6 months
        Do you use Velocity for work or play? Work
        Do you want to receive our newsletter? Yes
```

Listing 6.2 Sample output for the Velocity template version of the club application form.

Now that you have an idea of how content is output from a template, let's conclude this section with a quick look at how you can prevent content in a template from being processed. Often it is useful to leave yourself, or perhaps your colleagues, a note or two explaining the purpose of a bit of template code. Also, the ability to selectively disable sections of a template is frequently useful during debugging sessions. Finally, it is sometimes necessary to explicitly override Velocity's default behavior with regard to the handling of whitespace. Velocity supports such needs with a template commenting mechanism. Support is provided for both block and single-line comments. A block comment is started with the character sequence #* and terminated with the sequence *#; everything in between is discarded by the template engine. A single-line comment is initiated with the sequence ## and continues through the end of the line. Listing 6.3 provides a few examples of template comments.

In providing this initial description of a Velocity template, we have neglected several important topics. First, there is significantly more to Velocity references than we have so far let on. Furthermore, Velocity provides support for directives and macros, which allow more sophisticated content control directly from the template. Directives provide for flow control, file inclusion, and reference manipulation, while macros provide a powerful reuse mechanism for template code. We discuss these topics in detail in the next few chapters.

```
#*
 This is a block comment. It is being used to point out
 that this listing is intended to demonstrate the use of
 comments in Velocity templates.
*#

##This line is not rendered.

This part is rendered,## but this part is not.

If only the #*middle*# bit needs to be commented out, a
block comment will do the job.
```

Listing 6.3 Velocity comment examples.

The Context

In the previous section, we specified a reference to string mapping for our application template. However, we made no mention of the mechanism through which the Velocity references were tied to the string values. This is where Velocity's notion of a context comes into play. The context, represented on the application side by the Context interface defined in org.apache.velocity.context, serves as the go-between for application and template. The context is most easily viewed as a simple map that stores objects by key. More specifically, the context stores objects of type java.lang.Object, keyed by objects of type java.lang.String.

The value of the String used as the key is the same value that is used for the name of the reference, except that the reference is prefixed with a $. For example, a Java Object representing the string "John" might be keyed in the context with the Java String firstName, in which case the template could access the string "John" through the reference $firstName. In essence, the dynamic portion of a template's content is specified through the keys used to look up that content in the context. The $ prefix simply lets the template engine know that the following text potentially corresponds to a context key that requires special processing.

There are three ways in which a Velocity context can be populated with objects. First, Velocity itself may insert useful values into the context. For example, the current iteration count associated with the #foreach directive is made available by Velocity. Second, the #set directive allows a template to insert values directly into the context. Finally, and most important, Velocity's Context interface allows a programmer to populate the context with data needed by the view designer, using key names agreed upon by the programmer and the designer.

We address only the final case in this section.

In a typical application, the context is represented by an instance of org.apache.velocity.VelocityContext, which implements the Context interface. Creation of a context that stores the objects "John" and "Doe" keyed by "firstName" and "lastName", respectively, is achieved with the following code:

```
VelocityContext context = new VelocityContext();

context.put( "firstName", "John" );
context.put( "lastName", "Doe" );
```

Once created, a template would access the objects "John" and "Doe" using the references $firstName and $lastName, respectively. Although the objects in the context are already Java Strings in this case, it is quite acceptable that they be of some other type, such as Integer or Float. In such cases, Velocity uses the object's toString() method in order to generate a String representation for output. It is also possible for an object in a context to represent more than a simple value. This often occurs in cases where a template's requirements include advanced functionality available only through the methods of an object stored in the context. This last case is covered in detail when we discuss Velocity references in Chapter 7.

In addition to populating a context, the Context interface allows the programmer to query and further manipulate the context. The interface provides the following four additional methods:

```
boolean containsKey( java.lang.Object key )
java.lang.Object[] getKeys()
java.lang.Object remove( java.lang.Object key )
java.lang.Object get( java.lang.String key )
```

The containsKey() method allows the context to be checked for a specified key, returning true if the context contains an object associated with that key. The getKeys() method returns a list of all keys currently present in the context; note that the keys are returned as an Object array, rather than a String array. The remove() method removes the entry associated with the specified key from the context; the removed value is returned by the method. The get() method allows the programmer to access the object associated with the specified key.

Putting the Pieces Together

Now that you have a general understanding of the roles played in Velocity by the template and the context, let's put the pieces together in the form of a complete application for processing the Velocity template representing our Club Velocity membership application form. Since the real purpose of the application is to illustrate the basic structure of a Velocity application, let's try to keep application logic simple. In particular, the dynamic component of the final content is derived from hardcoded strings, where in a more realistic application that content would more likely be obtained from a database or otherwise generated on the fly.

Before taking a look at the application code, a summary of our goals seems in order. Using the template defined in Listing 6.1 as a starting point, let's develop an application that processes the template, replacing all of the references with appropriate text taken from a Velocity context. The final content--including the static content taken directly from the template and the dynamic content obtained from the context--is to be output by the application, resulting in a completed membership application form like that shown in Listing 6.2.

The source code for an application that meets these goals is shown in Listing 6.4. The code is representative of a general pattern common to most Velocity applications, and the comments placed sparsely throughout the code highlight this pattern. The pattern may be loosely viewed as a sequence consisting of six steps: template engine initialization, template inclusion, context creation, context population, template and context merging, and content rendering. Note that this is only a general pattern, and there is some flexibility. For example, it might be perfectly reasonable to read in the template after populating the context. Nonetheless, you shouldn't go too far wrong if you keep this pattern in mind.

```
import java.io.StringWriter;

import org.apache.velocity.Template;
import org.apache.velocity.VelocityContext;
import org.apache.velocity.app.Velocity;
import org.apache.velocity.exception.*;

public class ClubApp
{
  public static void main( String[] args )
  {
    // Initialize template engine
    try
    {
      Velocity.init();
    }
    catch( Exception x )
    {
      System.err.println( "Failed to initialize Velocity: " + x );
      System.exit( 1 );
    }
```

Listing 6.4 An application for processing the club membership form. (continues)

```
// Obtain a template
Template clubTemplate = null;

try
{
  clubTemplate = Velocity.getTemplate( "ClubApp.vm" );
}
catch( ResourceNotFoundException rnfX )
{
  System.err.println( "Template not found: " + rnfX );
  System.exit( 1 );
}
catch( ParseErrorException peX )
{
  System.err.println( "Failed to parse template: " + peX );
  System.exit( 1 );
}
catch( Exception x )
{
  System.err.println( "Failed to initialize template: " + x );
  System.exit( 1 );
}

// Create context
VelocityContext context = new VelocityContext();

// Populate context
context.put( "firstName", "John" );
context.put( "lastName", "Doe" );
context.put( "streetAddress", "123 Jane Ave." );
context.put( "city", "Azusa" );
context.put( "state", "CA" );
context.put( "zip", "91702" );
context.put( "phoneNumber", "626-555-1234" );
context.put( "emailAddress", "john@nodom.com" );
context.put( "occupation", "Web Developer" );
context.put( "otherInterests", "Hiking,Biking" );
context.put( "appType", "New" );
context.put( "useTime", "6 months" );
context.put( "useType", "Work" );
context.put( "wantNewsletter", "Yes" );

// Merge template and context
StringWriter writer = new StringWriter();

try
{
```

Listing 6.4 An application for processing the club membership form. (continues)

```
        clubTemplate.merge( context, writer );
      }
      catch( ResourceNotFoundException rnfX )
      {
        System.err.println( "Template not found on merge: " + rnfX );
        System.exit( 1 );
      }
      catch( ParseErrorException peX )
      {
        System.err.println( "Failed to parse template on merge: " + peX );
        System.exit( 1 );
      }
      catch( MethodInvocationException miX )
      {
        System.err.println( "Application method exception: " + miX );
        System.exit( 1 );
      }
      catch( Exception x )
      {
        System.err.println( "Failed to merge template: " + x );
        System.exit( 1 );
      }

      // Render merged content
      System.out.println( writer.toString() );
    }
  }
```

Listing 6.4 An application for processing the club membership form. (continued)

Now let's dissect this example and put the pieces under the microscope, so to speak. Starting with the imports, you see that java.io.StringWriter is pulled into the application. While the StringWriter class is not specifically required in the general case, the process of merging template and context does typically require an object of a class derived from java.io.Writer. For the purposes of the application under discussion, a StringWriter is appropriate. The first import from a Velocity package is org.apache.velocity.Template. The corresponding Template class provides an in-memory representation a template used by the application. Next, org.apache.velocity.VelocityContext is imported, providing a representation of the Velocity context via the corresponding VelocityContext class. The application then imports org.apache.velocity.app.Velocity, which provides the Singleton representation of the Velocity template engine. A non-Singleton implementation is also available through org.apache.velocity .app.VelocityEngine and will be discussed in Chapter 10. Finally, you import org.apache.velocity.exception.*, providing access to various Velocity exception classes.

With the imports out of the way, you next move to the code implementing the template processing. As mentioned earlier, this code follows a general pattern common to Velocity applications. The first element of that pattern is the initialization of the template engine. Using the Singleton model, this is as easy as invoking the static method Velocity.init(). If for any reason this method fails, a generic exception of type java.lang.Exception is thrown. If the non-Singleton model were to be used instead, you would create an instance of VelocityEngine and invoke its init() method.

After initializing the template engine, the application next obtains an in-memory representation of the template to be processed. As with template engine initialization, the manner in which this step is accomplished depends on whether a Singleton or non-Singleton model is being used. With the Singleton model, our template representation is obtained by invoking the static getTemplate() method from the Velocity class, which returns an instance of Template. This method takes as a parameter the name of the template file to be loaded, which in this case is ClubApp.vm. Note that while vm is the commonly accepted standard suffix for Velocity template files, you are not required to follow this convention.

If a non-Singleton model is instead used for template acquisition, the process remains much the same. The key difference is that getTemplate() would be invoked on an instance of VelocityEngine created and initialized in the first step. Regardless of the model used, it is necessary to address the same set of possible exceptions. This set includes ResourceNotFoundException, ParseErrorException, and Exception. The first two are Velocity exceptions specified in the org.apache.velocity.exception package. The last is the standard java.lang.Exception. The ResourceNotFoundException is thrown when Velocity is unable to locate the specified template. The ParseErrorException is thrown when Velocity is unable to parse the template. Finally, a generic Exception is thrown if any other problem occurs during template acquisition.

With a copy of the template in place, you can proceed to create and populate a context. You begin by constructing an instance of VelocityContext. Population of the context consists of calls to VelocityContext's put method, each of which provides a key and an associated Java Object. For a typical Velocity application, most of the processing will be centered on context population. It is here that the data and tools required for generation of dynamic content are made available to the template designer.

Now that you have template and context in hand, the next step is to merge these items. This causes the references in the template to be replaced with data obtained from the context. The merge is accomplished by calling the merge() method on the Template instance obtained earlier. Template's merge() method requires two arguments. The first is a context, which can be any object implementing the Context interface; in this case, you pass the instance of VelocityContext created and populated earlier in the application. The second required argument is an object of type java.io.Writer, or more specifically of a type derived from Writer. The Writer object is used as the destination of the processed template.

Finally, you render the output. Since you used a StringWriter for the merge operation, rendering involves no more than calling toString() on the Writer and sending its output to an appropriate location. The output looks like that shown in Listing 6.2.

What's Next

This chapter covered the basics of Velocity templates and contexts. We presented a sample application demonstrating the use of templates and contexts and discussed it in detail. Armed with this information, you should be ready to design basic templates and/or develop simple template-processing applications. However, a couple stumbling blocks remain in the path to utilizing Velocity for more advanced template-processing tasks. To clear the obstacles, we first need to take our discussion of Velocity references beyond the arm-waving explanations employed so far. That is the goal of our next chapter.

CHAPTER 7

Exploring References

In the previous chapter, we provided a brief introduction to Velocity references and even made use of such references in our club membership application template. However, we repeatedly deferred a detailed discussion of references in an attempt to ease the initial learning curve. Now that you have handle on what Velocity is about and how a basic application works, it is time to talk about references in detail. Until you have a reasonably good grasp of Velocity references, much of the power of Velocity remains beyond reach.

Reference Types

As we hinted in the previous chapter, there is much more to Velocity references than the ability to reference a simple string value stored in the context. A reference can in fact refer to any Java Object placed in the context. It is important to note that our use of Object refers to a true Java Object—that is, an instantiated object that satisfies the condition of being an instance of java.lang.Object. Neither primitive types nor purely static classes satisfy this condition and thus cannot be placed in the context.

We mentioned previously that the name of a Velocity reference is, minus the prefix, the same as the key used to store the referenced object in the context. However, this is not entirely true—or perhaps it would be more appropriate to say that this is not the whole truth. While all valid Velocity reference names do in fact include the name used for the context key, some correspond to more than a stringified version of the Context object and thus require more in the way of a name. In all, three distinct types of Velocity references exist, each with its own naming convention. We discuss the types—which include variables, methods, and properties—in the following sections.

Variables

All of the Velocity references we have so far encountered are of the *variable* variety. A reference of this type corresponds to a Java Object that implicitly provides a stringified representation of its value through the use of its toString() method. Given that the root of the Java class hierarchy, Java's Object class, provides a toString() implementation, any object in a Velocity context is fair game for a variable reference. Of course, the toString() implementation provided by the Object class returns only a string containing the name of the associated class and the hex representation of the object's hash code, which is unlikely to be of much use for anything other than debugging. A more practical example of a Velocity variable reference is one that refers to an instance of one of Java's numeric wrapper classes, such as Integer or Float.

While Java's wrapper classes are likely to be targets for Velocity variable references, such references are certainly not limited to instances of built-in Java classes. Just as Java classes like Integer and Float override toString() in order to provide a more appropriate and meaningful string representation, a developer may overload a custom class's toString() implementation to the same end. To get a better feeling for how this all works, let's take a look at an example that involves several variable references.

We'll start by defining a couple of custom classes that will highlight the relevance of the toString() method. Listings 7.1 and 7.2 define two trivial classes, each representing a single string value stored as a public data member; while using public member data is typically a bad idea, we do so here to underscore the fact that Velocity obtains its stringified representation through toString() rather than through direct member data access. As you can see from the two listings, the only significant difference in functionality is that the Override class overrides toString(), while the NoOverride class relies on the default toString() inherited from Object.

```
public class NoOverride
{
  public final String value = "toString() not overridden";
}
```

Listing 7.1 The NoOverride class definition.

```
public class Override
{
  public final String value = "toString() overridden";

  public String toString()
  {
    return (value);
  }
}
```

Listing 7.2 The Override class definition.

The template implemented for this example is shown in Listing 7.3. In addition to demonstrating variable references for our user-defined classes, the template includes variable references intended to map to a generic Java Object, a Java Integer object, and a Java Float object. When this template is processed using the code in Listing 7.4, the generated output looks like that shown in Listing 7.5. Note that aside from context population, the source in Listing 7.4 is nearly identical to that in Listing 6.4; the only other differences are in class and template (file and variable) naming. Except where there is an overriding need to do otherwise, we will limit the driver source for further examples to that demonstrating the manner in which the context is populated.

```
## A variable reference for a generic Java Object
Value of generic Object is $genericObject

## A variable reference for an Integer object
Value of Integer object is $integerObject

## A variable reference for a Float object
Value of Float object is $floatObject

## A variable reference for a custom object with no toString() override
Value of user object with default toString() is $userNoOverride

## A variable reference for a custom object with a toString() override
Value of user object with overridden toString() is $userOverride
```

Listing 7.3 The template for the variable reference example.

```
import java.io.StringWriter;

import org.apache.velocity.Template;
```

Listing 7.4 The driver code for the variable reference example. (continues)

```
import org.apache.velocity.VelocityContext;
import org.apache.velocity.app.Velocity;
import org.apache.velocity.exception.*;

public class VarRef
{
  public static void main( String[] args )
  {
    // Initialize template engine
    try
    {
      Velocity.init();
    }
    catch( Exception x )
    {
      System.err.println( "Failed to initialize Velocity: " + x );
      System.exit( 1 );
    }

    // Obtain a template
    Template varTemplate = null;

    try
    {
      varTemplate = Velocity.getTemplate( "VarRef.vm" );
    }
    catch( ResourceNotFoundException rnfX )
    {
      System.err.println( "Template not found: " + rnfX );
      System.exit( 1 );
    }
    catch( ParseErrorException peX )
    {
      System.err.println( "Failed to parse template: " + peX );
      System.exit( 1 );
    }
    catch( Exception x )
    {
      System.err.println( "Failed to initialize template: " + x );
      System.exit( 1 );
    }

    // Create context
    VelocityContext context = new VelocityContext();

    // Populate context
    context.put( "genericObject", new Object() );
```

Listing 7.4 The driver code for the variable reference example. (continues)

```
    context.put( "integerObject", new Integer( 10 ) );
    context.put( "floatObject", new Float( 3.1415 ) );
    context.put( "userNoOverride", new NoOverride() );
    context.put( "userOverride", new Override() );

    // Merge template and context
    StringWriter writer = new StringWriter();

    try
    {
      varTemplate.merge( context, writer );
    }
    catch( ResourceNotFoundException rnfX )
    {
      System.err.println( "Template not found on merge: " + rnfX );
      System.exit( 1 );
    }
    catch( ParseErrorException peX )
    {
      System.err.println( "Failed to parse template on merge: " +
peX );
      System.exit( 1 );
    }
    catch( MethodInvocationException miX )
    {
      System.err.println( "Application method exception: " + miX );
      System.exit( 1 );
    }
    catch( Exception x )
    {
      System.err.println( "Failed to merge template: " + x );
      System.exit( 1 );
    }

    // Render merged content
    System.out.println( writer.toString() );
  }
}
```

Listing 7.4 The driver code for the variable reference example. (continued)

```
Value of generic Object is java.lang.Object@cdedfd

Value of Integer object is 10
```

Listing 7.5 Output from the variable reference example application. (continues)

```
Value of Float object is 3.1415

Value of user object with default toString() is NoOverride@bf2d5e

Value of user object with overridden toString() is toString()
overridden
```

Listing 7.5 Output from the variable reference example application. (continued)

As you can see in Listing 7.5, the Velocity references corresponding to our NoOverride class, which lacks an overridden toString() method, result in output similar to that of the generic Java Object. This is because Velocity uses toString() to obtain the stringified value and pays no attention to the underlying member data itself. Since the toString() method used by our NoOverride class is in fact borrowed from the Java Object class, the similarity of the output is not surprising. In the case of our Override object, the variable reference results in precisely the value provided by Override's toString() method. Since the Java Integer and Float classes implement their own toString() methods in a manner appropriate for their respective types, the corresponding references generate equally appropriate output.

Getting back to reference names, a quick comparison of the keys used in the context population code (Listing 7.4) and the reference names used in the template (Listing 7.3) yields the following relationship:

```
genericObject    =>      $genericObject
integerObject    =>      $integerObject
floatObject      =>      $floatObject
userNoOverride   =>      $userNoOverride
userOverride     =>      $userOverride
```

It is clear that except for the $ prefix, the key and reference names are identical. This relationship is not a coincidence. In the case of variable references, our previous assertions regarding the relationship between key and reference names are entirely accurate. That is, a variable reference name is the context key prefixed with a $ (or a $! in the case of quiet notation, which we discuss later in this chapter).

More precisely, using Velocity's lingo, the name of a valid context key accessible via a variable reference must conform to VTL Identifier syntax. A *VTL identifier* is a string that begins with an alphabetic character and thereafter consists only of alphabetic characters, numeric characters, hyphens (-), and underscores (_). Characters are defined as alphabetic or numeric relative to the standard ASCII character set (i.e., alphabetic characters consist of upper and lower case A through Z, and numeric characters consists of 0 through 9). A Velocity variable reference, then, is just the corresponding key's VTL Identifier prefixed with a $ (or $!).

Methods

As with variable references, Velocity method reference names include a VTL Identifier prefixed with a $. However, in the case of method references, the name is further qualified by a VTL Method Body. The *VTL Method Body* consists of a VTL Identifier, an opening parenthesis, an optional comma-delimited argument list, and a closing parenthesis. A dot (.) separates the initial VTL Identifier from the VTL Method Body. Examples of method references include the following:

```
$date.changeTo( 2003, "March", 2 )
$car.newColor("Blue" )
$document.print()
```

The syntax and semantics of the portion of the reference name that precedes the initial dot are identical to those described for variable references. That is, this portion of the reference name contains the VTL Identifier that serves as the context key for the desired Context object. The remaining portion of the Velocity method reference provides the name of and arguments for a Java method implemented by the referenced Java object. In order for Velocity to access the referenced method, the method must be declared as public and further must be a member of a public class.

Velocity's method references are used in much the same way as its variable references. A method reference is placed at that point in the template where its action should be invoked. As intuition probably suggests, any given Velocity reference is processed after those references that occur earlier in the template and before those that occur later in the template. As such, evaluation of Velocity references should be considered a sequential process, with actions invoked by earlier references potentially affecting the behavior of later references.

When a method reference corresponds to a Java method that returns a value, the template processing proceeds in a manner similar to that employed for variable reference processing. After the Java method is executed, Velocity stringifies the return value by invoking that object's toString() method. Should the return value be a primitive type rather than a Java Object, Velocity first converts the value to the appropriate Java wrapper type (e.g., int is converted to Integer, boolean is converted to Boolean, and so forth). In either case, the resulting string replaces the method reference in the final template output.

In order to get a better feel for how Velocity's method references are used, let's put them to work in a simple example. Listing 7.6 provides a Java class representing some basic automobile specifications. The specifications include make, model, color, and year. Methods are provided for defining the value of each of these specifications. Additionally, a method is provided for displaying the defined values.

```
public class Auto
{
  public void defineType( String make, String model )
  {
    this.make  = make;
    this.model = model;
  }

  public void defineColor( String color )
  {
    this.color = color;
  }

  public void defineYear( Integer year )
  {
    this.year = year;
  }

  public String printSpecs()
  {
    return (color + " " + year + " " + make + " " + model);
  }

  private String make;
  private String model;
  private String color;
  private Integer year;
}
```

Listing 7.6 An automobile specification class.

The code necessary for populating a context with an instance of our Auto class looks like this:

```
context.put( "car", new Auto() );
```

The instance of Auto might then be accessed and manipulated by the template shown in Listing 7.7. This template uses Velocity method references to define the automobile specifications by way of the object's defineType(), defineColor(), and defineYear() methods. Then, the object's printSpecs() method is invoked, again by way of a method reference, in order to obtain a string containing the defined automobile specifications. The string is added to the template output, as seen in Listing 7.8.

```
## Define the make model of the automobile
Defining automobile type...$car.defineType( "Chevrolet", "Cavalier")

## Define the color of the automobile
Defining automobile color...$car.defineColor( "Blue" )

## Define the year of the automobile
Defining automobile year...$car.defineYear( 1997 )

## Display the automobile specifications
$car.printSpecs()
```

Listing 7.7 The automobile specification template.

```
Defining automobile type...

Defining automobile color...

Defining automobile year...

Blue 1997 Chevrolet Cavalier
```

Listing 7.8 Results from processing the automobile specifications template.

One important aspect of Velocity method references that we have so far deftly sidestepped is that of parameter type. Any value inserted into, or extracted from, a Velocity template is handled as if it were a string. As we mentioned previously, any non-string value inserted into a template, via a variable reference or method reference return value, is implicitly stringified using the corresponding object's toString() method. However, things are not quite so straightforward when it comes to extracting values from the template—as happens when Velocity processes the arguments provided by method references.

Being only a template language, as opposed to a high-level programming language, the Velocity template syntax does not provide a sophisticated typing mechanism. As such, the Velocity template engine expects all method reference parameters to be strings. String values are specified explicitly in templates by quoting the string value with either single quotes (e.g., ‘stringValue’) or double quotes (e.g., “stringValue”). Velocity also supports implicit string specification for the case of integer values in the range supported by Java's Integer type; it is not necessary to quote such values. This support does not extend either to integer types outside the range of Integer (e.g., long) or to other numeric types (e.g., float, double); proper handling of such parameter values requires methods on the Java side that accept String values and provide their own user-defined type conversions. Enhanced support for numeric types is likely to find its way into future versions of Velocity.

Properties

Velocity property references are essentially an extension to Velocity method references that address a particular class of methods. Using introspection, Velocity offers an alternate interface for public Java methods that have names starting with either set or get. This alternate interface allows the template to access such methods as if they were instead ordinary object properties, resulting in template code that is cleaner and more readable. Where a Velocity method reference might require that a template designer access a piece of data using something like $obj.getValue(), a property reference allows the same piece of data to be accessed with $obj.Value.

The functionality of the Velocity property mechanism goes a bit further than that implied by our brief example. In addition to providing an alternate interface, it does so in a case-insensitive manner. Upon encountering $obj.Value in a template, Velocity would first look for a method named getValue() and, if that were not found, it would look for a method named getvalue(). In other words, the property reference would initially be treated in a manner equivalent to that of the method reference $obj.getValue(). If Velocity were unable to match the reference to an appropriate Java method, it would next consider the property reference as equivalent to the method reference $obj.getvalue() and once again try to find a corresponding Java method. Likewise, the property reference $obj.value would first be treated as equivalent to $obj.getvalue() and then, if necessary, $obj.getValue().

In addition to eliminating issues of case, the property mechanism supports the alternate interface for objects implementing get() methods, such as those specified by the following prototypes:

```
Object get( Object key );
String get( String key );
```

The first prototype is identical to that specified by Java's Map class, correctly indicating that Velocity's property references are applicable to objects of any class that implements the Map interface, assuming those objects do in fact key their entries with strings. The second prototype likely provides what is a more appropriate prototype for a user-defined implementation, given that everything taken from the template and returned to the template is either explicitly or implicitly handled as a string.

As we did for Velocity's variable and method references, we now present a simple example demonstrating the use of property references. We again use the Auto class introduced in the last section; however, the printSpecs() method is now replaced with three new methods, each of which returns one piece of what printSpecs() previously provided. The new methods are named getType(), getColor(), and getYear(), and they return the automobile make and model, color, and year, respectively. The getYear() method returns an object of type Integer, which as previously discussed is implicitly converted to a string by way of its toString() method.

```
public class Auto
{
  public void defineType( String make, String model )
  {
    this.make  = make;
    this.model = model;
  }

  public void defineColor( String color )
  {
    this.color = color;
  }

  public void defineYear( Integer year )
  {
    this.year = year;
  }

  public String getType()
  {
    return (make + " " + model);
  }

  public String getColor()
  {
    return (color);
  }

  public Integer getYear()
  {
    return (year);
  }
```

Listing 7.9 Our revised Auto class with support for the property reference interface. (continues)

```
    private String make;
    private String model;
    private String color;
    private Integer year;
}
```

Listing 7.9 Our revised Auto class with support for the property reference interface. (continued)

The template implemented for our property reference example is shown in Listing 7.10. The first half of the template, in which the values for the automobile specifications are defined, is identical to that used for the method reference example (Listing 7.7). The latter half of the template demonstrates three techniques for accessing the Auto object's properties. With the first, the property names begin with uppercase letters, matching the case used for the corresponding Java methods. With the second, the property names begin with lowercase letters. With the last, the property values are obtained through the equivalent method references. As shown in Listing 7.11, the output is the same regardless of the technique used. Velocity's property references simply provide an alternate interface to the template designer; behind the scenes, the same Java methods are invoked in the same manner.

```
## Define the make and model of the automobile
Defining automobile type...$car.defineType( "Chevrolet", "Cavalier")

## Define the color of the automobile
Defining automobile color...$car.defineColor( "Blue" )

## Define the year of the automobile
Defining automobile year...$car.defineYear( 1997 )

## Display the automobile specifications (upper case properties)
$car.Color $car.Year $car.Type

## Display the automobile specifications (lower case properties)
$car.color $car.year $car.type

## Display the automobile specifications (method references)
$car.getColor() $car.getYear() $car.getType()
```

Listing 7.10 A template demonstrating the use of property references.

```
Defining automobile type...

Defining automobile color...

Defining automobile year...

Blue 1997 Chevrolet Cavalier

Blue 1997 Chevrolet Cavalier

Blue 1997 Chevrolet Cavalier
```

Listing 7.11 Results from processing the automobile specification template.

Instead of providing separate property access methods, suppose our Auto class implemented a key-based approach to property access. If implemented in a manner similar to that shown in Listing 7.12, Velocity's introspection would provide continued support for the property references defined in the previous example. In processing an occurrence of $car.Type, Velocity would check for a Java method capable of handling a call to get("Type"). Such a method, if found, would be invoked only if Velocity's introspection failed to find both getType() and gettype(). The same resolution would be carried out for $car.Color and $car.Year. Given that the string comparisons in our get() implementation are carried out with equalsIgnoreCase(), the property references $car.type, $car.color, and $car.year would also remain valid.

```
public String get( String item )
{
  if ( item.equalsIgnoreCase( "type" ) )
  {
    return (make + " " + model);
  }
  else
  if ( item.equalsIgnoreCase( "color" ) )
  {
    return (color);
  }
  else
  if ( item.equalsIgnoreCase( "year" ) )
  {
    return (year.toString());
  }
  else
  {
    return ("");
  }
}
```

Listing 7.12 A key-based implementation of property access for the Auto class.

Formal Reference Notation

So far in our examples and discussion, we have limited ourselves to the use of Velocity's shorthand, or informal, reference notation. Velocity also provides a formal notation, which some people argue improves template readability. Regardless of your preference, it is important to understand the formal notation, because it is sometimes required in order to avoid ambiguity in your templates. For example, suppose you have a need to produce a series of URLs of the form http://www.my.site/pageN.html, where the *N* in pageN.html corresponds to a page number that is to be generated dynamically (e.g., page2.html, page99.html). An attempt to provide the page number through a Velocity variable reference, using the shorthand notation, would result in template code similar to http://www.my.site/page$number.html. This template code is problematic in that $number.html looks just like a Velocity property reference for an html property associated with the $number object. Having no way to determine your intent, Velocity just assumes a reference. If a reference is incorrectly assumed, chance are that the reference either will fail to resolve or will resolve to an unintended property. In either case, the final result is likely to be undesirable output.

If we instead use a Velocity method reference to generate the page numbers for our URLs, we run into a similar problem. The template code now looks something like http://www.my.site/page$number.getNext().html. From Velocity's perspective, this is a request for the html property associated with the object returned by the $number.getNext() method reference. Again, this almost certainly results in undesirable output. If a Velocity property reference is used in place of the method reference, the template code becomes http://www.my.site /page$number.next.html. Since $number.next is equivalent to $number.getNext(), the template processing would fail in the same manner as that described for the method reference.

The easiest way to avoid the template-processing issues associated with the ambiguity introduced by Velocity's shorthand notation is to apply Velocity's formal reference notation. The formal notation clearly delimits the reference, providing Velocity with sufficient information to determine your intent in cases where it might otherwise be ambiguous. The reference is delimited with curly braces ({}) and the $ prefix remains outside the braces. Otherwise, the reference syntax remains the same. The URL template code we have been discussing in this section may be rewritten using formal notation as follows:

```
http://www.my.site/page${number}.html
http://www.my.site/page${number.getNext()}.html
http://www.my.site/page${number.next}.html
```

Quiet Notation

We mentioned earlier in this chapter that Velocity references may be prefixed with a $!, in addition to the standard $ prefix that we have so far adhered to in our examples. The $! provides what Velocity refers to as *quiet notation*. Quiet notation affects the manner in which the template engine processes references that it is unable to resolve. In most cases, Velocity treats a standard reference—one prefixed with $—as static content if it is unable to locate an appropriate object or method through the provided context. This is illustrated by the first three lines of text in Listing 7.14, which is the result of processing the template in Listing 7.13 using an empty context. In contrast, the final three lines of text in Listing 7.14, which correspond to the template lines incorporating quiet notation, show no evidence of associated references. Velocity's quiet notation in effect replaces unresolved references with empty strings (i.e., "") where they would otherwise be treated as ordinary static content.

```
## Standard variable reference notation
This variable reference is loud...$object.

## Standard method reference notation
This method reference is loud...$object.getValue().

## Standard property reference notation
This property reference is loud...$object.Value.

## Quiet variable reference notation
This variable reference is quiet...$!object.

## Quiet method reference notation
This method reference is quiet...$!object.getValue().

## Quiet property reference notation
This property reference is quiet...$!object.Value.
```

Listing 7.13 A template illustrating the use of both standard and quiet reference notation.

```
This variable reference is loud...$object.

This method reference is loud...$object.getValue().

This property reference is loud...$object.Value.
```

Listing 7.14 The template output demonstrating the difference between standard and quiet reference notation. (continues)

```
This variable reference is quiet....

This method reference is quiet....

This property reference is quiet....
```

Listing 7.14 The template output demonstrating the difference between standard and quiet reference notation. (continued)

Although our example used the shorthand reference notation, quiet notation is equally valid when combined with Velocity's formal reference notation. Implemented using formal reference notation, the template in Listing 7.13 would look like that shown in Listing 7.15. The output generated by the two templates is identical, assuming the absence of a valid context entry. The important thing to note when combining quiet and formal notation is that the ! character is placed outside the curly braces.

```
## Standard variable reference notation
This variable reference is loud...${object}.

## Standard method reference notation
This method reference is loud...${object.getValue()}.

## Standard property reference notation
This property reference is loud...${object.Value}.

## Quiet variable reference notation
This variable reference is quiet...$!{object}.

## Quiet method reference notation
This method reference is quiet...$!{object.getValue()}.

## Quiet property reference notation
This property reference is quiet...$!{object.Value}.
```

Listing 7.15 The template from Listing 7.13 implemented using formal reference notation.

Escaping References

While discussing quiet notation in the previous section, we demonstrated that template content that looks like a Velocity reference but does not resolve to a Context object or method is treated as static context where quiet notation is not employed. This behavior is often useful where the nature of a template requires static content that, by coincidence, looks like a Velocity reference. For example, many scripting languages prefix their variables with a $. If tasked to write code generation templates for such a language, knowing that the language's variables will typically be passed through as-is is likely to eliminate a significant amount of tedious work. However, note that this technique is not guaranteed to work. In some cases Velocity will force an entity prefixed with a $ to be treated as a reference, regardless of the contents of the context. An example is ${foo:bar}, which Velocity attempts to treat as a reference, resulting in a parse error since the colon is not allowed by the VTL Identifier syntax.

So how might a special case such as ${foo:bar} be handled? Or more generally, how do you explicitly prevent Velocity from interpreting as a reference something that looks like a reference? Typically, the simplest solution is to *escape* the reference. This is accomplished by inserting a backslash (\) before the reference's $ prefix.

To further illustrate the nature of the problem, consider the template shown in Listing 7.16. The first section of the template provides a brief description of naming for Velocity's variable reference. The static content includes $email and $name, which should appear as-is in the final output. If the context lacked objects corresponding to these reference-like strings, Velocity would produce the desired output, and all would be well. However, the second part of the template provides contact information, which is generated dynamically. As it turns out, the dynamic portion of the template also makes use of $name and $email, but in this case they are intended as true Velocity references rather than as static content.

```
## Description of names used for standard, shorthand variable
references
Velocity variable references are built upon the VTL identifiers
used to key the associated objects in the context. For example,
an object keyed with the string 'email' would be referenced from
the template with $email. Likewise, an object keyed with the
string 'name' would be referenced with $name.

## Contact information
For more on this topic, contact $name at $email.
```

Listing 7.16 A template that illustrates the need to escape references.

If the context contains objects keyed with name and email, then Velocity replaces all occurrences of $name and $email with the corresponding object values. If on the other hand the context does not contain objects keyed with either name or email, then Velocity doesn't replace any of the occurrences of $name and $email. Clearly, neither action provides the desired result. The solution is to escape the occurrences of $name and $email wherever Velocity should treat them as simple static content. This is illustrated in Listing 7.17. Assuming that the context included the string "John" keyed with "name" and doe@my.site keyed with "email", the processed template would produce the output shown in Listing 7.18.

```
## Description of names used for standard, shorthand variable references
Velocity variable references are built upon the VTL identifiers
used to key the associated objects in the context. For example,
an object keyed with the string 'email' would be referenced from
the template with \$email. Likewise, an object keyed with the
string 'name' would be referenced with \$name.

## Contact information
For more on this topic, contact $name at $email.
```

Listing 7.17 A template using escaped references.

```
Velocity variable references are built upon the VTL identifiers
used to key the associated objects in the context. For example,
an object keyed with the string 'email' would be referenced from
the template with $email. Likewise, an object keyed with the
string 'name' would be referenced with $name.

For more on this topic, contact John at doe@my.site.
```

Listing 7.18 Output produced by the template in Listing 7.17.

The fact that a backslash serves to escape a Velocity reference raises the question of what to do when you actually want a literal backslash to precede a reference. In other words, how do you escape an escape? The answer is to add yet more backslashes. The number of backslashes required depends both on how many literal backslashes are required and whether the reference itself is to be escaped. Velocity processes the backslashes from left to right, with each pair of backslashes being reduced to a single backslash. If after processing the leading backslashes, one pair at a time, a single backslash remains, the reference is escaped; otherwise, the reference is processed as usual. That is, an odd number of backslashes results in the reference being escaped, while an even number results in the reference being replaced by the value of its underlying Context object. Illustrating this behavior, Listing 7.19 provides a template that prefixes a given reference with varying numbers of backslashes, and Listing 7.20 shows the final output generated by this template.

```
## Escaping a reference for which a corresponding context object exists
$object.getValue()
\$object.getValue()
\\$object.getValue()
\\\$object.getValue()
\\\\$object.getValue()
\\\\\$object.getValue()
\\\\\\$object.getValue()
```

Listing 7.19 A template showing the use of varying numbers of backslash reference escapes.

```
formal
$object.getValue()
\formal
\$object.getValue()
\\formal
\\$object.getValue()
\\\formal
```

Listing 7.20 Output produced by the template in Listing 7.19.

Should your template make use of a reference that is not guaranteed to have a corresponding Context object—or something that just looks like a reference but is intended as a literal—you need to be aware that Velocity complicates matters with regard to leading backslashes. The current behavior of 1.3.1 depends on whether there are an even or odd number of backslashes. When the number of backslashes is even, all of the backslashes are treated as literals, with nothing escaped. In contrast, when the number of backslashes is odd, each pair starting from the left is treated as an escaped backslash, resulting in one backslash in the output. The final backslash is treated as a literal. This is illustrated in Listings 7.21 and 7.22.

```
## Escaping a reference for which no corresponding context object exists
$noobject.getValue()
\$noobject.getValue()
\\$noobject.getValue()
\\\$noobject.getValue()
\\\\$noobject.getValue()
\\\\\$noobject.getValue()
\\\\\\$noobject.getValue()
```

Listing 7.21 A template showing the use of varying numbers of backslashes preceding references with no associated Context objects.

```
$noobject.getValue()
\$noobject.getValue()
\\$noobject.getValue()
\\$noobject.getValue()
\\\\$noobject.getValue()
\\\$noobject.getValue()
\\\\\\$noobject.getValue()
```

Listing 7.22 Output produced by the template in Listing 7.21.

What's Next

In this chapter, we provided an in-depth treatment of Velocity references, including variable, method, and property references. We also examined Velocity's formal and quiet notations and reference escaping. At this point, you should have most of the information that you need in order to work with Velocity references. In the next chapter, we build on our knowledge of references and extend the power and functionality of templates by introducing directives. Velocity's directives take template design to the next level, allowing the template designer access to a minimal set of constructs similar to those found in many programming languages.

CHAPTER 8

Using Directives

In the previous chapter, we nailed down the role of references in Velocity templates. In addition to discussing the ability to obtain values directly through variable and property references, we also covered method references, which allow template designers to manipulate and access data through custom Java methods that operate on referenced Context objects. Method references provide a great deal of power and a range of functionality limited only by the Java language itself and what it is capable of returning in the form of a string. Although this functionality is likely sufficient to support anything that might reasonably be expected in terms of template processing, Velocity takes its template language a step further and provides shortcuts for many common tasks. This is where Velocity directives come into play.

Directives provide support for controlling template processing flow, insertion and manipulation of context values, inclusion of parsed and unparsed text, and template code reuse through macros. As with references, Velocity directives are identified by a special prefix character that causes the subsequent text to be interpreted in a special manner. In the case of directives, the prefix character is the pound sign (#). Velocity currently supports a total of 10 directives, some of which are meaningful only when used in combination with others. In this chapter, we cover each of the Velocity directives.

#stop

The first directive that we present, #stop, is intended primarily for debugging. When the template engine encounters this directive, it terminates execution and returns control to the calling program. More specifically, the process of merging context and template terminates at the point of the #stop directive. This process corresponds to the call to stopTemplate's merge method in Listing 8.1. With the exception of some changes in naming and a couple of additional print statements, the driver code in Listing 8.1 is identical to that used in the previous chapter. Also as in the previous chapter, you should assume that the code, except where noted, is used with only trivial modifications for all other examples in this chapter.

```
import java.io.StringWriter;

import org.apache.velocity.Template;
import org.apache.velocity.VelocityContext;
import org.apache.velocity.app.Velocity;
import org.apache.velocity.exception.*;

public class Stop
{
  public static void main( String[] args )
  {
    // Initialize template engine
    try
    {
      Velocity.init();
    }
    catch( Exception x )
    {
      System.err.println( "Failed to initialize Velocity: " + x );
      System.exit( 1 );
    }

    // Obtain a template
    Template stopTemplate = null;

    try
    {
      stopTemplate = Velocity.getTemplate( "Stop.vm" );
    }
    catch( ResourceNotFoundException rnfX )
    {
      System.err.println( "Template not found: " + rnfX );
      System.exit( 1 );
    }
    catch( ParseErrorException peX )
    {
      System.err.println( "Failed to parse template: " + peX );
      System.exit( 1 );
```

Listing 8.1 The driver program used for the #stop directive example. (continues)

```
    }
    catch( Exception x )
    {
      System.err.println( "Failed to initialize template: " + x );
      System.exit( 1 );
    }

    // Create context
    VelocityContext context = new VelocityContext();

    // Populate context
    context.put( "before", "before the stop directive" );
    context.put( "after", "after the stop directive" );

    // Merge template and context
    StringWriter writer = new StringWriter();

    try
    {
      System.out.println( "***** Starting merge *****" );
      stopTemplate.merge( context, writer );
      System.out.println( "***** Returning from merge  *****" );
    }
    catch( ResourceNotFoundException rnfX )
    {
      System.err.println( "Template not found on merge: " + rnfX );
      System.exit( 1 );
    }
    catch( ParseErrorException peX )
    {
      System.err.println( "Failed to parse template on merge: " +
peX );
      System.exit( 1 );
    }
    catch( MethodInvocationException miX )
    {
      System.err.println( "Application method exception: " + miX );
      System.exit( 1 );
    }
    catch( Exception x )
    {
      System.err.println( "Failed to merge template: " + x );
      System.exit( 1 );
    }

    // Render merged content
    System.out.println( writer.toString() );
  }
}
```

Listing 8.1 The driver program used for the #stop directive example. (continued)

Applying the code shown in Listing 8.1 to the template shown in Listing 8.2 demonstrates the effect of Velocity's #stop directive. This is illustrated in Listing 8.3, where you can see from the program's output that the #stop directive caused the call to merge to return before the template was fully processed. Template content prior to the #stop directive was processed normally, including proper reference handling, while template content subsequent to the #stop directive was not processed at all. The program's non-template related output (i.e., the messages noting the start and stop of the merge) demonstrates that #stop does not introduce any sort of error condition, but instead simply causes the merge process to terminate early and the associated method to return normally.

```
## Start processing
=== Start of template ===

The portion of the template preceding the stop directive is
processed normally.

This is $before.

## Stop processing
#stop

The portion of the template following the stop directive is
not processed.

This is $after.
```

Listing 8.2 A template using the #stop directive.

```
***** Starting merge *****
***** Returning from merge  *****
=== Start of template ===

The portion of the template preceding the stop directive is
processed normally.

This is before the stop directive.
```

Listing 8.3 Results from processing the template in Listing 8.2.

#include

The #include directive performs precisely the task that its name implies. It allows the template designer to include content external to the template file.

More specifically, it allows for the inclusion of static content from one or more external sources. The content is included at the point where the #include directive occurs, effectively replacing the directive in the output. As an example, consider the template shown in Listing 8.4. Except for the three daily specials, the template consists of only static content. Supposing that the specials are likely to change daily based only on the whim of the chef, we plan for the specials to be recorded in simple text files and implement #include directives to retrieve the contents of those files. If the files were defined as shown in Listing 8.5, the output resulting from the processed template would look like that shown in Listing 8.6.

```
## Generic welcome
Welcome to Gem's Bar and Grill!

We are conveniently located at the corner of 5th and Ives
in beautiful lower downtown.

Our three specials of the day are as follows:
## Present today's specials
#include( "special-1.txt" )
#include( "special-2.txt" )
#include( "special-3.txt" )

## Generic info
We are open from 4:00 P.M. to 2:00 A.M. daily.

Call 555-1234 for more information.
```

Listing 8.4 A template using #include directives.

```
special-1.txt:  Quesadilla Pie — $7.95

special-2.txt:  Gem's Famous Cheeseburger — $5.95

special-3.txt:  Soup and Salad — $4.95
```

Listing 8.5 File definitions used for the #include examples.

```
Welcome to Gem's Bar and Grill!

We are conveniently located at the corner of 5th and Ives
in beautiful lower downtown.
```

Listing 8.6 Results from processing the template in Listing 8.4. (continues)

```
Our three specials of the day are as follows:
  Quesadilla Pie – $7.95
  Gem's Famous Cheeseburger – $5.95
  Soup and Salad – $4.95

We are open from 4:00 P.M. to 2:00 A.M. daily.

Call 555-1234 for more information.
```

Listing 8.6 Results from processing the template in Listing 8.4. (continued)

While there is not much more to be said about the services provided by Velocity's #include directive, the directive's syntax warrants further discussion. In our daily special example, each include directive specifies a single file by way of a string literal representation of the corresponding file's name. The #include directive allows you to expand on this approach in two ways. First, you can use a Velocity reference in place of a string literal to specify the file you want to include. If for example the context was populated using the code shown in Listing 8.7, the template in Listing 8.4 could be rewritten as shown in Listing 8.8 without any change in the output generated during template processing.

```
// Populate context with file names used by #include
context.put( "special-1", "special-1.txt" );
context.put( "special-2", "special-2.txt" );
context.put( "special-3", "special-3.txt" );
```

Listing 8.7 Java code that populates the context with filenames used by the #include directive.

```
## Generic welcome
Welcome to Gem's Bar and Grill!

We are conveniently located at the corner of 5th and Ives
in beautiful lower downtown.

Our three specials of the day are as follows:
## Present today's specials
#include( $special-1 )
#include( $special-2 )
#include( $special-3 )

## Generic info
We are open from 4:00 P.M. to 2:00 A.M. daily.

Call 555-1234 for more information.
```

Listing 8.8 A template demonstrating the use of Velocity references with the #include directive.

The second manner in which the #include directive allows you to extend the syntax demonstrated in our first example involves the number of files provided to the directive. Instead of repeating the directive for each included file, whether using a string literal or a reference, you can specify multiple files with a single #include directive. The three #include directives in each of Listings 8.4 and 8.8 could, respectively, be rewritten equivalently as follows:

```
#include( "special-1.txt" "special-2.txt" "special-3.txt" )
#include( $special-1 $special-2 $special-3 )
```

We have so far neglected one important piece of information regarding the use of Velocity's #include directive, namely the manner in which it finds the specified files. Although the name of the file is provided to the directive directly, no mention is made of the file's location relative to the overall directory structure. Velocity handles this ambiguity by assuming that all filenames are specified relative to a template root, which by default is the directory from which the application is being run. This default template root location may be overridden through Velocity's runtime configuration properties, as we discuss in Chapter 10, "Taking Control of Velocity."

#parse

Velocity's #parse directive is quite similar to its #include directive in that both provide for the inclusion of content taken from an external file located in the template root. The primary distinguishing feature between the two directives is that while #include treats its content as static, #parse treats its content as yet another template to be processed relative to the current context. In other words, the #parse directive allows you to nest templates within templates. To get a feel for how the #parse directive might be used, let's consider an enhancement to the daily special example presented in the previous section. Suppose that management wants all of the prices to be pulled from the store's database rather than being hardcoded into the included files.

The first step is to modify the context population code so that the current prices are obtained and inserted into the context. This is shown in Listing 8.9, where the variables qPiePrice, cBurgerPrice, and sSaladPrice represent prices obtained from the store's database; each value is keyed by a string that matches the respective variable name.

```
// Populate context
context.put( "qPiePrice", qPiePrice );
context.put( "cBurgerPrice", cBurgerPrice );
context.put( "sSaladPrice", sSaladPrice );
```

Listing 8.9 Our modified application code that inserts the daily special prices into the context.

Next, we create new files representing the daily specials. These files are really just modifications of those defined in Listing 8.5. The new files have been renamed to reflect that they now contain template content, and the prices have been replaced with Velocity variable references. The resulting files are defined in Listing 8.10.

```
special-1.vm:  Quesadilla Pie – $qPiePrice

special-2.vm:  Gem's Famous Cheeseburger – $cBurgerPrice

special-3.vm:  Soup and Salad – $sSaladPrice
```

Listing 8.10 Files definitions used for #parse examples.

Finally, we update the template shown in Listing 8.4, replacing the #include directives with #parse directives and changing the filenames as appropriate. The new template is shown in Listing 8.11, and the resulting output is identical to that shown in Listing 8.6.

```
## Generic welcome
Welcome to Gem's Bar and Grill!

We are conveniently located at the corner of 5th and Ives
in beautiful lower downtown.

Our three specials of the day are as follows:
## Present today's specials
#parse( "special-1.vm" )
#parse( "special-2.vm" )
#parse( "special-3.vm" )

## Generic info
We are open from 4:00 P.M. to 2:00 A.M. daily.

Call 555-1234 for more information.
```

Listing 8.11 A template using #parse directives.

As with the #include directive, filenames may be provided via Velocity references. However, unlike the #include directive, the #parse directive does not support multiple arguments. So while we might legitimately replace the #parse lines in Listing 8.11 with something like

```
#parse( $special-1 )
#parse( $special-2 )
#parse( $special-3 )
```

using a single #parse such as

```
#parse( $special-1 $special-2 $special-3 )
```

would not generate the desired results.

The #parse directive also differs from the #include directive in terms of nesting and recursion, neither of which makes sense in the context of an #include. *Nesting* refers to placing a #parse directive inside a file that is itself included by way of a #parse directive. *Recursion* refers to a special case of nesting in which a #parse directive references its own file. By default,Velocity limits the #parse directive to at most 10 levels of nesting; however, this default may be overridden through Velocity's runtime configuration properties, as you'll learn in Chapter 10.

As an example of #parse nesting and recursion, consider the following template, which is named Myself.vm:

```
Before parse directive.
#parse( "Myself.vm" )
After parse directive.
```

Assuming that the maximum parse depth is overridden and set to a value of 3, this template would generate the following output:

```
Before parse directive.
Before parse directive.
Before parse directive.
After parse directive.
After parse directive.
After parse directive.
```

Each time the file is processed, the first line is output and then #parse causes the template engine to in effect start processing a new copy of the file. This repeats until the last #parse directive is processed or the maximum parse depth is reached; it is always the latter in the case of recursion. Then, as the template engine returns from each #parse directive, it resumes processing where it left off, generating the last line in our simple template.

#set

Unlike Velocity's other directives, which act upon a template directly, the #set directive affects the context associated with a template. You can use the #set directive either to update an existing context entry or to create a new entry. The entries, whether new or updated, are immediately available to the template; however, they become available to the underlying application only after the template and context are merged. To illustrate the fundamentals of the #set directive, let's dive right into a simple example. Assume that we have an existing context entry that holds the string value "oldValue" keyed with the string "existing". Suppose that, from a template, we want to change the value of this entry from "oldValue" to "newValue" and add a new context entry with a key of "new" and a value of "newEntry". The template in Listing 8.12 satisfies these requirements, as you can see in the resulting output (Listing 8.13).

```
## Before set directives
The initial value keyed by "existing" is $existing.
The initial value keyed by "new" is $!new.

#set( $existing = "newValue" )
#set( $new = "newEntry" )

## After set directives
The final value keyed by "existing" is $existing.
The final value keyed by "new" is $!new.
```

Listing 8.12 A template that uses the #set directive to update one entry and add another.

```
The initial value keyed by "existing" is oldValue.
The initial value keyed by "new" is .


The final value keyed by "existing" is newValue.
The final value keyed by "new" is newEntry.
```

Listing 8.13 Results from processing the template in Listing 8.12.

Note that while the template seemingly has immediate access to the updated and new values, this is not the case for the underlying application. In reality, all template-initiated changes to the context occur during the merge phase. Since during the merge context changes are carried out in the same order as they are encountered in the template, references in the template receive the appropriately updated values. However, the underlying application doesn't know anything about these changes until after the fact. Consider, for example, the Java code shown in Listing 8.14. This code prints the values of the "existing" and "new" context entries before and after the call to merge. When the underlying application is run, this code generates the following output:

```
Before merge: oldValue/null
After merge: newValue/newEntry
```

```
System.out.println( "Before merge: " + context.get( "existing" )
                 + "/" + context.get( "new" ) );

setTemplate.merge( context, writer );

System.out.println( "After merge: " + context.get( "existing" )
                 + "/" + context.get( "new" ) );
```

Listing 8.14 Code querying the context before and after the merge of a template using #set directives.

In introducing the #set directive in the previous example, we limited ourselves to its simplest usage, namely that of assigning a string literal to a variable reference. While all forms of the #set directive adhere to the general #set(reference = value) syntax introduced in the first example, the diversity of the reference and value types allowed by the #set directive greatly enhances its power and usefulness. Starting with the left-hand side of the equal sign, the reference provided to the #set directive can be either a variable reference or a property reference. We have already seen an example #set with a variable reference, so let's take a look at one using a property reference.

As we discussed in Chapter 7, property references are tied to introspection. In that chapter, we provided examples where introspection uncovered get methods that allowed object property values to be read through property references. In a similar manner, Velocity also allows the use of property references for modification of object property values through set methods of the form setValue(value). As an example, consider the SetObj class in Listing 8.15, which provides setValue() and getValue() methods for access to its value property. Assuming an instance of this class is stored in the context with the key setObj, the property reference setObj.value can be combined with the #set directive to update the value property. The template code would look like this:

```
#set( $setObj.value = "some value" )
```

```
public class SetObj
{
  public void setValue( String value )
  {
    this.value = value;
  }

  public String getValue()
  {
    return (value);
  }

  private String value;
}
```

Listing 8.15 A simple class providing a set and get method for access to its single property.

Moving on to the right side of the #set directive's equal sign, we find that the value may be provided using a variety of types and operations. The types include string literals, integer literals, references, range operators, array lists, and Boolean values. Note that the #set directive does not allow you to assign a null, regardless of value type; if an attempt is made to assign from something that returns a null (e.g., a method reference), the value of the reference on the left-hand side remains unchanged. The operations supported by the #set directive include simple arithmetic and Boolean evaluation. We have already seen examples involving string literal values, so let's start with references.

The #set directive supports values of all three types of Velocity references: variable, property, and method. This is demonstrated in the template shown in Listing 8.16, where it is assumed that the context contains two instances of the SetObj class from Listing 8.15. The template starts out by creating a variable reference holding the value "A value". It then uses this variable reference to set the value property associated with the setObjA context object. The setObjA context object is then used to set the value property of the setObjB context object, first with a property reference and then with a method reference. At each step, the template outputs the value "A value".

```
## Create a variable reference
#set( $varRef = "A value"" )
```

Listing 8.16 A template demonstrating the use of variable, property, and method references as values for the #set directive. (continues)

```
## Use a variable reference as the value
#set( $setObjA.value = $varRef )
$setObjA.value

## Use a property reference to set the value
#set( $setObjB.value = $setObjA.value )
$setObjB.value

## Use a method reference to set the value
#set( $setObjB.value = $setObjA.getValue() )
$setObjB.value
```

Listing 8.16 A template demonstrating the use of variable, property, and method references as values for the #set directive. (continued)

Separately, we have looked at the use of string literals and references within the #set directive, but what if you would like to combine the two in a single directive? This is not a problem. Simply include the reference inside the double quotes ("") enclosing the string literal. Velocity will automatically interpolate the contents of a double-quoted value; the string literal portion will be passed on as is and the reference will be processed in the usual manner. If on the other hand you need to include a string literal that only looks like a reference, use single quotes ('') to enclose the value. Velocity will interpret the single quotes as a request to skip interpolation of the value.

Next, let's consider #set directive values built from range operators and array lists. The range operator takes the form [*m*..*n*], where *m* and *n* are either literal integers or references that correspond to integer values. Like the range operator, an array list is defined with square brackets; however, its contents are comma-delimited and allowed to take on values of any type supported by the #set directive, including ranges and even other array lists. A template implementing both range and array lists is shown in Listing 8.17, and its corresponding output appears in Listing 8.18.

This template first uses the #set directive to create a range using integer literals and then creates a second range using variable references holding integer values. It then proceeds to use the #set directive to create an array list using a string literal, an integer literal, a range, a Boolean value, and variable reference. At various points in the template, the newly created references are queried for information regarding their content and properties. The referenced objects behave as instances of Java's ArrayList class, and thus we adhere to the ArrayList interface when working with the new range and list references.

```
## Set range with literals
#set( $range1 = [0..9] )

#set( $m = 1 )
#set( $n = 10 )

## Set range with references
#set( $range2 = [$m..$n] )

## Use ArrayList interface to access first and last
First value of range2: $range2.get( 0 )
Last value of range2 : $range2.get( 9 )

## Build list with a string literal, numeric literal,
## boolean value, and variable reference
#set( $list = ["string", 2, [2..-5], false, $m] )

## Use ArrayList interface to access index of some value
Index of $m     : $list.indexOf( 1 )
Index of false : $list.indexOf( false )
Index of 2      : $list.indexOf( 2 )
Index of string: $list.indexOf( "string" )

## Get the size and fourth element of the nested range
Size of nested range: $list.get( 2 ).size()
Fourth element of nested range: $list.get( 2 ).get( 3 )
```

Listing 8.17 A template that uses range operators and array lists with the #set directive.

```
First value of range2: 1
Last value of range2 : 10


Index of 1     : 4
Index of false : 3
Index of 2      : 1
Index of string: 0

Size of nested range: 8
Fourth element of nested range: -1
```

Listing 8.18 Results from processing the template in Listing 8.17.

Next on the list of supported #set directive value types is the Boolean type. As you might expect, the acceptable values are limited to true and false. If the values were all that Velocity provided, the type wouldn't buy much for the template designer since it is easy enough to store a Boolean value with a string or number. However, Velocity also provides support for the Boolean operations AND, OR, and NOT. As with many programming languages, Velocity uses short-circuit evaluation for its Boolean operations, meaning that it evaluates only as much of an expression as is necessary to determine the result. For example, if the first element a Boolean AND is false, then there is no need to evaluate further since the result of the AND must be false. Likewise, a Boolean OR where the first element is true must evaluate to true, so there is no need to consider the second element.

In Velocity templates, the Boolean AND, OR, and NOT operations are represented by the symbols &&, ||, and !, respectively, and Boolean values are represented by the literals true and false. Parentheses are allowed in Boolean expressions for the purpose of grouping, and references representing Boolean values are allowed anywhere that a Boolean literal is allowed. We've shown a template demonstrating various Boolean operations in Listing 8.19 and the corresponding output in Listing 8.20.

```
## Initialize some references with boolean values
#set( $bValA = true )
#set( $bValB = false )
#set( $bValC = false )

## Perform some boolean operations
#set( $taf = $bValA && $bValB )
true AND false = $taf

#set( $tanf = $bValA && !$bValB )
true AND NOT false = $tanf

#set( $tof = $bValA || $bValC )
true OR false = $tof

#set( $ntof = !$bValA || $bValC )
NOT true OR false = $ntof

#set( $paoa = ($bValA && $bValB) || (!$bValC && !$bValB) )
(true AND false) OR (NOT false AND NOT false) = $paoa
```

Listing 8.19 A template demonstrating the use of Boolean values and operations in #set directives.

```
true AND false = false

true AND NOT false = true

true OR false = true

NOT true OR false = false

(true AND false) OR (NOT false AND NOT false) = true
```

Listing 8.20 Results from processing the template in Listing 8.19.

Finally we come to the last value type supported by Velocity's #set directive: integer literals. The range of integers supported is the same as that represented by Java's Integer class, which includes –2147483648 through 2147483647. Values outside this range result in integer overflow. Only standard base-10 integer notation is allowed for integer values; attempts to provide values making use of decimal points, scientific notation, or other bases result in template parse errors.

In addition to allowing the template designer to store integer values, the #set directive provides for simple arithmetic operations. The operations include addition, subtraction, multiplication, integer division, and modulus. Velocity template code represents these operations with the symbols +, -, *, /, and %, respectively. Standard operator precedence applies, and parentheses are allowed for expressing precedence explicitly. References representing integer values that meet the criteria for Velocity's numeric literals may be used interchangeably with numeric literals in arithmetic expressions. The template in Listing 8.21 demonstrates the use of integer literals and integer operations with the #set directive, including cases of integer overflow. Listing 8.22 shows the output generated by this template.

```
## Set maximum and minimum Integer values
#set( $max = 2147483647 )
#set( $min = -2147483648 )

## Demonstrate overflow
#set( $maxo = $max + 1 )
$max + 1 = $maxo
#set( $mino = $min - 1 )
$min - 1 = $mino
```

Listing 8.21 A template demonstrating the use of integer literals and operations in #set directives. (continues)

```
## Addition
#set( $add = 1 + 1 )
1 + 1 = $add
## Subtraciton
#set( $sub = 1 - 2 )
1 - 2 = $sub
## Multiplication
#set( $mult = 2 * 2 )
2 * 2 = $mult
## Integer division
#set( $div = 10 / 6 )
10 / 6 = $div
## Modulus
#set( $mod = 10 % 6 )
10 % 6 = $mod
## Compound expression
#set( $comp = ((7 / 3) * 3) + (7 % 3) )
((7 / 3) * 3) + (7 % 3) = $comp
```

Listing 8.21 A template demonstrating the use of integer literals and operations in #set directives. (continued)

```
2147483647 + 1 = -2147483648
-2147483648 - 1 = 2147483647

1 + 1 = 2
1 - 2 = -1
2 * 2 = 4
10 / 6 = 1
10 % 6 = 4
((7 / 3) * 3) + (7 % 3) = 7
```

Listing 8.22 Results from processing the template in Listing 8.21.

#end

The #end directive is used to signal the end of a block of template code. It is meaningful only when combined with certain other Velocity directives, including #if, #foreach, and #macro. When the template engine encounters an #end directive, it considers the preceding #if, #foreach, or #macro directive to be complete. You'll see examples of the #end directive at work when we discuss those directives that rely on #end.

#if

As its name implies, Velocity's #if directive provides support for conditional template code processing. In its simplest incarnation, the #if directive begins a block of conditional template code and the #end directive terminates that block. If the associated condition evaluates to true, the block is processed and the results are inserted into the output. In contrast, if the condition evaluates to false, the block is ignored with regard to the output. A condition is considered to be true if it either evaluates to a Boolean value of true or is a reference that corresponds to a non-null value; otherwise, it evaluates to false. A template that demonstrates some simple uses of the #if directive is shown in Listing 8.23; the corresponding output appears in Listing 8.24.

```
## Trivial example with boolean literal
#if ( true )
  The condition literal is true!
#end

## Examples using boolean conditions
#set( $condition = true )
#if( $condition )
  The condition reference is true!
#end

#set( $condition = false )
#if( $condition )
  This test is never output! The condition reference is false.
#end

## Example using non-boolean condition
#set( $refValue = "A string" )
#if( $refValue )
  A string is true!
#end

## Example using non-existent (null) condition
#if ( $nullValue )
  This text is never output! Reference is null.
#end
```

Listing 8.23 A template demonstrating simple uses of the #if directive.

```
The condition literal is true!

The condition reference is true!


A string is true!
```

Listing 8.24 Results from processing the template in Listing 8.23.

In the previous example, we limited ourselves to conditions consisting of simple references and Boolean literals. However, the #if directive also supports expressions that evaluate to a Boolean value. Such expressions include those built upon Boolean and relational operators. We discussed the Boolean operators earlier; they include AND (&&), OR (||), and NOT (!). The relational operators include less-than, greater-than, less-than-equal, greater-than-equal, not-equal, and equal, represented in Velocity templates by <, >, <=, >=, !=, and ==, respectively. The relational operators operate only on integer literals and references corresponding to integer values that meet the criteria of Velocity's integer literals. As usual, you may use parentheses in expressions to explicitly state evaluation precedence. The template in Listing 8.25 demonstrates the use of Boolean, relational, and mixed expressions in #if directives.

```
## Example using boolean operators
#if ( ($bValA && !$bValB) || $bValB )
  Boolean expression evaluates to true.
#end

## Examples using relational operators
#if ( $iVal < 1 ) less-than #end
#if ( $iVal > 1 ) greater-than #end
#if ( $iVal <= 1 ) less-than-equal #end
#if ( $iVal >= 1 ) greater-than-equal #end
#if ( $iVal != 1 ) not-equal #end
#if ( $iVal == 1 ) equal #end

## Example mixing boolean and relational operators
#if ( ($iVal >= 1) && (!($iVal == 1) || $bValB) )
  The expression evaluates to true.
#end
```

Listing 8.25 A template demonstrating Boolean and relational expressions used for #if directive conditions.

While relational and Boolean operators provide the power to express quite complex conditions, such conditions often come at the expense of readability and maintainability. In many cases, the complexity of a condition can be more clearly and easily expressed by taking advantage of the fact that Velocity supports the nesting of #if directives. Consider, for example, the template in Listing 8.26. The first #if directive represents the conjunction of four individual conditions. While the compound condition is perfectly valid, understanding its overall meaning requires a bit of effort. Also, by the nature of its complexity, it is more susceptible to the introduction of errors during code maintenance. The second #if directive—or more accurately the nested block of #if directives—defines exactly the same overall condition, but it does so with four simplified conditions that are easier to both read and maintain. For any given set of values for $x, $y, $allow, and $sleeping, both approaches behave in the same manner.

```
## Single complex condition
#if ( ($x < 5) && ($y < 3 || $y >= 9) && $allow && !$sleeping )
  Take action
#end

## Complex condition rewritten as four simple nested conditions
#if ( $x < 5 )
  #if ( $y < 3 || $y >= 9 )
    #if ( $allow )
      #if ( !$sleeping )
        Take action
      #end
    #end
  #end
#end
```

Listing 8.26 A template demonstrating nested #if directives.

#else

The #else directive is valid only when used in conjunction with Velocity's #if directive. It serves a dual role, terminating one block of template code and initiating another. In its first role, it behaves in a manner similar to a simple #if directive's associated #end directive, providing the closing delimiter for the block of template code processed when the #if directive's condition evaluates to true. In its second role, it serves as the opening delimiter for a block of template code processed when the #if directive's condition evaluates to false. In short, the #else directive's purpose is to specify an alternate template code block for cases where an #if condition is not satisfied. The alternate block is terminated by an #end directive. The template in Listing 8.27 provides an example of the #else directive in action. Its output is shown in Listing 8.28.

```
## An if/else with a true condition
#set( $condition = true )

#if ( $condition )
  With a condition of $condition, we get the 'if' block.
#else
  With a condition of $condition, we get the 'else' block.
#end

## Try one with a false condition
#set( $condition = false )

#if ( $condition )
  With a condition of $condition, we get the 'if' block.
#else
  With a condition of $condition, we get the 'else' block.
#end
```

Listing 8.27 A template demonstrating the use of #else directives.

```
  With a condition of true, we get the 'if' block.


  With a condition of false, we get the 'else' block.
```

Listing 8.28 Results from processing the template in Listing 8.27.

#elseif

Not surprisingly, Velocity's #elseif directive serves as a combination of the #else and #if directives. Where the #else directive provides what amounts to an unconditional alternative to an #if directive's template code block, the #elseif directive allows for conditional alternatives. As with the #else directive, the #elseif directive serves two roles, namely a closing delimiter on a previous template code block and an opening delimiter for an alternate block. The alternate block is processed only if the condition associated with the #elseif directive evaluates to true. In the simplest cases, the #end directive is used to terminate the block associated with an #elseif directive. Listing 8.29 shows a template implemented with #elseif directives. This template is essentially the same as that shown in Listing 8.27, but the #else directives are replaced with #elseif directives specifying conditions that are the complement of the conditions of their associated #if directives. As illustrated by Listing 8.30, this template behaves in the same manner as that of Listing 8.27.

```
## An if/elseif with a true condition
#set( $condition = true )

#if ( $condition )
  With a condition of $condition, we get the 'if' block.
#elseif ( !$condition )
  With a condition of $condition, we get the 'elseif' block.
#end

## Try one with a false condition
#set( $condition = false )

#if ( $condition )
  With a condition of $condition, we get the 'if' block.
#elseif (!$condition )
  With a condition of $condition, we get the 'elseif' block.
#end
```

Listing 8.29 A template demonstrating the use of #elseif directives.

```
  With a condition of true, we get the 'if' block.


  With a condition of false, we get the 'elseif' block.
```

Listing 8.30 Results from processing the template in Listing 8.29.

While the template in Listing 8.29 clearly demonstrates the use of Velocity's #elseif directive, it doesn't necessarily show what advantages the directive provides over the simpler #else directive. The first advantage is that the condition associated with #elseif is not by definition tied to the condition of the corresponding #if. In contrast, the condition implicitly associated with the #else directive is by definition the complement of its corresponding #if's condition, assuming that there are no associated #elseif's. The second advantage is that multiple #elseif directives may be associated with a single #if directive. In this case, the conditions of the #elseif's are evaluated in order with the first that evaluates to true determining which alternate block of template code is processed. All other blocks associated with the overall #if construct are ignored.

When multiple #elseif directives occur in a single #if construct, each #elseif serves to terminate the code block of the previous #elseif, or the previous #if in the case of the first #elseif. If explicit conditions are to be associated with each alternative, then the end of the block of the last #elseif is delimited with an #end directive. If on the other hand an unconditional alternative is necessary for cases where all of the explicit conditions evaluate to false, then an #else directive may be used to delimit the block of the last #elseif and introduce the default alternative. As usual, the code block introduced by the #else directive is terminated with an #end directive. An example demonstrating multiple #elseif directives, with and without final #else directives, is shown in Listing 8.31.

```
#set( $isDawn = false )
#set( $isNoon = false )
#set( $isDusk = false )

## Multiple #elseif directives
#if ( $isDawn )
  The sun is rising.
#elseif ( $isNoon )
  The sun is overhead.
#elseif ( $isDusk )
  The sun is setting.
#end

## Multiple #elseif directives with closing #else directive
#if ( $isDawn )
  The sun is rising.
#elseif ( $isNoon )
  The sun is overhead.
#elseif ( $isDusk )
  The sun is setting.
#else
  What time is it?
#end
```

Listing 8.31 A template demonstrating the use of multiple #elseif directives, without and with a closing #else directive.

As with simple #if directives, nesting is allowed. In general, any #if construct, consisting of all the code from the initial #if to its matching #end—including any #elseif and #else directives—may be nested inside any other #if, #elseif, or #else directive code block. The template in Listing 8.32 demonstrates the nesting of #if constructs within #if, #elseif, and #else directives. The outer construct first checks to see whether $red is true. If not, it moves on to a test of $blue. If neither is true, it defaults to the block associated with its #else directive. The outer construct selected determines which inner construct is to be processed. For example, if it turned out that $red was true, the template engine would then process the first #if's inner block, evaluating $blue, and if necessary $yellow, in order to determine the template's output. All other inner constructs would be ignored. Similar processing would occur for the other outer-block alternatives, were they to be selected instead. Velocity does support multiple levels of nesting, though this is not shown in the listing.

```
#if ( $red )                      ## outer
  #if ( $blue )                     ## inner
    Purple
  #elseif ( $yellow )               ## inner
    Orange
  #else                             ## inner
    Red and What?
  #end                              ## inner
#elseif ( $blue )                 ##outer
  #if ( $yellow )                   ## inner
    Green
  #else                             ## inner
    Blue and What?
  #end                              ## inner
#else                             ## outer
  #if ( $yellow )                   ## inner
    We only mix yellow with red or blue
  #end                              ## inner
#end                              ## outer
```

Listing 8.32 A template demonstrating the use of nested #if, #elseif, and #else directives.

#foreach

Velocity's #foreach directive provides the template designer with the ability to process the same block of template code multiple times. More accurately, it provides the ability to iterate over a list of items, processing the associated block of code once for each item in the list. The #foreach directive itself begins the block, and as with the #if related directives, an #end directive terminates the code block. The #foreach directive takes the form #foreach (*REF* in *LIST*), where *LIST* corresponds to the list of items iterated over and *REF* corresponds to a Velocity variable reference that refers to the current list item. The number of times the #foreach directive's associated code block is processed by the template engine is equal to the size of *LIST*. The item to which *REF* refers changes on each iteration, moving sequentially from the first to the last item.

There is some flexibility in the manner in which the #foreach directive's *LIST* is specified. The template in Listing 8.33 demonstrates two of the simpler cases.

In the first, *LIST* is provided via the range operator, resulting in #foreach iterating over the list 1, 2, 3, 4, 5. In the second, *LIST* is provided by way of an array list, resulting in iteration over the list "one", "two", "three", "four", "five". The output generated when this template is processed is shown in Listing 8.34.

```
Iterating over a range...
#foreach ( $item in [1..5] )
  On this iteration, \$item refers to the value $item.
#end

Iterating over an array list...
#foreach ( $item in ["one", "two", "three", "four", "five"] )
  On this iteration, \$item refers to the value $item.
#end
```

Listing 8.33 A template demonstrating the use of #foreach directives.

```
Iterating over a range...
  On this iteration, $item refers to the value 1.
  On this iteration, $item refers to the value 2.
  On this iteration, $item refers to the value 3.
  On this iteration, $item refers to the value 4.
  On this iteration, $item refers to the value 5.

Iterating over an array list...
  On this iteration, $item refers to the value one.
  On this iteration, $item refers to the value two.
  On this iteration, $item refers to the value three.
  On this iteration, $item refers to the value four.
  On this iteration, $item refers to the value five.
```

Listing 8.34 Results from processing the template in Listing 8.33.

In addition to specifying fixed lists for the #foreach directive using range operators and array lists, Velocity allows you to provide the list by way of the context associated with the template. To use a context object as the #foreach list, the object must either correspond to a Java Object array (i.e., Object[]) or an object that implements one of a number of Java interfaces. The allowable interfaces include Collection, Map, Iterator, and Enumeration. The template shown in Listing 8.35 includes an example of each option. With a context populated as shown in Listing 8.36, the output generated by the template appears as shown in Listing 8.37.

```
## Object Array
Iterating over Object array...
#foreach ( $elem in $objectArray )
  The element is $elem on this iteration.
#end

## Map Interface
Iterating over Hashtable values...
#foreach ( $value in $hashtable )
  The value is $value on this iteration.
#end

## Collection Interface
Iterating over Hashtable keys...
#foreach ( $key in $hashtable.keySet() )
  The key is $key on this iteration.
#end

## Enumeration Interface
Iterating over Vector elements...
#foreach ( $elem in $vector.elements() )
  The element is $elem on this iteration.
#end

## Iterator Interface
Iterating over LinkedList elements...
#foreach ( $elem in $linkedList.listIterator() )
  The element is $elem on this iteration.
#end
```

Listing 8.35 A template demonstrating the use of the #foreach directive with lists taken from the context.

```
    // Create and initialize context objects
    Object[] objAr = new Object [3];
    objAr[0] = "0";
    objAr[1] = new Integer( 1 );
    objAr[2] = "2";

    Hashtable hash = new Hashtable();
    hash.put( "A", new Integer( 65 ) );
    hash.put( "B", new Integer( 66 ) );
    hash.put( "C", new Integer( 67 ) );
```

Listing 8.36 Context population code used with the template in Listing 8.35 to generate the output shown in Listing 8.37. (continues)

```
    Vector vec = new Vector();
    vec.add( "Hickory" );
    vec.add( "Dickory" );
    vec.add( "Dock" );

    LinkedList list = new LinkedList();
    list.add( "Red" );
    list.add( "Green" );
    list.add( "Blue" );

    // Populate context
    context.put( "objectArray", objAr );
    context.put( "hashtable", hash );
    context.put( "vector", vec );
    context.put( "linkedList", list );
```

Listing 8.36 Context population code used with the template in Listing 8.35 to generate the output shown in Listing 8.37. (continued)

```
Iterating over Object array...
  The element is 0 on this iteration.
  The element is 1 on this iteration.
  The element is 2 on this iteration.

Iterating over Hashtable values...
  The value is 65 on this iteration.
  The value is 67 on this iteration.
  The value is 66 on this iteration.

Iterating over Hashtable keys...
  The key is A on this iteration.
  The key is C on this iteration.
  The key is B on this iteration.

Iterating over Vector elements...
  The element is Hickory on this iteration.
  The element is Dickory on this iteration.
  The element is Dock on this iteration.

Iterating over LinkedList elements...
  The element is Red on this iteration.
  The element is Green on this iteration.
  The element is Blue on this iteration.
```

Listing 8.37 Output generated by the template in Listing 8.35 when using the context defined in Listing 8.36.

As you can see in the Hashtable list output in Listing 8.37, the order in which list items are iterated over is not necessarily the same order in which they were inserted into the list. The #foreach directive will step through the list in order, moving from the first to the last list element; however, the order itself is determined by the container, just as it is when the same type of iteration is performed directly in Java code.

In the previous examples, we made no attempt to explicitly distinguish between iterations. We just let the current list item reference speak for itself. However, it is frequently useful to know which iteration—such as when it is necessary to label output or take special actions on certain iterations. Although you could use the #set directive to initialize and increment a loop counter, this approach is rather tedious. Velocity addresses this issue by providing a special variable reference that serves as a loop counter for the #foreach directive. By default, this variable is named $velocityCount, but the name may be overridden via Velocity's runtime configuration. The template in Listing 8.38 provides an example of using Velocity's built-in loop counter. Listing 8.39 shows the corresponding output.

```
## Track the iteration with Velocity's loop counter
#foreach ( $outer in [-1..1] )
  Iteration $velocityCount of outer loop: $outer
  #foreach ( $inner in ["one", "two"] )
    Iteration $velocityCount of inner loop: $inner
  #end
#end
```

Listing 8.38 A template demonstrating the use of Velocity's loop counter reference.

```
    Iteration 1 of outer loop: -1
      Iteration 1 of inner loop: one
      Iteration 2 of inner loop: two
    Iteration 2 of outer loop: 0
      Iteration 1 of inner loop: one
      Iteration 2 of inner loop: two
    Iteration 3 of outer loop: 1
      Iteration 1 of inner loop: one
      Iteration 2 of inner loop: two
```

Listing 8.39 Results from processing the template in Listing 8.38.

Besides simply demonstrating Velocity's loop counter, Listings 8.38 and 8.39 highlight two other important aspects of the #foreach directive. The first is that Velocity supports nested #foreach directives; it also supports nesting of other directives, though that is now shown in this example. The second is that the loop counter is scoped to the current #foreach directive. In effect, when the template engine moves from an outer #foreach to an inner #foreach, the loop count for the outer directive is saved and a new counter is initialized for the inner directive. When control returns to the outer directive, its saved value is restored to the counter.

#macro

Velocity's #macro directive provides a mechanism for template code reuse. It serves much the same purpose as the #parse directive but provides significantly more flexibility and control. Instead of importing and processing all of the template code contained by an arbitrary file, the #macro directive provides a syntax for specifying and naming a block of template code, including support for input parameters. The block may be specified either in a macro library or inline in a regular template file. Once defined, the code block is accessed using normal Velocity directive syntax. Since Chapter 9, "Introducing Velocimacros," is dedicated to the #macro directive, we provide only a quick taste here. Listing 8.40 illustrates a simple example of an inline #macro directive. A macro named sayHi is defined inline in the template file and invoked as #sayHi(). The generated output is, of course, none other than the ubiquitous Hello world.

```
## Define inline macro for this template
#macro( sayHi )
  Hello world
#end

## Invoke the macro using normal directive syntax
#sayHi()
```

Listing 8.40 A template demonstrating the use of the #macro directive.

Escaping Directives

Sometimes there is a need to prevent the template engine from processing a directive. An obvious example is the case of dynamic content that discusses Velocity template syntax. In such a case, it is frequently necessary to treat as literals entities that look like Velocity directives. As with Velocity's references, this is accomplished with the use of a backslash (\) escape character. In fact, the process of escaping directives is essentially identical to that we already discussed for references in Chapter 7, including escaping the escape character and differences in behavior between cases where the reference/directive is and isn't defined. Recall that binding is from left to right, with each pair of escape characters collapsing to a single backslash, though the behavior is somewhat more erratic in the case where the directive (or macro) is not defined. Listings 8.41 and 8.42 provide a template and its corresponding output, respectively, that summarize the behavior of directive escaping.

```
## Valid directive
Output for valid directive with varying numbers of escapes.
#include( "info.txt" )
\#include( "info.txt" )
\\#include( "info.txt" )
\\\#include( "info.txt" )
\\\\#include( "info.txt" )
\\\\\#include( "info.txt" )

## Undefined directive/macro
Output for undefined directive/macro with varying numbers of escapes.
#xinclude( "info.txt" )
\#xinclude( "info.txt" )
\\#xinclude( "info.txt" )
\\\#xinclude( "info.txt" )
\\\\#xinclude( "info.txt" )
\\\\\#xinclude( "info.txt" )
```

Listing 8.41 A template demonstrating the use of directive escapes.

```
Output for valid directive with varying numbers of escapes.
Included information.
#include( "info.txt" )
\Included information.
\#include( "info.txt" )
\\Included information.
\\#include( "info.txt" )

Output for undefined directive/macro with varying numbers of escapes.
#xinclude( "info.txt" )
\#xinclude( "info.txt" )
\\#xinclude( "info.txt" )
\\\#xinclude( "info.txt" )
\\#xinclude( "info.txt" )
\\\\\#xinclude( "info.txt" )
```

Listing 8.42 Results from processing the template in Listing 8.41.

What's Next

In this chapter, we provided a detailed discussion of Velocity directives, which greatly extend the template-processing power available to template designers. We offered numerous examples to demonstrate how you can use these directives to control processing flow, insert content, manipulate the context, and reuse blocks of template code. The last directive, #macro, was only briefly introduced. It is this directive to which we devote the next chapter.

CHAPTER 9

Introducing Velocimacros

In the previous chapter, we discussed all of Velocity's directives, including the #macro directive. However, we provided only a brief introduction to the #macro directive since it is interesting enough to warrant its own chapter. Here, we resume our discussion of #macro directives, or *Velocimacros* as they are more affectionately known. We discuss argument passing, macro libraries, runtime configuration, and other topics associated with Velocimacros.

Argument Passing

When we introduced the #macro directive in Chapter 8, we presented a simple Hello World example. The template used for that example defines an inline Velocimacro that outputs *Hello world* each time it is invoked. This macro is defined so that no arguments are allowed in the macro invocation. Note that the #macro directive itself always requires at least one argument, the first of which specifies the name used to invoke the macro. However, the invocation of a macro takes zero or more arguments, depending on its specification.

In order to allow the passing of arguments to a Velocimacro, you need only provide the #macro directive with a reference name for each argument to be passed. The names are provided as arguments to the #macro directive, following the macro name and separated by whitespace. Each reference name can then be used in the macro's code block in the same manner as any other Velocity variable reference. As with #foreach and the #if related directives, the code block is terminated with an #end directive. As an example, let's improve on the Velocimacro in Listing 8.40 by providing the ability to say *hello* to a particular person, rather than the world in general. The new and improved macro is shown in Listing 9.1. When processed, the template generates the string "Hello Arthur!" followed by the string "Hello Zaphod!".

```
## Define inline macro for this template
#macro( sayHiTo $who )
  Hello $who!
#end

## Invoke the macro using normal directive syntax
#sayHiTo( "Arthur" )
#sayHiTo( "Zaphod" )
```

Listing 9.1 A template demonstrating the #macro directive with support for argument passing.

For a Velocimacro to be successfully invoked, the number of arguments in the invocation must match exactly the number specified by the macro definition. For example, if the macro in Listing 9.1 were called as #sayHiTo() or #sayHiTo("Zaphod" "Beeblebrox"), the invocation would be ignored. It follows that Velocimacros do not provide support for default arguments; neither do Velocimacros support overloading. As such, there is no particularly clean way to handle cases where a Velocimacro is intended to carry out a specific action that only varies subtly based on argument number. In most such cases, multiple, uniquely named macro definitions are required.

Although our examples have so far only demonstrated the use of string literals as input parameters, Velocimacros also support integer literals, Booleans, range operators, array lists, and Velocity references. Listing 9.2 shows a template demonstrating macro definitions and invocations involving all of these types. The first Velocimacro expects a string literal, an integer literal, and a Boolean. The second expects a range and an array list. The last expects a Velocity reference. Note that the argument lists for both the macro definitions and invocations are space delimited, rather than comma delimited as is the case with many common programming languages. The macros simply output the values of the provided arguments, as seen in Listing 9.3.

```
## Define Velocimacros
## (string literal - integer literal - boolean)
#macro( sib $string $int $bool )
  The string is $string.
  The integer is $int.
```

Listing 9.2 A template demonstrating the #macro directive used with various argument types. (continues)

```
  The boolean is $bool.
#end

## (range - array list)
#macro( ra $range $arrayList )
  #foreach ( $val in $range ) $val #end

  #foreach ( $val in $arrayList ) $val #end

#end

## (Velocity reference)
#macro( r $vref )
  The reference correspond to $vref
#end


## Invoke Velocimacros
#sib( "Hello" 42 true )

#ra( [-9..-1] ["favorite", "color"] )

#set( $color = "Blue. No! Yellow!" )
#r( $color )
```

Listing 9.2 A template demonstrating the #macro directive used with various argument types. (continued)

```
  The string is Hello.
  The integer is 42.
  The boolean is true.

   -9  -8  -7  -6  -5  -4  -3  -2  -1
   favorite  color

  The reference correspond to Blue. No! Yellow!
```

Listing 9.3 Results from processing the template in Listing 9.2.

While argument handling for most of the types supported by Velocimacros is straightforward and clearly illustrated by the previous example, the use of Velocity references as input arguments requires further discussion. References used for macro input are not limited to variable references, but may also include Velocity method and property references. Although this is certainly a handy feature, some care is required to obtain the desired results. The trick to using these references correctly is in understanding that they are passed by name. That is, the reference is not evaluated until after it is received by the Velocimacro. In order to clarify this notion, start by considering the FromFive class shown in Listing 9.4. This class simply initializes an int property to the value of 5 and decrements that value each time it is requested through the class's getNext() method.

```
public class FromFive
{
  public FromFive()
  {
    nextValue = 5;
  }

  public Integer getNext()
  {
    return (new Integer( nextValue-- ));
  }

  public String toString()
  {
    return (String.valueOf( nextValue ));
  }

  private int nextValue;
}
```

Listing 9.4 The FromFive class, which generates a sequence of decreasing integer values.

Next, assume that our application maintains a Velocity context populated with three instances of the FromFive class that are keyed with the strings methodRef, propRef, and varRef. If this application then processes the template shown in Listing 9.5, the output will appear as that shown in Listing 9.6. As the output demonstrates, the value associated with the $ref reference in the countDown Velocimacro changes each time it is evaluated for the cases of method and property reference input. This is due to the fact that in these two cases $ref stores the names $methodRef.getNext() and $propRef.next, respectively, rather than the values those references evaluate to. In effect, $ref simply becomes an alias for the provided method or property reference. Although not as obvious, the same is in fact true for the variable reference $varRef; the associated output differs only due to the fact that FromFive's toString() method does not decrement the value of an object's nextValue property. If toString() were modified to behave in the same manner as getNext(), then passing $varRef to the countDown Velocimacro would also result in decrementing output.

```
## Evaluate provided reference six times.
#macro( countDown $ref )
  $ref.. $ref.. $ref.. $ref.. $ref.. $ref
#end

## Call countDown with a method reference
#countDown( $methodRef.getNext() )

## Call countDown with a property reference
#countDown( $propRef.next )

## Call countDown with a variable reference
#countDown( $varRef )
```

Listing 9.5 A template demonstrating the use of all three types of Velocity references with the #macro directive.

```
  5.. 4.. 3.. 2.. 1.. 0

  5.. 4.. 3.. 2.. 1.. 0

  5.. 5.. 5.. 5.. 5.. 5
```

Listing 9.6 Results from processing the template in Listing 9.5.

If it is necessary to pass by value the result of evaluating a Velocity reference, the easiest solution is generally to use the #set directive to capture the value in an independent variable reference and then pass that reference. As an example of this approach, consider the template in Listing 9.7. This template's inline macro definitions are unchanged from those in Listing 9.5; however, we changed the invocations to emulate pass-by-value behavior. Note that the new template only emulates pass-by-value by way of the #set directive. Underneath the wrappers, the call is still pass-by-name.

```
## Evaluate provided reference six times.
#macro( countDown $ref )
  $ref.. $ref.. $ref.. $ref.. $ref.. $ref
#end

## Call countDown with the value of a method reference
#set( $methodValue = $methodRef.getNext() )
#countDown( $methodValue )
```

Listing 9.7 A template demonstrating emulated pass-by-value behavior with a #macro directive. (continues)

```
## Call countDown with the value of a property reference
#set( $propValue = $propRef.next )
#countDown( $propValue )

## Call countDown with the value of a variable reference
#set( $varValue = $varRef )
#countDown( $varValue )
```

Listing 9.7 A template demonstrating emulated pass-by-value behavior with a #macro directive. (continued)

Inline vs. Library Macros

So far all of our Velocimacro examples have focused on inline definitions, since this approach is most convenient for simple examples. While inline definitions are perfectly appropriate in many cases, the fact that they are inline inherently limits their power in terms of code reuse. The scope of an inline Velocimacro is limited to the template file in which it is defined; more specifically, it is limited to that part of the template file that follows the macro definition. Therefore, other template files may not access such a macro. Attempts to pull a Velocimacro definition from one template into the scope of another by way of either the #include or #parse directive will fail. The #include directive imports only static content, so #macro directives would lose any special meaning. The #parse directive does process the included text as normal template code, but it does so at runtime. In contrast, Velocimacro calls are determined when the template is first parsed by the template engine, well before any #parse directives have a chance to import external Velocimacro definitions.

So how do you share Velocimacros across multiple templates while avoiding a lot of tedious copy and paste? The answer lies with Velocity's support for macro libraries. This feature allows you to create multiple macro libraries that applications may register through one of the available Velocimacro properties. Once such a library is registered, any template processed by the application may invoke the Velocimacros from that library. We discuss the Velocimacro properties later in this chapter and Velocity's property system in general in Chapter 10, "Taking Control of Velocity." For now, suffice it to say that through the property system, files containing #macro directives can serve as Velocimacro libraries accessible to any and all templates.

If your Velocimacro library needs are modest, there is probably no reason to bother with the Velocity property system at all. By default, the template engine assumes that any file with the name VM_global_library.vm that is located in an application's directory is to be interpreted as a macro library for that application. For example, if our template from Listing 9.5 is broken up into two files, as shown in Listings 9.8 and 9.9, the output generated will remain the same (see Listing 9.6). The only requirement is that the Velocimacro library be named VM_global_library.vm.

```
## Evaluate provided reference six times.
#macro( countDown $ref )
  $ref.. $ref.. $ref.. $ref.. $ref.. $ref
#end
```

Listing 9.8 A macro library containing the Velocimacro originally defined in Listing 9.5. If Velocity defaults are assumed, this file must be named VM_global_library.vm.

```
## Call countDown with the value of a method reference
#countDown( $methodRef.getNext() )

## Call countDown with the value of a property reference
#countDown( $propRef.next )

## Call countDown with the value of a variable reference
#countDown( $varRef )
```

Listing 9.9 The template from Listing 9.5 after moving its Velocimacro to a macro library.

Velocimacro Properties

Velocity provides a number of configurable properties that affect the behavior of Velocimacros. We discuss how these properties are set in Chapter 10, but for now let's examine the relevant names, descriptions, and default settings.

velocimacro.library

The library property is the one that we referred to in the previous section. This property defines the names of the files that are to comprise an application's Velocimacro library. The names are taken relative to the currently configured template path. If multiple files are to be included in the library, then they are provided as a comma-separated list. The default value of the library property is VM_global_library.vm.

velocimacro.permissions.allow.inline

The permissions.allow.inline property specifies whether inline Velocimacro definitions are allowed--that is, whether a Velocimacro macro may be defined in a non-library template file. If this property is set to false, inline Velocimacro definitions result in logged warning messages and are ignored by the template engine. The default value for permissions.allow.inline is true.

velocimacro.permissions.allow.inline.to.replace.global

The permissions.allow.inline.to.replace.global property specifies whether an inline Velocimacro is allowed to override a library Velocimacro with the same name. This is, of course, meaningful only if the permissions.allow.inline property is true; otherwise, inline definitions aren't even permitted. If the permissions.allow.inline.to.replace.global property is set to true, library Velocimacros with the same names as inline Velocimacros are hidden by the inline versions. If the property is set to false, library Velocimacros are protected from both accidental and intentional replacement by inline Velocimacros. The default value for this property is false.

velocimacro.permissions.allow.inline.local.scope

The permissions.allow.inline.local.scope property specifies whether templates should provide private namespaces with regard to Velocimacros. When this property is set to true, private namespaces are enabled, and inline Velocimacro definitions are visible only to the defining template. Private namespace support also results in a template's namespace being searched first whenever a Velocimacro definition is required. This latter feature allows a local Velocimacro definition to override any other definition defined outside of the template. The default value for the permissions.allow.inline.local.scope property is false.

velocimacro.context.localscope

The context.localscope property specifies the manner in which the #set directive affects the Velocity context when used within a Velocimacro. When this property is set to true, the Velocimacro in effect receives its own local context. Objects keyed into the context of the caller are not visible to the Velocimacro, and changes made to the context from within the Velocimacro do not propagate back to the caller. In contrast, a value of false places the caller's context in a scope that is both accessible to and modifiable from a Velocimacro. The default value for the context.localscope property is false.

velocimacro.library.autoreload

The library.autoreload property specifies whether a modified Velocimacro library is automatically reloaded when one of its macros is invoked. If the property is set to true, each call to a library Velocimacro will result in the corresponding library being checked for modifications. If it is discovered that such a library has been modified since last being loaded, Velocity will automatically reload the library. If the property is set to false, Velocimacro libraries are not checked for modifications once loaded. The default value for the library.autoreload property is false. The reload functionality provided by this property is primarily intended for testing and debugging. If you find that you need to enable this property, it is likely that you also need to disable the resource loader cache; we discuss the property controlling this cache in the next chapter.

velocimacro.messages.on

The messages.on property specifies whether the template engine should generate additional informational log messages regarding inline Velocimacros. When this property is set to true, additional messages are generated. When set to false, the messages are suppressed. The default value for the messages.on property is true.

Nesting and Recursion

So far, all of our Velocimacro examples have been limited to cases not requiring nesting or recursion. Nesting, which is simply a case of calling one Velocimacro from within another, is frequently useful in terms of code reuse. Without the ability to nest macros, template code would need to be duplicated each time a common task is performed by a Velocimacro. Recursion, which is a special case of nesting where a Velocimacro calls itself, is less frequently needed; however, there are certain types of problems for which recursion provides a very elegant solution. Fortunately, Velocimacros support both nesting and recursion. An example of both is illustrated in Listing 9.10. The recurs Velocimacro calls itself the number of time specified by its $depth argument. The writeABC macro demonstrates Velocimacro nesting by calling the getA and getBC Velocimacros, the second of which in turn calls the getB and getC Velocimacros. Listing 9.11 shows the output generated by these macros.

```
## A recursive Velocimacro
#macro( recurs $depth )
  Entering at level $depth
  #set( $depth = $depth - 1 )
    #if ( $depth > 0 )
      #recurs( $depth )
```

Listing 9.10 A template demonstrating the use of nesting and recursion of Velocimacros. (continues)

```
    #end
  #set( $depth = $depth + 1 )
  Leaving from level $depth
#end

## Nesting of Velocimacros
#macro( getA ) A #end
#macro( getB ) B #end
#macro( getC ) C #end
#macro( getBC )
  #getB()#getC()
#end
#macro( writeABC )
  #getA()#getBC()
#end

#recurs( 3 )

#writeABC()
```

Listing 9.10 A template demonstrating the use of nesting and recursion of Velocimacros. (continued)

```
Entering at level 3
Entering at level 2
Entering at level 1
Leaving from level 1
Leaving from level 2
Leaving from level 3

 A  B  C
```

Listing 9.11 Results from processing the template in Listing 9.10.

What's Next

In this chapter, we extended our discussion of Velocity directives with a more in-depth treatment of the #macro directive, or Velocimacro. We covered argument passing, macro libraries, nesting and recursion, and Velocimacro properties. At this point, you should have a reasonably good understanding of Velocity's contexts and template language, including references and directives. You should now have the tools needed to develop reasonably sophisticated templates. However, there remain a few more aspects of Velocity's functionality that you will want to know about in order to get the most out of what Velocity offers. That is the subject of our next chapter.

CHAPTER 10

Taking Control of Velocity

In previous chapters, we discussed the core components of the Velocity Template Language and the role played by the Velocity context in template processing. While these chapters provide the information necessary to design and implement sophisticated template-based applications, they omit, or at best only hint at, a number of additional Velocity features that really let you take control of template processing. In this chapter, we introduce those features, which include runtime configuration, events, whitespace management, and context chaining.

Initializing the Runtime Configuration

While discussing Velocimacros in Chapter 9, we introduced a number of Velocity properties that affect the manner in which Velocimacros are handled by the template engine. Later in this chapter, we introduce yet more Velocity properties that affect other aspects of the runtime system, but first let's discuss how such properties are specified and passed to the Velocity runtime.

In previous examples, we initialized the runtime by simply calling the static method Velocity.init(). This results in the Velocity runtime engine being initialized with default Velocity properties specified in the org/apache/ velocity/runtime/defaults/velocity.properties distribution file. These default properties provide a reasonable configuration that is adequate for many, if not most, applications. However, for cases where you need to exert more control over the manner in which the template engine behaves, Velocity offers three techniques for customizing the runtime configuration. Regardless of the technique used, the runtime always starts with the base configuration specified by the velocity.properties file. Therefore, you only have to concern yourself with those properties you need to change or add to the base configuration.

The first technique that we discuss for custom configuration of the Velocity runtime is one that mirrors the technique used for the default configuration. This approach involves creating a runtime configuration file that uses the same syntax as the velocity.properties file. Using this syntax, you set a Velocity property by providing its name and value, separated by an equal sign. Where multiple values are provided for a property that supports them, you use commas to delimit the values. As for all customization techniques, the properties in this file may either override or add to the default configuration. The file is passed to the runtime by invoking an overloaded version of the Velocity engine's init() method that takes a filename as an argument. For example, suppose that you are testing some new Velocimacros that are defined in files named tags.vm and labels.vm. You would like to make these libraries visible to the runtime, eliminate the possibility of the macros being overridden in a template file, and enable Velocimacro library auto-reloading to facilitate debugging. To this end, you create a file named custom.properties, shown in Listing 10.1. The properties specified by this file are then passed to the runtime by providing the name of the file to the Velocity engine's initialization method, as shown in Listing 10.2.

```
## Specify the names of our custom libraries
velocimacro.library = tags.vm, labels.vm

## Disable inline Velocimacro definitions
velocimacro.permissions.allow.inline = false

## Enable Velocimacro library auto-reloading
velocimacro.library.autoreload = true
```

Listing 10.1 A custom Velocity runtime configuration file.

```
// Initialize template engine
try
{
  Velocity.init( "custom.properties" );
}
catch( Exception x )
{
  System.err.println( "Failed to initialize Velocity: " + x );
  System.exit( 1 );
}
```

Listing 10.2 An example of runtime initialization using a custom configuration file.

If it is important to provide an application with more control over the specification of Velocity properties, or if the ability to easily read and write the properties is desirable, the technique we discuss next might be preferable. This technique involves the use of a java.util.Properties object. If building up the Properties object at runtime, the object's setProperty() method is used to add entries for Velocity properties. This method expects two parameters of type String: the property key and the property value. The Velocity property name is used as the key, and the value of the Velocity property--in the form of a string literal--is used for the value argument. Note that we use the term *property* here to describe two distinct entities. Relative to the Java Properties object, it refers to a generic property with no inherent relationship to Velocity. In all other cases, we are referring to properties that define the runtime configuration of the Velocity template engine.

If we were to modify the template engine initialization shown in Listing 10.2 so that it used a Java Properties object to configure the runtime identically to that specified by the file in Listing 10.1, the code would look something like that shown in Listing 10.3. Notice that the Properties object is passed to the Velocity engine using yet another overloaded version of the init() method. If the ability to simply and efficiently read and write configuration files is also of importance, you can take advantage of the load() and store() methods provided by the Java Properties class. This approach offers advantages over Velocity's file-based configuration in that modifications and additions to the read properties are straightforward, writing out the properties requires little effort, and the files use a native Java format.

```
Properties customProps = new Properties();

// Specify the names of our custom libraries
customProps.setProperty( "velocimacro.library", "tags.vm, labels.vm" );

// Disable inline Velocimacro definitions
customProps.setProperty( "velocimacro.permissions.allow.inline", "false" );

// Enable Velocimacro library auto-reloading
customProps.setProperty( "velocimacro.library.autoreload", "true" );

// Initialize template engine
try
{
  Velocity.init( customProps );
}
catch( Exception x )
{
```

Listing 10.3 An example of runtime initialization using a Java Properties object. (continues)

```
    System.err.println( "Failed to initialize Velocity: " + x );
    System.exit( 1 );
  }
```

Listing 10.3 An example of runtime initialization using a Java Properties object. (continued)

Finally, if the primary goal of runtime configuration customization is fine-grain control over Velocity properties based on application runtime conditions, then this last technique might be the best choice. This technique is based around the Velocity engine's own setProperty() method; this method has nothing to do with the Properties class setProperty() method discussed for the last technique, though it is used in a similar manner. The template engine's setProperty() method takes two parameters: a String specifying the property name and an Object representing the corresponding value. A getProperty() method is also available for querying current property settings. There is even a clearProperty() method for cases where it is necessary to remove a Velocity property altogether. Once all relevant Velocity properties are set, the runtime is configured by invoking the Velocity engine's no-argument init() method. Continuing with the example used for the first two techniques, Listing 10.4 contains a version using Velocity's setProperty(). As with the other techniques, this setProperty() approach builds on a default configuration specified by the velocity.properties file.

```
// Specify the names of our custom libraries
Velocity.setProperty( "velocimacro.library", "tags.vm, labels.vm" );

// Disable inline Velocimacro definitions
Velocity.setProperty( "velocimacro.permissions.allow.inline", "false" );

// Enable Velocimacro library auto-reloading
Velocity.setProperty( "velocimacro.library.autoreload", "true" );

// Initialize template engine
try
{
  Velocity.init();
}
catch( Exception x )
{
  System.err.println( "Failed to initialize Velocity: " + x );
  System.exit( 1 );
}
```

Listing 10.4 An example of runtime initialization using the Velocity engine's setProperty() method.

Whatever technique you use, ensure that you have specified all of your Velocity property modifications and additions before invoking the engine's init() method in any of its forms. While invoking init() more than once does no harm, further calls have no effect on the runtime configuration. After the first call, you are stuck with the resulting configuration.

More Velocity Properties

Now that we have covered the various ways in which Velocity's runtime configuration properties may be specified, let's take a closer look at more of those properties. We group the Velocity properties discussed here into five general categories: directives, encoding, logging, resource management, and miscellaneous. We discussed a sixth category, Velocimacros, in Chapter 9.

Directive Properties

The following properties affect the behavior of certain Velocity directives.

directive.foreach.counter.name

The directive.foreach.counter.name property specifies the VTL Identifier used to name the #foreach directive's loop counter. When prefixed with a $, this identifier serves as the Velocity variable reference that allows the template designer access to a #foreach directive's current iteration count. By default, this count starts at 1 and is incremented once with each iteration. The value of the directive.foreach.counter.name property defaults to velocityCount, with the corresponding variable reference specified as $velocityCount. If the template designer instead wants to access the count through a reference named $myCount, a value of myCount can be assigned to the property.

directive.foreach.counter.initial.value

The directive.foreach.counter.initial.value property specifies the initial value used for the #foreach directive's loop counter. This is the value that is provided by a loop counter reference (see the directive.foreach.counter.name property) accessed from within a #foreach block during the first iteration over that block. At the beginning of each subsequent iteration, the value is incremented by one. The default value for the directive.foreach.counter.initial.value property is 1. Template designers familiar with C++ and Java for loops might prefer zero-based counters, which can be achieved by setting the value of the property to 0.

directive.include.output.errormsg.start

The directive.include.output.errormsg.start property specifies the text that precedes the error message resulting from an invalid input parameter being passed to the #include directive. An undefined Velocity reference is an example of the type of parameter that will trigger this sort of error message. The error message prefix specified by this property is output only if the directive.include. output.errormsg.end property is also defined. The default value for the directive.include.output.errormsg.start property is the string “<!– include error :”.

directive.include.output.errormsg.end

The directive.include.output.errormsg.end property specifies the text that follows the error message resulting from an invalid input parameter being passed to the #include directive. An undefined Velocity reference is an example of the type of parameter that will trigger this sort of error message. The error message suffix specified by this property is output only if the directive.include.output.errormsg.start property is also defined. The default value for the directive.include.output.errormsg.end property is the string “see error log –>”.

directive.parse.max.depth

The directive.parse.max.depth property specifies the maximum depth to which #parse directives may be nested. A value of 1 essentially disables the #parse directive since a template containing a #parse directive is already at a depth of at least 1. Each increment of this property beyond 1 allows one additional level of nesting for #parse directives. Although the primary purpose of this property is to prevent runaway recursion, the depth limit applies equally to general #parse nesting that involves no recursion. The default value for the directive. parse.max.depth is 10.

Encoding

The following properties specify encodings to be associated with templates and data used by certain tools associated with the Velocity template engine.

input.encoding

The input.encoding property is used to specify the encoding of templates processed by the template engine. Once set, all template input is assumed to adhere to the specified encoding. The default value for the input.encoding property is ISO-8859-1. The supported encodings depend on the underlying Java character set support. See the documentation for the Java Charset class for more information.

output.encoding

The output.encoding property is used to specify an encoding that should be associated with the output stream. This is not a general-purpose Velocity property and is currently intended only for use with the VelocityServlet class and the Anakia project. For the general case, encoding may be specified directly by initializing the output Writer appropriately before using it in the merge process. The default value for the output.encoding property is ISO-8859-1.

Logging

The following properties affect the behavior of the logging system used by Velocity.

runtime.log

The runtime.log property specifies the path to Velocity's log file. By default, this path is specified relative to the location of the application; this can be overridden with the file.resource.loader.path property, which we discuss later. The default value for the runtime.log property is velocity.log. If you have been working through the examples, you are probably already familiar with this file, which is generated each time you run a Velocity application.

runtime.log.logsystem

The runtime.log.logsystem property specifies an object to which Velocity should hand off logging tasks. In order to use an object in this manner, it is necessary that the corresponding class implement the org.apache.velocity.runtime.log.LogSystem interface. This property is intended primarily for cases where Velocity's logging needs to be integrated with a custom application logging class. There is no default for this property. Also, note that since the property's value is an object rather than a string, it cannot be specified directly using either a configuration file or a Java Properties object.

runtime.log.logsystem.class

The runtime.log.logsystem.class property specifies the class that the runtime is to instantiate for handling Velocity's logging services. The value of this property may consist of a comma-delimited list of classnames. The runtime engine steps through the list of names in the order provided and tries to find a matching class. The first match determines the class instantiated for Velocity logging. The default value for the runtime.log.logsystem.class property is org.apache.velocity.runtime.log.AvalonLogSystem,org.apache.velocity.runtime.log.SimpleLog4J logSystem. Logging may be disabled by providing a value of org.apache.velocity.runtime.log.NullLogSystem.

runtime.log.error.stacktrace

The runtime.log.error.stacktrace property specifies whether a stack trace should be generated and logged when the Velocity runtime engine logs an error. Although support for the property itself exists, the associated functionality is not yet implemented. The default value for the runtime.log.error.stacktrace property is false.

runtime.log.warn.stacktrace

The runtime.log.warn.stacktrace property specifies whether a stack trace should be generated and logged when the Velocity runtime engine logs a warning. Although support for the property itself exists, the associated functionality is not yet implemented. The default value for the runtime.log.warn.stacktrace property is false.

runtime.log.info.stacktrace

The runtime.log.info.stacktrace property specifies whether a stack trace should be generated and logged when the Velocity runtime engine logs an informational message. Although support for the property itself exists, the associated functionality is not yet implemented. The default value for the runtime.log.info.stacktrace property is false.

runtime.log.invalid.references

The runtime.log.invalid.references property specifies whether invalid Velocity references found in a template should be logged. If this property is set to true, invalid references result in the generation of warning messages. If false, invalid references are ignored with regard to the log file. The default value for the runtime.log.invalid.references property is true.

Resource Management

The following properties affect the behavior of Velocity's resource management system.

resource.manager.class

The resource.manager.class property specifies the class instantiated to handle Velocity's resource management tasks. This class must implement the org.apache.velocity.runtime.resource.ResourceManager interface. The default value for this property is org.apache.velocity.runtime.resource.ResourceManagerImpl.

resource.manager.cache.class

The resource.manager.cache.class property specifies the class instantiated to handle resource-caching requests on behalf of the resource manager. This class must implement the org.apache.velocity.runtime.resource.ResourceCache interface. The default value for this property is org.apache.velocity.runtime.resource.ResourceCacheImpl.

resource.manager.logwhenfound

The resource.manager.logwhenfound property specifies whether or not the resource manager should log an information message each time it locates a given resource for the first time. The default value for this property is true, which enables the logging of such messages.

resource.loader

The resource.loader property associates a name with a particular resource loader. This name is used only as a label to further define the resource loader's behavior via Velocity properties. In the following subsections, we use the string *<loader>* when referring to this name. The velocity.properties file defines only one resource loader, which it names *file*, and the corresponding property names are those listed in the following subsections with *<loader>* replaced by *file*. We discuss resource loaders in a bit more detail later in this chapter.

<loader>.resource.loader.description

The resource.loader.description property specifies a textual description of the resource loader. This property is informational in nature and does not actually affect the functionality of the resource loader. The velocity.properties file provides a value of Velocity File Resource Loader for the file.resource.loader.description property.

<loader>.resource.loader.class

The resource.loader.class property specifies the class instantiated for loading the associated resource type. This class extends Velocity's org.apache.velocity.runtime.resource.loader.ResourceLoader class, and provides the resource type specific functionality. The velocity.properties file provides a value of org.apache.velocity.runtime.resource.loader.FileResourceLoader for the file.resource.loader.class property.

<loader>.resource.loader.path

The resource.loader.path property specifies a root directory for resources of the associated type. Any locations provided for these resources are considered to be relative to this root. The velocity.properties file provides a value of . for the file.resource.loader.path property; this establishes an application's directory as the root relative to which file resources such as templates and log files are located.

<loader>.resource.loader.cache

The resource.loader.cache property specifies whether or not the loader should cache certain resources. The velocity.properties file provides a value of false for the file.resource.loader.cache property. This prevents the file resource loader from caching templates, which is often preferred for development and debugging. For production, a value of true is generally a better choice.

<loader>.resource.loader.modificationCheckInterval

The resource.loader.modificationCheckInterval property specifies the interval, in seconds, between checks for modifications to cached resources. This property is meaningful only if the corresponding resource.loader.cache property is set to true. A negative value for the resource.loader.modificationCheckInterval property disables checks altogether. The velocity.properties file provides a value of 2 for the file.resource.loader.modificationCheckInterval property.

Miscellaneous

The following properties affect miscellaneous aspects of Velocity's runtime behavior.

runtime.interpolate.string.literals

The runtime.interpolate.string.literals property specifies whether or not the template engine should interpolate string literals. Affected literals include double-quoted strings occurring on the right side of the equal sign in #set directives, as parameters to reference methods, as Velocimacro parameters, and as general parameters to other Velocity directives. If the property is set to false, such strings are not interpolated. They are instead treated equivalently to single-quoted strings, which are never interpolated. The default value for the runtime.interpolate.string.literals property is true.

parser.pool.size

The parser.pool.size property specifies the size of the parser pool created by the runtime at startup. This is the minimum number of parsers that are made available to the Velocity engine. If additional parsers are required, they are created as needed, but never added to the pool. The default value of the parser.pool.size property is 20.

Resource Loaders

While discussing Velocity properties, we introduced a number of properties that affect resource loaders without really defining the notion of a resource loader. Here we rectify that omission. A Velocity *resource* is simply an input to the template engine. Such inputs include regular templates, Velocimacro libraries, and plain text requested through #include directives. A *resource loader* is simply an entity that knows how to obtain such resources from a particular source. All of the examples so far presented in this book have depended on Velocity's file resource loader, which is implemented by its FileResourceLoader class. Likewise, the default properties we presented while discussing Velocity's resource management focused on configuration of the file resource loader. However, in addition to the hooks required for creating custom resource loaders, Velocity provides complete support for three other resource loader types: JAR, Classpath, and DataSource.

The JAR resource loader, implemented by Velocity's JarResourceLoader class, obtains its resources from JAR files. The resource loader properties we described for the file resource loader are all applicable to the JAR resource loader, with the exception that the resource.loader.path property for the JAR resource loader is expressed using JAR URL syntax; see the documentation for Java's JarURLConnection class for more information regarding this syntax.

The Classpath resource loader, implemented by Velocity's ClasspathResourceLoader class, obtains its resources through the ClassLoader from sources in the CLASSPATH. The sources may be zip files, JAR files, or directories. This resource loader is especially useful when working with servlets. The only resource loader properties relevant to this loader are resource.loader.description and resource.loader.class. Only resource.loader.class is required.

The DataSource resource loader, implemented by Velocity's DataSourceResourceLoader class, obtains its resources via physical data source connections obtained through a Java DataSource object. An obvious example is a case where Velocity templates and related resources are obtained from a relational database. This resource loader uses all of the resource loader properties, except for resource.loader.path. It also supports several other properties that are unique to this type of loader. For more information regarding these properties, see the Velocity's API documentation for its DataSourceResourceLoader class. This resource loader requires J2EE and is not included in the standard Velocity build.

Events

To provide finer control over template processing, Velocity supports limited user intervention at the event-handling level. There are three types of events for which Velocity allows the user to intervene in the processing. The first results when an attempt is made to assign a null to a Velocity reference via the #set directive. The second results when a Java method invoked through a Velocity method or property reference throws an exception. The third results each time the value corresponding to a Velocity reference is inserted into the output stream. Velocity provides event-handler interfaces for each of these cases, named NullSetEventHandler, MethodExceptionEventHandler, and ReferenceInsertionEventHandler, respectively.

The handler method specified by the NullSetEventHandler interface is passed strings representing the left- and right-hand sides of the #set directive's equal sign and is expected to return a boolean value indicating whether or not the event should be logged. The handler method specified by the MethodExceptionEventHandler interface is passed a Class object representing the class of the throwing method, a String representing the name of the throwing method, and the exception thrown. The method returns an object that replaces the value that would have been returned had the Velocity method or reference not thrown an exception. The handler method specified by the ReferenceInsertionEventHandler interface is passed a String representing the name of the reference being processed and an Object representing its value. The Object returned by the method is inserted into the output stream using its toString() method.

As an example of Velocity event handling, consider the Java class definition shown in Listing 10.5. This class defines three methods that help demonstrate Velocity's event-handling features. The first purposely returns a null that will be used in a #set directive, the second throws a generic exception, and the third provides a default value for output stream insertion.

```
public class EventGen
{
  public String getNull()
  {
```

Listing 10.5 A Java class that assists in the creation of Velocity events. (continues)

```
    return (null);
  }

  public void throwException() throws Exception
  {
    throw new Exception();
  }

  public String toString()
  {
    return "toString() handled by EventGen";
  }
}
```

Listing 10.5 A Java class that assists in the creation of Velocity events. (continued)

Next consider the template in Listing 10.6 and the event-handling class in Listing 10.7. The template triggers all three events for which user intervention is supported by assigning a null in a #set directive, invoking a method that throws an exception, and inserting the value of a reference into the output stream. The event-handling class defines methods that allow user intervention for each of the three events. The null assignment results in an informational message and no log entry. The exception results in an informational message being inserted into the output stream, and the reference insertion event results in the value of the $eventGen reference being overridden.

```
## Trigger a NullSetEventHandler response
#set( $ref = $eventGen.getNull() )

## Trigger a MethodExceptionEventHandler response
$eventGen.throwException()

## Trigger a ReferenceInsertionEventHandler response
$eventGen
```

Listing 10.6 A template that generates all three of the Velocity events that allow user intervention.

```
import org.apache.velocity.app.event.NullSetEventHandler;
import org.apache.velocity.app.event.MethodExceptionEventHandler;
import org.apache.velocity.app.event.ReferenceInsertionEventHandler;
```

Listing 10.7 A Velocity event-handling class that handles all three of the Velocity events that allow user intervention. (continues)

```
public class EventHan implements NullSetEventHandler,
                                 MethodExceptionEventHandler,
                                 ReferenceInsertionEventHandler
{
  // NullSetEventHandler method
  public boolean shouldLogOnNullSet( String lhs, String rhs )
  {
    System.out.println( "From app: choosing not to log "
                        + lhs + " = " + rhs );
    return (false);
  }

  // MethodExceptionEventHandler method
  public Object methodException( Class claz,
                                 String method, Exception e )
  {
    String msg = e + " thrown by " + claz + ":" + method;

    return (msg);
  }

  // ReferenceInsertionEventHandler method
  public Object referenceInsert( String reference, Object value )
  {
    Object insertValue = value;

    if ( reference.equals( "$eventGen" ) )
    {
      insertValue = "toString() handled by EventHan";
    }

    return (insertValue);
  }
}
```

Listing 10.7 A Velocity event-handling class that handles all three of the Velocity events that allow user intervention. (continued)

All that remains is to inform the Velocity runtime of your intent to intervene in the event handling. This is accomplished through the use of Velocity's Event-Cartridge class. This class allows you to register your event handlers and attach the EventCartridge to a Velocity context. The code for accomplishing this last step is shown in Listing 10.8, and Listing 10.9 shows the result of executing the application.

```
// Create context
VelocityContext context = new VelocityContext();

// Populate context
context.put( "eventGen", new EventGen() );

// Setup event handler
EventCartridge eventCart = new EventCartridge();

eventCart.addEventHandler( new EventHan() );

eventCart.attachToContext( context );

// Merge template and context
```

Listing 10.8 Java code demonstrating event-handler registration and context attachment using Velocity's EventCartridge class.

```
From app: choosing not to log $ref = $eventGen.getNull()

java.lang.Exception thrown by class EventGen:throwException

toString() handled by EventHan
```

Listing 10.9 Results from processing the template in Listing 10.6.

Context Chaining

All of the examples that we have thus far explored have made use of only a single Velocity context. For many tasks this is sufficient, but there is nothing preventing the use of multiple contexts in a single application. If multiple contexts are to be used independently in an application, nothing new is required. Each is created and used in the same manner as the first. However, there are cases where it is convenient to combine multiple contexts so that an aggregate Velocity context is available to the merge process. Velocity supports such aggregation through what it refers to as *context chaining*.

Context chaining is in effect a technique for wrapping one context with another. All objects in the original context whose keys are not duplicated by entries inserted into the wrapping context remain available in the aggregate. If on the other hand entries with keys that duplicate those in the original context are inserted into the wrapped context, then the original entries are hidden. While these entries become inaccessible from the aggregate context, they remain intact and fully accessible from the original context.

Context chaining is accomplished through an overloaded VelocityContext constructor. The overloaded constructor takes another VelocityContext object as an input parameter, and it is this object that is wrapped by the newly created context. Such chaining is most frequently used for sharing tools and layering data. In the first case, a single context is populated with a number of tools, or general helper classes. This context is then used with the overloaded VelocityContext constructor to create additional contexts. The result is that each new context contains the tool set without the need to manually insert tools one by one into each new context.

In the case of data layering, an initial context is created and populated with core data. Then this context is used with the overloaded VelocityContext constructor to create a new context. The new context is populated with additional data and, if appropriate, used to create yet another context. This process is repeated as many times as is necessary. This technique is useful for cases where an aggregate data set is built from individual sets, where data in a later set may need to override data in an earlier set. It is also useful for cases where a core data set will remain the same across multiple templates but minor enhancements may be required for each individual template processed.

Managing Whitespace

When it comes to template design, the goals of template readability and desired output format are often at odds. Many people have a tendency to use whitespace, such as indentation and blank lines, to improve the readability of source code. There is a natural tendency to do the same with template code, especially where directives come into play. Unfortunately, whitespace plays a critical role in templates, as opposed to general source code where whitespace is largely ignored. Expecting a template engine to make its own decisions regarding which whitespace is important and which is not is questionable at best.

To get a better feeling for the nature of the problem, consider the template shown in Listing 10.10. This template prints out the names of a number of colors using various Velocity directives. The desired output is shown in Listing 10.11, but the actual output looks like that shown in Listing 10.12. The discrepancy comes about from the attempt to improve the readability of the template. Whitespace resulting from indentation and extra carriage returns slips into the template output.

```
#macro( write $list )
    #foreach( $color in $list )
        $color
    #end
#end

red
green

#set( $favorite = "blue" )
$favorite

#if ( $likeViolet )
    violet
#else
    purple
#end

#write( ["orange","yellow","brown"] )
```

Listing 10.10 A template that demonstrates the effects of whitespace formatting for readability.

```
red
green
blue
purple
orange
yellow
brown
```

Listing 10.11 The desired output for the template that lists color names.

```
red
green

blue

    purple

            orange
            yellow
            brown
```

Listing 10.12 The output generated for the template in Listing 10.10.

Unfortunately, there is currently no good solution to this problem. The options are to abandon readability altogether, as demonstrated by the modified template in Listing 10.13, make heavy use of VTL comments to filter out whitespace (as shown in Listing 10.14), or to settle on some compromise between these two approaches. Because whitespace handling is a frequently discussed topic on the Velocity lists, the future may bring better solutions.

```
#macro( write $list )
#foreach( $color in $list )
$color
#end
#end
red
green
#set( $favorite = "blue" )
$favorite
#if ( $likeViolet )
violet
#else
purple
#end
#write( ["orange","yellow","brown"] )
```

Listing 10.13 A modified version of the Listing 10.10 template that does away with attempts to improve readability.

```
#macro( write $list )
#**##foreach( $color in $list )
#*    *#$color
#**##end
#end
##
red
green
##
#set( $favorite = "blue" )
$favorite
##
#if ( $likeViolet )
#**#violet
#else
#**#purple
#end
##
#write( ["orange","yellow","brown"] )
```

Listing 10.14 A modified version of the Listing 10.10 template that uses VTL comments to filter whitespace.

Singleton vs. Non-Singleton

Velocity provides two approaches to obtaining instances of the Velocity engine. The legacy model, which we have used for all of our examples so far, is based on the Singleton pattern. Using this model, there is only one shared instance of the Velocity engine in the JVM. This is sufficient for most cases and provides certain advantages in terms of resource sharing. However, Velocity also supports a non-Singleton model that is sometimes more appropriate. The non-Singleton model allows for multiple Velocity engines to exist simultaneously in the JVM. This approach is especially useful for cases where multiple runtime configurations are required. The only difference between the two models in terms of instantiation and initialization is the manner in which the Velocity engine is obtained. With the Singleton model, the Velocity engine is obtained implicitly by invoking static methods on the Velocity class. With the non-Singleton model, the Velocity engine is obtained explicitly by instantiating a VelocityEngine object.

What's Next

In this chapter, we explained how to get the most out of your Velocity programming. In the next chapter, we explore the interaction of Velocity and XML as well as a tool called Anakia to make the marriage easy to manage.

CHAPTER 11

Velocity, XML, and Anakia

Extensible Markup Language (XML) has been one of the most talked about technologies in the past few years. The potential of this technology might have been overstated in the beginning, but no doubt exists about its power to fully characterize data in a text-based format. In this chapter, we look at two XML topics and how they relate to Velocity: accessing XML data from a DOM object within a Velocity template and using Anakia to handle XML data translations.

Accessing XML in Velocity Templates

As you probably know, Sun has taken great pains to provide Java developers with the tools they need to deal with XML data. At first, XML had little support, and products like JDOM (an open source API) and Xerces (from the Apache Software Foundation) were developed so that developers could work with XML data. Soon afterward, Sun offered additional packages that could be used with Java 1.3. With the release of Java 1.4, Sun built the XML support directly into the language.

If you want to use XML in your Velocity templates, you need to process the XML file within the controller Java class and attach the necessary information to the Context object. Let's look at an example. First, take a look at the XML file in Listing 11.1. The goal is to have the Velocity controller read in this XML file and parse it into an object that can be supplied with a Velocity template. Listing 11.2 shows an example controller for handling the XML.

```
<?xml version="1.0"?>

<cds>
 <cd>
  <title>2112</title>
  <artist>Rush</artist>
 </cd>
</cds>
```

Listing 11.1 An XML document.

```
import java.util.Vector;
import javax.servlet.http.*;
import org.apache.velocity.Template;
import org.apache.velocity.context.Context;
import org.apache.velocity.servlet.VelocityServlet;
import org.apache.velocity.exception.*;
import org.apache.xerces.parsers.*;

public class VelocityServletExample extends VelocityServlet {
  public Template handleRequest( HttpServletRequest request,
                                 HttpServletResponse response,
                                 Context context ) {

    try {
      SAXBuilder builder = new SAXBuilder(
        "org.apache.xerces.parsers.SAXParser" );
      Document root = builder.build("cds.xml");

      VelocityContext context = new VelocityContext();
      context.put("root", root );
    }  catch(Exception e){
      e.printStackTrace();
    }

    Template template = null;
    try {
      template = getTemplate("displayxml.vm");
    } catch( Exception e ) {
      System.out.println("Error " + e);
    }
    return template;
  }
}
```

Listing 11.2 The Velocity controller.

At this point, the servlet in Listing 11.2 resembles any of the controller servlets you've seen in previous chapters. The only change relates to the XML file. We assume that the XML in Listing 11.1 is stored in a file called cds.xml and is located in the same directory as the servlet.

The first task is to pull the actual document into the application and parse it into a format that you can easily manipulate. If you are familiar with XML processing, you know that there are two primary ways to parse a text-based XML document and turn it into a data structure that can be used in an application: SAX and DOM. Ultimately, it doesn't matter which method you use; however, SAX is better for large documents.

For this controller, we chose to use the SAXParser class found in Xerces. Xerces is a XML parser package under the Apache umbrella of products; you can find it at http://xml.apache.org/xerces2-j/index.html. Using Xerces is quite easy. First, instantiate a new SAXBuilder object and specify that you want to use one of the parsers in the Xerces family. As you can see in Listing 11.2, we're using the SAXParser class. The SAXBuilder class allows you to pass raw XML and produce a Document object in return. The Document object is a data structure representation of the XML. This is important because you know that any type of object can be added to the Velocity context and passed to a template.

In the code, you attach the XML data structure to the context under the reference name of "root". Next, the controller loads the template called displayxml.vm and returns the template to the VelocityServlet process. The displayxml.vm template (Listing 11.3) does all of the output work.

```
<html>
<body>
  CD title is  $root.getChild("cds").getChild("cd").getChild("title").get-
Text()
  CD artist is  $root.getChild("cds").getChild("cd").getChild("artist").get-
Text()

  </body>
</html>
```

Listing 11.3 The displayxml.vm template file.

The template in Listing 11.3 is designed to pull the artist and title values from the XML processed by the controller. As you can see, you're using normal XML methods to access the data within the data structure. Because Velocity gives you complete access to the objects in the context, you can use any methods defined on the Document class type as well as its parent type, Node.

For example, you can use the getChildNodes() method to return a NodeList object with all of the <cd> elements--that is, NodeList list = $root.getChild("cds").getChildNodes();. You can use the #foreach directive to walk through the nodes and display information about each one.

Velocity and Anakia

The process we just described is the foundation for the Anakia project (supplied as part of the Velocity download). Anakia is an Ant task designed to convert XML into an output medium of your choosing using Velocity templates instead of Extensible Stylesheet Language (XSL). The code for the Ant task can be found in the class org.apache.velocity.anakia.AnakiaTask, and you can find a full example in the /examples/anakia directory of the distribution.

The Ant Build Task

Let's look at the example before you attempt your own. As we mentioned earlier, Anakia is basically an Ant task that merges an XML document with Velocity templates. The Ant task is shown in Listing 11.4.

```
<project name="build-site" default="docs" basedir=".">
    <property name="docs.src" value="../xdocs"/>
    <property name="docs.dest" value="../docs"/>

    <target name="prepare">
        <available classname="org.apache.velocity.anakia.AnakiaTask"
        property="AnakiaTask.present"/>
    </target>

    <target depends="prepare" name="prepare-error"
unless="AnakiaTask.present">
        <echo>
            AnakiaTask is not present! Please check to make sure that
            velocity.jar is in your classpath.
        </echo>
    </target>

    <target name="docs" depends="prepare-error" if="AnakiaTask.present">
        <taskdef name="anakia" classname="org.apache.velocity.anakia.Anaki-
aTask"/>
        <anakia basedir="${docs.src}" destdir="${docs.dest}/"
             extension=".html" style="./site.vsl"
             projectFile="./stylesheets/project.xml"
```

Listing 11.4 The Anakia Ant task. (continues)

```
            excludes="**/stylesheets/**"
            includes="**/*.xml"
            lastModifiedCheck="false"
            velocityPropertiesFile="velocity.properties">
        </anakia>

        <copy todir="${docs.dest}/images" filtering="no">
            <fileset dir="${docs.src}/images">
                <include name="**/*.gif"/>
                <include name="**/*.jpeg"/>
                <include name="**/*.jpg"/>
            </fileset>
        </copy>
    </target>
</project>
```

Listing 11.4 The Anakia Ant task. (continued)

The Ant task attempts to locate the AnakiaTask class as well as set up the directories for the source and the destination files. In the example cases, the /xdocs directory contains the source and /docs contains the destination files. Table 11.1 explains the elements within the Ant task.

Table 11.1 Anakia Ant Task Definitions

TASK NAME	DEFINITION
<basedir>	The path to the XML files to be processed.
<destdir>	The path where the output from the templates and XML files will be placed.
<extension>	The extension that will be applied to the output file. The file will take the filename of the input XML file along with this extension.
<style>	The path to XSL stylesheets files.
<projectFile>	The path to the project file for the conversion (if one is used). You can use the projectFile to provide navigation.
<excludes>	An element that describes file or directories that are not to be processed.
<includes>	An element that describes files or directories that are to be processed.
<lastModifiedCheck>	An element that determines whether last-modified dates are processed. Set to true by default.
<templatePath>	The path to your VXL template file.
<velocityPropertiesFile>	The path to the velocity.properties file.

Source Documents

The example program contains two source documents. The first, called index.xml, is found in the /xdocs directory, and it appears in Listing 11.5. The second document, called index.xml, is found in the /xdocs/about directory and is used as a link within the root-level index document.

```
<?xml version="1.0" encoding="UTF-8"?>
<document>
  <properties>
    <author email="jon@latchkey.com">Jon S. Stevens</author>
    <title>The Jakarta Project</title>
  </properties>
  <body>
  <section name="Section 1">
    <p>This is an example template that gets processed.</p>
    <img src="/images/velocity.gif" width="329" height="105"/>
    <table border="1">
    <tr>
      <td>It even has a table in it!</td>
    </tr>
    </table>
    <h3>And an h3 tag</h3>
  </section>
  <section name="Section 2">
    <p> here is another section </p>
  </section>
  <section name="section 3">
    <p>
      <a href="./about/index.html">A link to a sub page</a>
    </p>
  </section>
  </body>
</document>
```

Listing 11.5 The index.xml source document.

The XML document shown in Listing 11.5 provides the information that you want applied to a Velocity template. As you can see, it includes traditional HTML tags as well as user-defined tags. The user-defined tags are the ones that will be matched against the Velocity template when the Anakia Ant task combines the two documents. Note that there is even a link on the page to another file called index.html.

In some cases, you might want to have a project file that describes the navigation to place on the output. For the example provided with Velocity, the projectFile looks like the following. When the projectFile is processed, the

<menu> elements are used as entries in a navigation menu on the left part of the HTML page.

```
<?xml version="1.0" encoding="ISO-8859-1"?>
<project name="Jakarta Site"
 href="http://jakarta.apache.org/">
<title>Jakarta Site</title>
<body>
  <menu name="Home">
     <item name="Front Page" href="/index.html"/>
  </menu>

  <menu name="About">
     <item name="About" href="/about/index.html"/>
  </menu>
</body>
</project>
```

Now let's take a look at the Velocity template to see what the various tags will produce.

Anakia Velocity Stylesheets

Listing 11.6 is the example template designed to process the index.xml file in Listing 11.5. The template takes advantage of many Velocity features we've covered, including directives and macros. Let's walk through the processing that takes place within the template. First, note that Anakia provides various context references to the template automatically. We discuss these variables in the next section. In order to understand the template, you must familiarize yourself with a few of them:

- **$xpath**–A list of all nodes in the supplied XML
- **$root**–The root of the parsed XML
- **$project**–The root of the project file

The template begins with local definitions that will be used in the template itself. Next, a call is made to the macro called document(). The template is basically made up of many different macros, each designed to output a specific part of the XML document to its HTML representation. The Anakia Ant task doesn't know about the macros in the template file, so things have to be started with a call to one of them. In this case, the document() macro defines the main part of the HTML output.

As you start to look at the code for the document() macro, you will find that it consists of all the primary HTML tags you might expect to see in a Web page. The first difference is found in the <title> elements. The value for the title is obtained with the following code:

```
$root.getChild("properties").getChild("title").getText()
```

This code uses the $root reference found in the Velocity context that relates to the XML document you are using as input to the template to find the properties element with its child title. It gets the text associated with the title element and outputs it in the new page being created. Look back at the XML data and you'll see that the output from the getText() call will be "The Jakarta Project". Next, the macro begins to build a table on the page. The left part of the table is a navigation menu, and the right part displays the information found in the input XML. (As you'll recall, the navigation menu is built from the projectFile we discussed earlier.)

To build the navigation menu, the document() macro calls the makeProject() macro. The makeProject() macro finds all of the menu items in the project XML and outputs a list of them in order. When the makeProject() macro is finished, control returns to the document() macro.

The left part of the table created by the document() macro consists of all the section elements found in the input XML. The various parts of the element are extracted, as well as information from the subelements, to produce the information for the table. Finally, all of the closing HTML tags are sent to the output, and the result is a complete Web page, as shown in Listing 11.7. Figure 11.1 shows how the final Web page looks when used in a browser.

```
## Defined variables
#set ($bodybg = "#ffffff")
#set ($bodyfg = "#000000")
#set ($bodylink = "#525D76")
#set ($bannerbg = "#525D76")
#set ($bannerfg = "#ffffff")
#set ($tablethbg = "#039acc")
#set ($tabletdbg = "#a0ddf0")

<!-- start the processing -->
#document()
<!-- end the processing -->

## This is where the macros live

#macro ( makeProject )
 #set ($menus = $xpath.applyTo("body/menu", $project))
 #foreach ( $menu in $menus )
   <strong>$menu.getAttributeValue("name")</strong>
     <ul>
     #foreach ( $item in $menu.getChildren() )
       #set ($name = $item.getAttributeValue("name"))
       <li>
```

Listing 11.6 The example stylesheet. (continues)

```
          #projectanchor($name $item.getAttributeValue("href"))
        </li>
      #end
      </ul>
  #end
 #end

 #macro ( image $value )
   #if ($value.getAttributeValue("width"))
     #set ($width=$value.getAttributeValue("width"))
   #end
   #if ($value.getAttributeValue("height"))
     #set ($height=$value.getAttributeValue("height"))
   #end
   #if ($value.getAttributeValue("align"))
     #set ($align=$value.getAttributeValue("align"))
   #end
   <img src="$relativePath$value.getAttributeValue("src")"
     width="$!width" height="$!height" align="$!align">
 #end

 #macro ( projectanchor $name $value )
   <a href="$relativePath$value">$name</a>
 #end

 #macro ( metaauthor $author $email )
   <meta name="author" value="$author">
   <meta name="email" value="$email">
 #end

 #macro (document)
 <html>
   <head>
     <title>
       $root.getChild("properties").getChild("title").getText()
     </title>
   </head>
   <body bgcolor="$bodybg" text="$bodyfg" link="$bodylink">
     <table border="1">
       <tr>
         <td>#makeProject()</td>
         <td>
             #set ($allSections = $xpath.applyTo("body/section",
               $root))
             #foreach ( $section in $allSections )
               #foreach ( $item in $section.getChildren() )
                 #if ($item.getName().equals("img"))
```

Listing 11.6 The example stylesheet. (continues)

```
                #image ($item)
             #else
                $xmlout.outputString($item)
             #end
           #end
         #end
     </td>
   </tr>
  </table>
 </body>
</html>
#end
```

Listing 11.6 The example stylesheet. (continued)

```
<!-- Content Stylesheet for Site -->
<!-- start the processing -->
<!--================== -->
<!-- Main Page Section -->
<!--================== -->
<html>
  <head>
    <meta http-equiv="Content-Type"
      content="text/html; charset=iso-8859-1"/>
    <meta name="author" value="Jon S. Stevens">
    <meta name="email" value="jon@latchkey.com">
    <title>The Jakarta Project</title>
  </head>
  <body bgcolor="#ffffff" text="#000000" link="#525D76">
    <table border="1">
       <tr>
         <td>
            <strong>Home</strong>
            <ul>
              <li>    <a href="./index.html">Front Page</a></li>
            </ul>
            <strong>About</strong>
            <ul>
              <li>    <a href="./about/index.html">About</a></li>
            </ul>
         </td>
         <td>
           <p>
             This is an example template that gets processed.
           </p>
           <img src="./images/velocity.gif" width="329"
```

Listing 11.7 The completed Web page. (continues)

```
              height="105" align="">
            <table border="1">
              <tr>
               <td>
                 It even has a table in it!
               </td>
              </tr>
            </table>
            <h3>And an h3 tag</h3>
            <p> here is another section </p>
            <p><a href="./about/index.html">A link to a sub page</a></p>
          </td>
        </tr>
     </table>
   </body>
 </html>
 <!-- end the processing -->
```

Listing 11.7 The completed Web page. (continued)

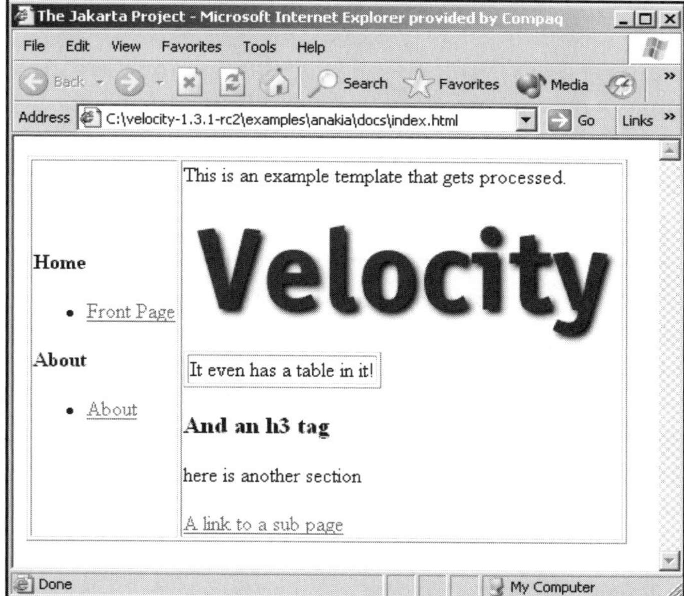

Figure 11.1 The Web page output.

Context References

When the Anakia Ant task combines the template with the XML, it adds a few references to the context so that the Velocity template has data to work with.

You've already seen a few of the objects that will be in the context. Table 11.2 describes all of the possible objects.

Table 11.2 Anakia Context References

OBJECT NAME	DESCRIPTION
$root	This reference's value is the root element of your XML document.
$project	This is the root element of your project.xml file.
#escape.getText($string)	This object can be used to convert text into escaped HTML text. Thus, quote, <, >, and & will be converted to the ", <, >, and & strings.
$relativePath	This represents the path to your input XML file based on the baseDir within the Ant task.
$xpath.applyTo(" ", $root)	This represents the ability to apply the first element to all of the nodes supplied in the second parameter tree.
$data	This represents a java.util.Date object.

Note that you can use the XPath expressions with any of the element references. For example, you can use $root.selectNodes("cds/cd") to get a list of nodes matching the <cd> element type.

Outputting XML Using Velocity

If you have data in a database or produced by a servlet application, you might encounter a situation where you want to output XML to the user either in a Web browser or as a file. Consider the CD application you developed earlier in this chapter. This application provides the ability to add CDs and query against the records in a database. For the most part, you either query against a single artist or display the tracks of a specific CD. It's quite possible that you will want to produce the output in an XML format, and since we are discussing XML in this chapter, let's show you how to do that.

For this section, we consider two different situations: XML for our artist query and a full report of all CDs in the database.

The Artist Query XML

If you recall, our CD application utilizes a control servlet to interpret the various submit buttons on the main screen. For the artist query form, the submit button calls the control servlet, passing a value of obtain. The servlet executes the code shown in Listing 11.8.

```
else if (req.getParameter("submit").equals("obtain")) {
      try {
        if (cdHome == null) {
          context.put("message", "Sorry we had an error");
        } else {
          Collection cds = cdHome.findByArtist(req.getParameter("artist"));
          context.put ("cds", cds);
          try {
            template = getTemplate("displaycds.vm");
          } catch( Exception e ) {
            e.printStackTrace();
          }
        }
      } catch(Exception e) {
        e.printStackTrace();
      }
    }
```

Listing 11.8 The artist query code.

Very simply, the code calls a query associated with the CD Bean, and a collection is returned and displayed by the displaycds.vm Velocity template. Let's change the code a little to accommodate an additional submit value of obtainxml, which has the effect of pulling the same information from the database; however, instead of using the displaycds.vm template, it uses the producecdxml.vm Velocity template. The new code appears in Listing 11.9.

```
else if ((req.getParameter("submit").equals("obtain")) ||
          (req.getParameter("submit").equals("obtainxml"))) {
      try {
        if (cdHome == null) {
          context.put("message", "Sorry we had an error");
        } else {
          Collection cds = cdHome.findByArtist(req.getParameter("artist"));
          context.put ("cds", cds);
          try {
            if (req.getParameter("submit").equals("obtainxml")) {
            template = getTemplate("producecdxml.vm");
          } else {
            template = getTemplate("displaycds.vm");
          } catch( Exception e ) {
```

Listing 11.9 The artist query code with XML output. (continues)

```
            e.printStackTrace();
          }
        }
      } catch(Exception e) {
        e.printStackTrace();
      }
    }
```

Listing 11.9 The artist query code with XML output. (continued)

As you can see, you want to enter the block of code as either the obtain or the obtainxml submit button values are passed to the servlet. All of the same CDs are returned from the query, but depending on the submit value, either the producecdxml.vm or displaycds.vm Velocity template is used.

To use the code, you first have to define producecdxml.vm. Listing 11.10 shows the template.

```
<?xml version="1.0" ?>
<cds>
#foreach($value in $cds)
  <cd id="$value.id">
    <title>$value.title</title>
  </cd>
#end
</cds>
```

Listing 11.10 The producecdxml.vm Velocity template.

The Velocity template shown in Listing 11.10 produces an XML file for the artist query. Notice how the ID of the CD and the title are captured as an attribute and element, respectively.

The Full CD Report XML

In the previous example, all of the output was generated on the user's browser--but what if you want to download an XML file with all of the CDs in the database? You can do this by making a few changes to the code. Let's add a button on the main CD screen that will call the control servlet requesting a full report of the CD database. Use the following code:

```
<form action="http://localhost:8080/cd/cdVelocityHandler" method="post">
  <input type="submit" name="submit" value="fullreport"> -
  download 'report.txt' to your local system
</form>
```

When the user clicks on the FullReport button, control is passed to the servlet, where the fullreport value is recognized. The code in Listing 11.11 is then executed.

```
else if (req.getParameter("submit").equals("fullreport")) {
      try {
        if (cdHome == null) {
          context.put("message", "Sorry we had an error");
        } else {
          Collection cds = cdHome.findAllCDs();
          context.put ("cds", cds);
          try {
            res.setContentType("APPLICATION/OCTET-STREAM");
            res.setHeader("Content-Disposition","attachment;
filename=report.txt");
            template = getTemplate("fullreport.vm");
          } catch( Exception e ) {
            e.printStackTrace();
          }
        }
      } catch(Exception e) {
        e.printStackTrace();
      }
```

Listing 11.1 The fullreport code.

Note two changes from Listing 11.11. The first is a new query called findAllCDs(), added to the CDRecordBean class. The query is shown in Listing 11.12.

```
<query>
  <query-method>
    <method-name>findAllCDs</method-name>
  </query-method>
  <ejb-ql>SELECT o FROM CDTable o</ejb-ql>
</query>
```

Listing 11.12 The CDRecordBean All CD query.

The second change consists of these two lines of code:

```
Res.setContentType("APPLICATION/OCTET-STREAM");
res.setHeader("Content-Disposition","attachment;filename=report.txt");
```

This code is designed to tell the user's browser that the information that will be provided is in the form of a file called report.txt and that it is an attachment, so the Save As dialog box should be presented to the user. This is important because our Velocity template will be used to produce a downloadable file. Listing 11.13 shows the actual Velocity template.

```
<cds>
#foreach($value in $cds)
  <cd id="$value.id">
    <artist>$value.artist</artist>
    <title>$value.title</title>
  </cd>
#end
</cds>
```

Listing 11.13 The Velocity template for the XML output.

Now the user can browse the CD application index page and click on the Full-Report button. The code pulls all of the CDs from the database and formats them using the fullreport.vm Velocity file, as shown in Figure 11.2.

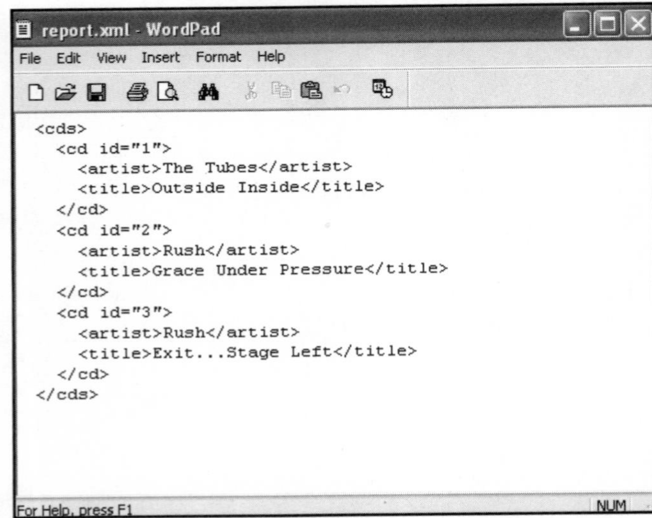

Figure 11.2 The XML output.

What's Next

In this chapter, we explored ways that you can use Velocity to process and use XML data. Developers can provide designers with a standard format for all data passed to the template, and designers can use a comprehensive set of methods to access the data. In the next chapter, we discuss how you can mix Velocity and servlets.

CHAPTER 12

Using Velocity with Servlets

As you've learned in previous chapters, Velocity is primarily used as a scripting language for the view component of a Model-View-Controller (MVC) paradigm. Servlets are one of the most common programming mechanisms for MVC under Java. By using servlets as the controller, Velocity as the view, and either servlets or JavaBeans as the model, you create an ideal environment for the development of comprehensive Web solutions. In this chapter, we show you how to use Velocity with servlets.

Using Servlets

Before you can start using Velocity with servlets, you must understand what servlets are and how they are used. If you are already familiar with them, you can move directly to the section "Extending Servlets with VelocityServlet."

In the early days of dynamic Web page development, server-side languages such as Active Server Pages (ASP) and JavaServer Pages (JSP) became available that you could embed in the HTML code. When a browser requested the Web page, the server parsed through the ASP/JSP page, executed the statements it found, and returned a pure HTML page to the user (barring any client-side JavaScript or VBScript). Mixing code and HTML is not easy, however, and the ASP and JSP server-side languages also have certain limitations, such as limited support across platforms and server support.

Servlets are a way to pull the code out of the HTML and place it at the server where it belongs. That way, you can write the logic using the full power of the

Java language. The servlets can be distributed across a farm of servers, and you can use templates to display information to the user.

A Common Format for Servlets

It is important that you know what a traditional servlet looks like before you go any further. Listing 12.1 shows a simple servlet.

```
import java.io.*;
import java.sql.*;
import javax.servlet.*;
import javax.servlet.http.*;
import javax.naming.*;

public class ViewAccount extends HttpServlet {
  public void init() throws ServletException {
  }

  public void doGet(HttpServletRequest request,
   HttpServletResponse response)
    throws IOException, ServletException {

    response.setContentType("text/html");
    PrintWriter out = response.getWriter();

    out.println("<HTML>");
    out.println("</HTML>");

    } catch (SQLException e) {
       e.printStackTrace();
    }
  }

  public void doPost(HttpServletRequest request,
HttpServletResponse response)
    throws ServletException, IOException {
    doGet(request, response);
  }
}
```

Listing 12.1 Traditional servlet code.

When a request comes from a Web browser, it will be either a POST or a GET. As you can see in the servlet code, there are methods for handling both the requests (although the doPost() method simply delegates to the doGet() method). Within the doGet() method are two important variables: request and response. The request object is responsible for transferring information from the user to the servlet. Typically, the information will be text that a user enters into input controls in an HTML form. The response object is responsible for configuring the HTML page that will be sent back to the user's Web browser. Information in the response object includes the type of page being returned (such as HMTL, XML, or an image). The response object also has a PrintWriter object associated with it, which is used to write information to the page returned to the user.

Servlets aren't hosted on ordinary Web servers but instead are hosted on *application servers*. Examples of these pieces of software include Tomcat, BOSS, and Resin. In most cases, the application server is used in conjunction with a Web server, like IIS or Apache. When the Web server gets a request for a servlet, the request is forwarded to the application server and executed. The application server uses the Java compiler to create an executable image of the servlet, which is executed within a Java Virtual Machine (JVM). We see an example of this in the next section.

Extending Servlets with VelocityServlet

You can use the Velocity engine with servlets in a way that makes outputting information to the user using the Velocity Templating Language a simple task. To facilitate the use of servlets, you use a base class called VelocityServlet and a method called handleRequest()--instead of directly extending HttpServlet and the doGet()/doPost() methods as in the traditional servlet.

The handleRequest() method passes three parameters--HttpServletRequest, HttpServletResponse, and Context--to the code responding to a GET/POST request. The HttpServletRequest and HttpServletResponse objects are the same objects received in the doGet() and doPost() methods found in the traditional servlet code shown in Listing 12.1. The Context object is a context for the Velocity engine designed to be used with the servlet. We will place information in this Context object for the Velocity templates used to display a response to the user.

The handleRequest() method returns a Template object, which the method automatically merges with the passed-in Context object. Thus, the code within the handleRequest() method should do everything necessary to set up the Context object and return a Velocity object for the merge. If the Template object returned equates to null, the code won't perform a merge. In this situation, the code returns to the user's browser anything placed in the PrintWriter object of the response object, just like the traditional servlet code.

Basic Velocity Servlet Code

With the introduction of the handleRequest() method, let's look at an example (Listing 12.2) that produces simple output to a browser.

```
import java.util.Vector;
import javax.servlet.http.HttpServletRequest;
import javax.servlet.http.HttpServletResponse;
import org.apache.velocity.Template;
import org.apache.velocity.context.Context;
import org.apache.velocity.servlet.VelocityServlet;
import org.apache.velocity.exception.*;

public class VelocityServletExample extends VelocityServlet {
  public Template handleRequest( HttpServletRequest request,
                                 HttpServletResponse response,
                                 Context context ) {

    Vector v = new Vector();
    v.add("one");
    v.add("two");
    v.add("three");

    context.put("list", v);

    Template template = null;
    try {
      template = getTemplate("displaylist.vm");
    } catch( Exception e ) {
      PrintWriter out = response.getWriter();
      out.println("Error getting template");
    }
    return template;
  }
}
```

Listing 12.2 A Velocity servlet example.

The code in Listing 12.2, when called by a browser, instantiates a Vector object and places three String objects into it. The Vector object is placed in the context with the statement

```
context.put("list", v);
```

Notice that we have placed the entire Vector object into the context. Next, a Template object is declared and a call is made to the getTemplate(String) method to locate and load a template from the server's hard drive. If there is a problem obtaining the template file from the hard drive, the PrintWriter from the response object is obtained and an error message is written to it. The last operation performed by the code is to return the Template object. If the object is null because of an error, the system won't perform a merge; otherwise, the template read from the server is merged with the context. Listing 12.3 shows the Velocity template used in this example.

```
<?xml version="1.0" encoding="ISO-8859-1" ?>

<list>
#foreach( $value in $list )
  <number>$value</number>
#end
</list>
```

Listing 12.3 The displaylist.vm Velocity code.

The template in Listing 12.3 isn't HTML; we used XML to show that Velocity isn't limited to output in HTML format only. Important work is being performed in this example. Remember that the "list" key relates to a Vector object. The Velocity Templating Language code in the template uses the Vector in a #foreach loop. Recall from our definition of the #foreach directive that with List objects such as Vector the iterator is automatically extracted and used to obtain all of the individual objects in the List (or Vector, in this case).

Each of the objects from the Vector are extracted and placed in the reference $value. Since the String isn't a compound object, we can simply use it to output its value within the <number> element tags. Figure 12.1 shows an example of the output from our first Velocity servlet and its corresponding template.

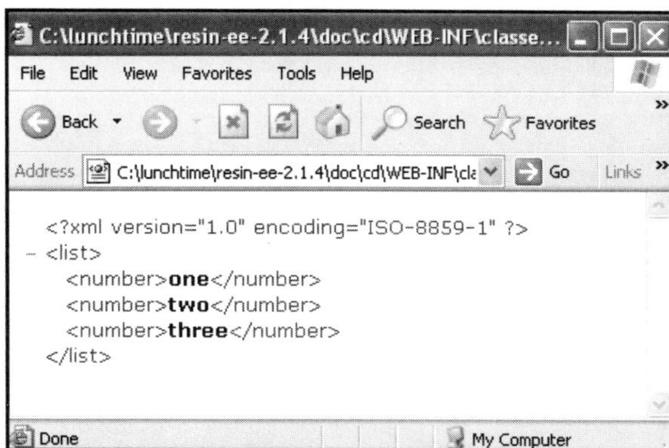

Figure 12.1 Output from the Velocity template.

Although the HttpServletRequest and HttpServletResponse objects are passed to the servlet code, they are also placed in the Context object as two constants:

- VelocityServlet.REQUEST—Stored as *req*
- VelocityServlet.RESPONSE—Stored as *res*

Each of the objects can be used in a Velocity template with code like the following, which extracts the value in a <form> input variable called username:

```
#set($username = $req.getParameter('username'))
```

Creating an MVC application

Our first servlet example for Velocity is quite simple, so let's make things a little more complex. In this section, you build an MVC application using servlets for the controller, Velocity templates for the view, and JavaBeans for the model. The application is a CD database where you have four possible operations:

- Adding a CD and returning a thank-you response
- Adding tracks for specific CDs and returning a thank-you response
- Obtaining all CDs by a specific artist
- Obtaining all tracks on a specific CD

Figure 12.2 shows the output produced when you add a new CD; Figure 12.3 shows the output produced when you search for all CDs by a specific artist. Figure 12.4 shows the output produced when you list all of the tracks on a specific CD.

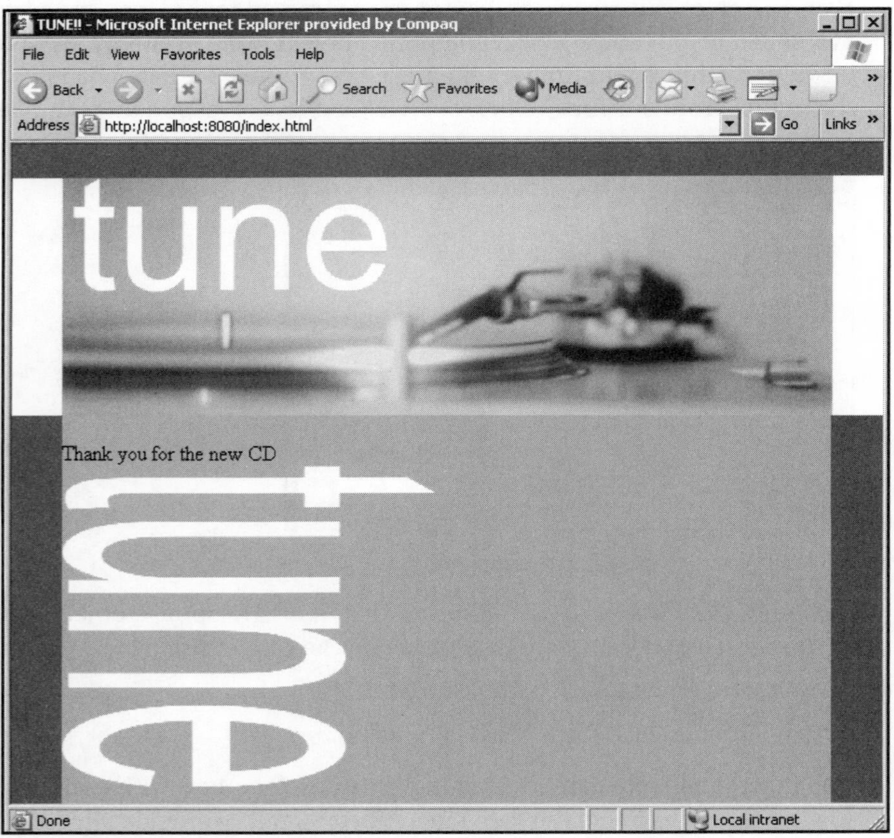

Figure 12.2 Adding a new CD.

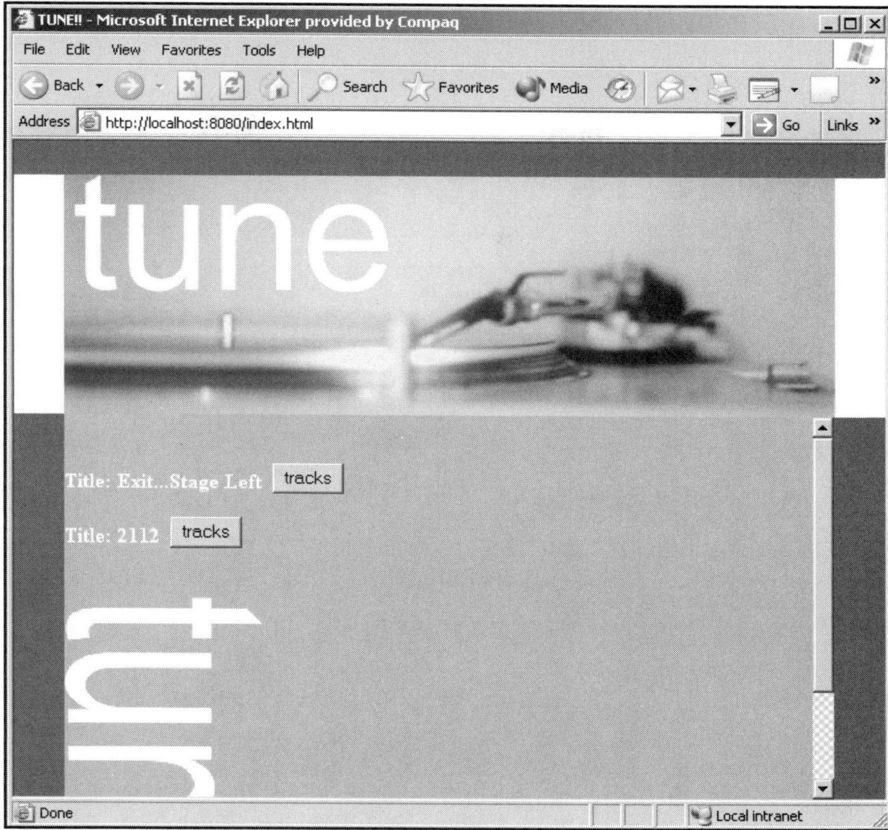

Figure 12.3 Listing all CDs for an artist.

The Database Structure

The application uses a database to hold the information about the CDs as well as the tracks. In the test environment, we chose MySQL but you could select another database vendor if you prefer. The following SQL create table commands show the schema for the CD and tracks tables that are placed in a database called products.

```
create table cd (
id int not null primary key auto_increment,
title varchar(128),
artist varchar(64),
tracks int);

create table tracks(
id int not null primary key auto_increment,
```

```
cd_id int,
name varchar(64),
length varchar(16));
```

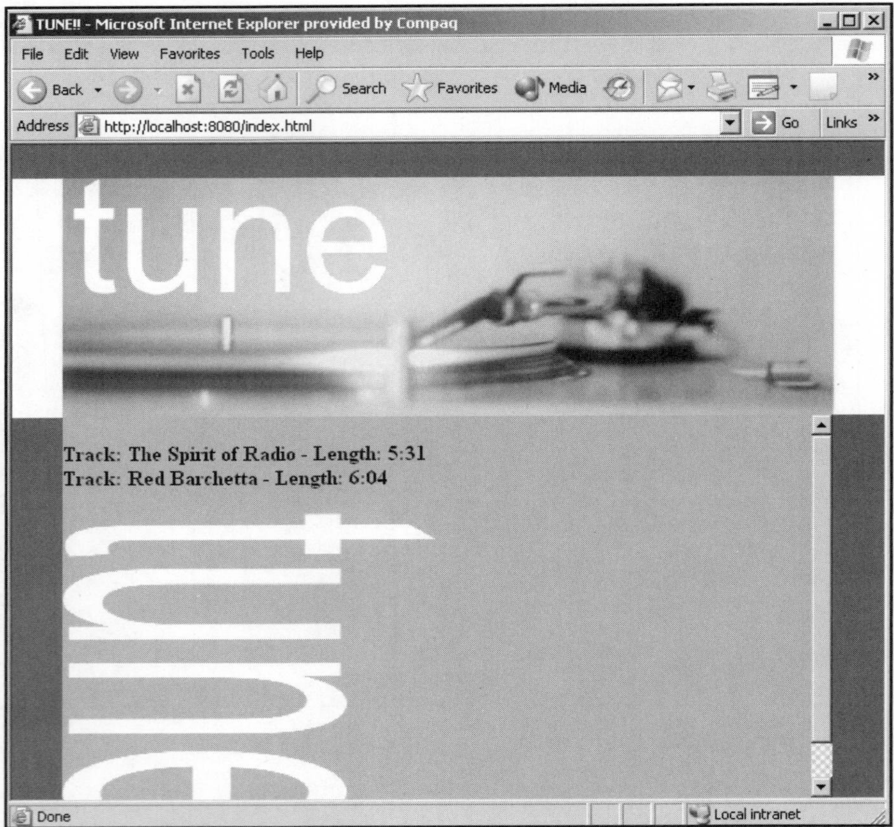

Figure 12.4 Listing all tracks on a CD.

Database Access

Our model components for the CD example are using entity EJBs to access the data within both the CD and tracks tables. The beans as well as the servlets are served to the user using an application server. For the test environment, we're using the Resin application server. The EJBs access the database through a Java Naming and Directory Interface (JNDI) resource reference. Listing 12.4 shows the <resource-ref> element that you add to the application server's configuration file. The element is fairly standard, except for the driver and URL for the database. If you are using another database vendor, you have to change both of these <init-param> elements.

```
<resource-ref>
  <res-ref-name>jdbc/ProductsDB</res-ref-name>
  <res-type>javax.sql.ConnectionPoolDataSource</res-type>
  <init-param driver-name="org.gjt.mm.mysql.Driver"/>
  <init-param url="jdbc:mysql://localhost:3306/products"/>
  <init-param user=""/>
  <init-param password=""/>
  <init-param max-connections="20"/>
  <init-param max-idle-time="30"/>
  <init-param max-active-time="1"/>
  <init-param max-pool-time="1"/>
  <init-param connection-wait-time="1"/>
</resource-ref>
```

Listing 12.4 The resin.config resource text.

The Model Code

At this point, you've created the database and included a JNDI reference that can be used by any of the code executing on the application server to access the database. It is now time to consider the entity beans that will be used to access the data in your tables. Since you have two tables, you need to build two entity EJBs. For our purposes, let's take advantage of Resin's *container-managed persistence (CMP)* model for beans, which focuses on the local instantiation of EJBs versus a remote invocation. What this means is that you will build entity EJBs that have to deal only with local interfaces, not remote ones, thus involving considerably less coding. Because this book is about Velocity, we show only the bean classes for the two entity EJBs; you can download all of the other files from the software Web site at www.wiley.com/compbooks/gradecki. First, let's look at the EJB file containing the bean definitions (Listing 12.5).

```
<ejb-jar>
  <enterprise-beans>
    <entity>
      <ejb-name>CDRecordBean</ejb-name>
      <local-home>cd.CDRecordHome</local-home>
      <local>cd.CDRecord</local>
      <ejb-class>cd.CDRecordBean</ejb-class>

      <prim-key-class>int</prim-key-class>
      <primkey-field>id</primkey-field>

      <persistence-type>Container</persistence-type>
```

Listing 12.5 The CDRecordBean EJB file. (continues)

```
      <reentrant>True</reentrant>

      <abstract-schema-name>CDTable</abstract-schema-name>
      <sql-table>cd</sql-table>

      <cmp-field><field-name>id</field-name></cmp-field>
      <cmp-field><field-name>title</field-name></cmp-field>
      <cmp-field><field-name>artist</field-name></cmp-field>
      <cmp-field><field-name>tracks</field-name></cmp-field>

      <query>
        <query-method>
          <method-name>findByArtist</method-name>
        </query-method>
        <ejb-ql>SELECT o FROM CDTable o WHERE o.artist like 
?1</ejb-ql>
      </query>
  </entity>

    <entity>
      <ejb-name>TracksRecordBean</ejb-name>
      <local-home>cd.TracksRecordHome</local-home>
      <local>cd.TracksRecord</local>
      <ejb-class>cd.TracksRecordBean</ejb-class>

      <prim-key-class>int</prim-key-class>
      <primkey-field>id</primkey-field>

      <persistence-type>Container</persistence-type>
      <reentrant>True</reentrant>

      <abstract-schema-name>TrackTable</abstract-schema-name>
      <sql-table>tracks</sql-table>

      <cmp-field><field-name>id</field-name></cmp-field>
      <cmp-field><field-name>cd_id</field-name></cmp-field>
      <cmp-field><field-name>name</field-name></cmp-field>
      <cmp-field><field-name>length</field-name></cmp-field>

      <query>
        <query-method>
          <method-name>findByCdID</method-name>
        </query-method>
        <ejb-ql>SELECT o FROM TrackTable o WHERE o.cd_id=?1</ejb-ql>
      </query>
    </entity>
  </enterprise-beans>
</ejb-jar>
```

Listing 12.5 The CDRecordBean EJB file. (continued)

The EJB file in Listing 12.5 shows how the two entity beans are defined, along with the primary key and all of the fields of each table. Both of the entity beans include a <query> element that allows data to be pulled from the tables using a field other than the primary key. To give you an idea of how entity beans are written using the Resin application server, consider the CDRecordBean class in Listing 12.6.

```
package cd;

import javax.ejb.*;

public abstract class CDRecordBean
  extends com.caucho.ejb.AbstractEntityBean {

  public abstract String getTitle();
  public abstract String getArtist();
  public abstract int getTracks();
  public abstract int getId();

  public abstract void setTitle(String title);
  public abstract void setArtist(String artist);
  public abstract void setTracks(int tracks);
  public abstract void setId(int id);


  public int ejbCreate(String title, String artist, int tracks)
    throws CreateException {
    setId(0);
    setTitle(title);
    setArtist(artist);
    setTracks(tracks);

    return 1;
  }

  public void ejbPostCreate(String title, String artist, int
tracks) {
    // since there are no relations, this is empty.
  }
}
```

Listing 12.6 The CDRecordBean class.

The CDRecordBean class in Listing 12.6 inherits from the class AbstractEntity-Bean, which is defined as a helper class from the makers of Resin. This helper class provides all the normal methods that an entity bean needs to implement with empty bodies. You only need to provide the methods actually used in your bean, thus cutting down on code clutter. Otherwise, the remaining code in the bean is used to define the fields of the table to which this bean relates. Listing 12.7 shows the bean class for TracksRecordBean.

```
package cd;

import javax.ejb.*;
import java.sql.*;

public abstract class TracksRecordBean
  extends com.caucho.ejb.AbstractEntityBean {

  public abstract int getId();
  public abstract int getCd_id();
  public abstract String getName();
  public abstract String getLength();

  public abstract void setId(int id);
  public abstract void setCd_id(int cd_id);
  public abstract void setName(String name);
  public abstract void setLength(String tracks);

  public int ejbCreate(int cd_id, String name, String length)
    throws CreateException {
    setCd_id(cd_id);
    setName(name);
    setLength(length);

    return 1;
  }

  public void ejbPostCreate(int cd_id, String name, String length) {
    // since there are no relations, this is empty.
  }
}
```

Listing 12.7 The TracksRecordBean class.

As we mentioned earlier, you can download the remaining files for the entity beans. All of the entity files are placed in the /classes directory of an application hosted by Resin.

The View Code

Now you need to consider how the output will look to the user using Velocity as your scripting language. This is where all of the magic takes place to provide your users with a pleasing experience. For this application, you have three Velocity templates:

- thanks.vm—A generic page for displaying thank-you messages to the user
- displaycd.vm—A page that displays a list of CDs for the user
- displaytracks.vm—A page that displays a list of tracks on a specific CD

First, let's look at the thanks.vm template, shown in Listing 12.8.

```
<HTML>
<HEAD>
    <TITLE></TITLE>
    <link rel="stylesheet" type="text/css" href="defaultpage.css">
</HEAD>
<BODY BGCOLOR="#F79C19" link="ffffff" alink="999999"
vlink="ffffff" topmargin="0" leftmargin="0" marginheight="0"
marginwidth="0">

<BR>
#if ($message)
  $message
#end
$thanks
<img src="/images/tune_big.gif" height="250" width=283></td></tr>

</table>
</BODY>
</HTML>
```

Listing 12.8 The thanks.vm template.

The thanks.vm template is actually part of a frameset that provides all the borders' look and feel. The template is placed in the *main*, or body, part of the frameset. Even with this, you still need to provide appropriate background colors and graphics to improve the appearance of the output. At the top of the template is the information for the background of the page, followed by the actual Velocity elements.

The first element is an #if directive surrounding the $message reference. The $message reference is designed to display a message in those cases where an error has occurred and you need to let the user know about it. The message is written only to the context when an error occurs, so there will be times when the reference won't be found in the context. If you didn't wrap the reference in an #if directive, the text string "$message" would be displayed instead. This wouldn't look very good, so the $if directive tests whether the $reference contains a value. If the $reference contains a value—meaning it was found in the context—you display the value in $message.

In case of an error, you still thank the user for attempting to enter a new CD or track. This output is generated using the $thanks reference.

Displaying CDs

Our application allows the user to search for all CDs in the database by a specified artist and get back a list of those CDs. A button appears next to each of the listed CDs that the user can click to list all of the tracks on that particular CD. The displaycd.vm template in Listing 12.9 handles these display tasks.

```
<HTML>
<HEAD>
    <TITLE></TITLE>
    <link rel="stylesheet" type="text/css" href="defaultpage.css">
</HEAD>
<BODY BGCOLOR="#F79C19" link="ffffff" alink="999999"
vlink="ffffff" topmargin="0" leftmargin="0" marginheight="0"
marginwidth="0">

<BR><BR>
<font color="ffffff">

#foreach($value in $cds)
<form action="http://localhost:8080/cd/cdVelocityHandler"
method="post">
  <b> Title: $value.title </b>
  <input type="hidden" name="id" value="$value.id">
  <input type="submit" name="submit" value="tracks">
</form>
#end

<BR>
<img src="/images/tune_big.gif" height="250" width="150">

</BODY>
</HTML>
```

Listing 12.9 The displaycd.vm template.

Just as with the thanks.vm template, you include some display HTML at the beginning of the template. All of the output for the CDs is displayed in the body of a frameset. After the HTML comes the Velocity code. Recall that there are two things you want the listing to do: include the title of all the CDs for that artist and display a button that the user can click to list the tracks on each CD.

Suppose that while working with your Web developers, you decide that the code pulling the CDs from the database will place a Collection object called $cds into the context. This Collection object will contain a number of CDRecordBean objects based on all of the CD rows pulled for a specific artist.

As you've already seen, the #foreach directive is designed to extract an iterator from objects that have them available. The Collection class is one such object, so each time through the loop, the $value reference will be a CDRecordBean entity object. Using the getter methods of the bean, the appropriate values are then extracted.

Most of the work occurs within the loop where the title of the CD pulled from the database is displayed. Notice that a <form> HTML tag surrounds the title. The <form> tag is used to display a button that the user can click to see the tracks on the CD.

After discussing the requirements for your application, you and the Web developers decide you want to have the ID from the CD table as the link to the tracks table. To do this, you create a hidden <input> element in the <form> element. Notice the hidden input uses a value of $value.id, which means you will be passing into the controller a different ID for each of the listed CDs.

Displaying Tracks

When a user clicks the Tracks button displayed by the displaycd.vm template, you want to display both the name of the track and the length of the song. Listing 12.10 shows the displaytracks.vm template, which handles these tasks. Again, this template contains the HTML tags necessary to display the look and feel of the template. After the HTML, you have another #foreach loop.

```
<HTML>
<HEAD>
    <TITLE></TITLE>
    <link rel="stylesheet" type="text/css" href="defaultpage.css">
</HEAD>
<BODY BGCOLOR="#F79C19" link="ffffff" alink="999999"
vlink="ffffff" topmargin="0" leftmargin="0" marginheight="0"
marginwidth="0">
#if ($message)
  $message
#end
<BR>

#foreach($value in $tracks)
  <b> Track: $value.name - Length: $value.length</b><BR>
#end

<br>
<img src="/images/tune_big.gif" height="250" width=283></td></tr>

</table>
</BODY>
</HTML>
```

Listing 12.10 The displaytracks.vm template.

At this point, your Web developer has indicated that you need another Collection object for all of the tracks on a CD. The Collection object, called $tracks, is placed in the context by the controller component.

The Controller Code

You have both the model and view components; now you need to build the controller component to tie these two components together. Listing 12.11 shows the Velocity servlet that will do the work.

```
import java.io.*;
import java.util.*;
import javax.servlet.*;
import javax.servlet.http.*;
import org.apache.velocity.Template;
import org.apache.velocity.context.Context;
import org.apache.velocity.servlet.VelocityServlet;
import org.apache.velocity.exception.*;
import javax.naming.*;
import javax.ejb.*;
import cd.*;

import org.apache.velocity.app.Velocity;

public class cdVelocityHandler extends VelocityServlet {
  private CDRecordHome cdHome = null;
  private TracksRecordHome tracksHome = null;


  protected Properties loadConfiguration(ServletConfig config )
        throws IOException, FileNotFoundException {
        Properties p = new Properties();

        String path =
          config.getServletContext().getRealPath("/");
        if (path == null) {
            System.out.println("
             Unable to get the current webapp root");
            path = "/";
        }

        p.setProperty(Velocity.FILE_RESOURCE_LOADER_PATH,
          path );
        return p;
    }
```

Listing 12.11 The controller servlet for the CD example. (continues)

```
public void init() throws ServletException {
  try {
    javax.naming.Context cmp = (javax.naming.Context)
      new InitialContext().lookup("java:comp/env/cmp");

    cdHome = (CDRecordHome) cmp.lookup("CDRecordBean");
    tracksHome = (TracksRecordHome)
      cmp.lookup("TracksRecordBean");

  } catch (NamingException e) {
    e.printStackTrace();
  }
}

public Template handleRequest( HttpServletRequest req,
  HttpServletResponse res, Context context ) {
  Template template = null;

  if (req.getParameter("submit").equals("new")) {
    try {
      if (cdHome == null) {
        context.put("message", "Sorry we had an error");
      } else {
        int tracks =
          Integer.parseInt(req.getParameter("tracks"));
        CDRecord cd =
         cdHome.create(req.getParameter("title"),
         req.getParameter("artist"), tracks);

        if (cd != null) {
          context.put("thanks",
            "Thank you for the new CD<BR>");
        } else {
          context.put("thanks",
            "We are sorry but your request failed<BR>");
        }
        try {
          template = getTemplate("thanks.vm");
        } catch( Exception e ) {
          e.printStackTrace();
        }
      }
    } catch(Exception e) {
      e.printStackTrace();
    }

  } else if (req.getParameter("submit").equals("obtain")) {
```

Listing 12.11 The controller servlet for the CD example. (continues)

```
    try {
      if (cdHome == null) {
        context.put("message", "Sorry we had an error");
      } else {
        Collection cds =
          cdHome.findByArtist(req.getParameter("artist"));
        context.put ("cds", cds);
        try {
          template = getTemplate("displaycds.vm");
        } catch( Exception e ) {
          e.printStackTrace();
        }
      }
    } catch(Exception e) {
      e.printStackTrace();
    }
  } else if (req.getParameter("submit").equals("tracks")) {
    try {
      if (tracksHome == null) {
        context.put("message", "Sorry we had an error");
      } else {
        int id = Integer.parseInt(req.getParameter("id"));
        Collection tracks = tracksHome.findByCdID(id);

        context.put ("tracks", tracks);
        try {
          template = getTemplate("displaytracks.vm");
        } catch( Exception e ) {
          System.out.println("Error " + e);
        }
      }
    } catch(Exception e) {
      e.printStackTrace();
    }
  } else if (req.getParameter("submit").equals("addtrack")) {
    try {
      if (tracksHome == null) {
        context.put("message", "Sorry we had an error");
      } else {
        int id= Integer.parseInt(req.getParameter("id"));
        TracksRecord track = tracksHome.create(id,
         req.getParameter("name"),
         req.getParameter("length"));

        if (track!= null) {
          context.put("thanks",
            "Thank you for the new track<BR>");
```

Listing 12.11 The controller servlet for the CD example. (continues)

```
          } else {
            context.put("thanks",
              "We are sorry but your request failed<BR>");
          }
          try {
            template = getTemplate("thanks.vm");
          } catch( Exception e ) {
            e.printStackTrace();
          }
        }
      } catch(Exception e) {
        e.printStackTrace();
      }

    } else {

    }

    return template;
  }
}
```

Listing 12.11 The controller servlet for the CD example. (continued)

The controller component is a Velocity servlet that uses the handleRequest() method of the VelocityServlet class. There are a few housekeeping steps you need to take in order for the servlet to be able to access both the Velocity template and the entity EJBs.

The Velocity templates are kept in the root directory of the servlet application, and the servlet must have access to that directory. To be sure the servlet can access the root directory of the application, set the FILE_RESOURCE_LOADER_PATH properties to be equal to the real path to the directory. You can do this in the loadConfiguration() method, which is called automatically before the handleRequest() method is called.

Next, you need to get access to the entity EJB home interfaces. You accomplish this in the init() method, which is called the first time the servlet is executed. The method obtains a naming.Context object for the comp/env/cmp JNDI reference. This reference is used to access the EJBs in the system. Next, you look up each of your beans and return an appropriate home object for both beans. These home objects will be used shortly to build entity beans.

In the handleRequest() method, the code checks to see which of the four operations defined for your application have been requested by the user. Let's take a look at these four operations.

Entering a New CD

When the user enters the title, artist, and total number of tracks for a new CD, the code must place the CD into the table. The code begins by making sure the home interface object is valid. If the object isn't valid, an error message is assigned to the "message" reference, which in turn is added to the context.

If the interface object is valid, the tracks string passed from the HTML <form> is converted to an integer. Next, the tracks and the rest of the values from the <form> are passed to the create() method of the CD bean's home interface. The result of the method call is either a null or a new entity EJB representing the row in the CD table. If the value from the method is not null, the "thanks" reference is set to a text string and added to the Context object. Otherwise, a failure message is added to the Context.

In either case, a Template object is set to the value returned from the getTemplate() method using the filename thanks.vm. If no exceptions occur, the new Template object is returned from the handleRequest() method and the user sees the appropriate output.

Entering a New CD Track

The code for adding a new CD track for the tracks database is basically the same as the code for adding a new CD. However, the track interface is used instead. In a production system, you must make certain that the CD for which the track is being added appears in the CD table.

Listing CDs by Artist

Getting a list of CDs by a particular artist is a little different from adding a CD because you need to query the database. You will remember that the EJB files for the two entity EJBs in the application each defined a <query> element. In the case of the CD table, our defined query returns all of the rows in the CD table by a specific artist.

The code calls the query using the findByArtist(String) method. The value returned from this method is a Collection object containing zero or more entity objects from the CD table. Regardless of the number of objects in the collection, it is added to the context using the command

```
context.put ("cds", cds);
```

After the Collection object is added to the context, the displaycds.vm template is pulled from the server's hard drive and the Template object is returned for display to the user.

Listing CD Tracks

When a user wants to display the tracks of a specific CD, the code takes the ID passed from the <form> in the ID variable and passes it to the findByCdID(int) method. This method executes the <query> element found in the EJB file for the TracksRecordBean. The result of the method is a collection containing the tracks for the specified CD. The collection is added to the context as the $tracks reference.

Advanced Servlet Functionality

For the VelocityServlet base class, numerous additional methods can be overridden. These methods are as follows:

- Properties loadConfiguration(ServletConfig)—A method that allows additional properties to be added to the servlet's properties. The properties currently defined in the Velocity runtime are:

  static java.lang.String--COUNTER_INITIAL_VALUE—The initial counter value in #foreach directives.

  static java.lang.String--COUNTER_NAME—The initial counter name in #foreach directives.

  static java.lang.String--DEBUG_PREFIX—-Log message prefixes.

  static java.lang.String--DEFAULT_RUNTIME_DIRECTIVES—-Default runtime directives.

  static java.lang.String--DEFAULT_RUNTIME_PROPERTIES—Default runtime properties.

  static java.lang.String--ENCODING_DEFAULT—The default encoding type.

  static java.lang.String--ERROR_PREFIX—Error message prefixes.

  static java.lang.String--ERRORMSG_END—The ending tag for error messages triggered by passing a parameter that is not allowed in the #include directive.

  static java.lang.String--ERRORMSG_START—The starting tag for error messages triggered by passing a parameter that is not allowed in the #include directive.

  static java.lang.String--FILE_RESOURCE_LOADER_CACHE—The public handle for turning the caching on in the FileResourceLoader.

  static java.lang.String--FILE_RESOURCE_LOADER_PATH—The public handle for setting a path in the FileResourceLoader.

  static java.lang.String--INFO_PREFIX—Information message prefixes.

static java.lang.String--INPUT_ENCODING—The character encoding for the templates.

static java.lang.String--INTERPOLATE_STRINGLITERALS—The switch for the interpolation facility for string literals.

static java.lang.String--LOGSYSTEM_LOG4J_EMAIL_BUFFER_SIZE--log4J configuration.

static java.lang.String--LOGSYSTEM_LOG4J_EMAIL_FROM—log4J configuration.

static java.lang.String--LOGSYSTEM_LOG4J_EMAIL_SERVER—log4J configuration.

static java.lang.String--LOGSYSTEM_LOG4J_EMAIL_SUBJECT—log4J configuration.

static java.lang.String--LOGSYSTEM_LOG4J_EMAIL_TO—log4J configuration.

static java.lang.String--LOGSYSTEM_LOG4J_FILE_BACKUPS—log4J configuration.

static java.lang.String--LOGSYSTEM_LOG4J_FILE_SIZE—log4J configuration.

static java.lang.String--LOGSYSTEM_LOG4J_PATTERN—log4J configuration.

static java.lang.String--LOGSYSTEM_LOG4J_REMOTE_HOST—log4J configuration.

static java.lang.String--LOGSYSTEM_LOG4J_REMOTE_PORT—log4J configuration.

static java.lang.String--LOGSYSTEM_LOG4J_SYSLOGD_FACILITY—log4J configuration.

static java.lang.String--LOGSYSTEM_LOG4J_SYSLOGD_HOST—log4J configuration.

static int--NUMBER_OF_PARSERS—The number of parsers you want to create.

static java.lang.String--OUTPUT_ENCODING—Encoding for the output stream.

static java.lang.String--PARSE_DIRECTIVE_MAXDEPTH—The maximum recursion depth allowed for the #parse directive.

static java.lang.String--PARSER_POOL_SIZE—The total number of parsers in the pool.

static java.lang.String--RESOURCE_LOADER—The key used to retrieve the names of the resource loaders that you want to use.

static java.lang.String--RESOURCE_MANAGER_CACHE_CLASS—A class implementing the resource manager cache.

static java.lang.String--RESOURCE_MANAGER_CLASS—A class implementing the resource manager.

static java.lang.String--RESOURCE_MANAGER_LOGWHENFOUND—Used to determine whether the finding of a resource is logged.

static java.lang.String--RUNTIME_LOG—Location of the Velocity log file.

static java.lang.String--RUNTIME_LOG_ERROR_STACKTRACE—The stack trace output for error messages.

static java.lang.String--RUNTIME_LOG_INFO_STACKTRACE—Stack trace output for informational messages.

static java.lang.String--RUNTIME_LOG_LOGSYSTEM—An externally provided logger.

static java.lang.String--RUNTIME_LOG_LOGSYSTEM_CLASS—A class of log system you want to use.

static java.lang.String--RUNTIME_LOG_REFERENCE_LOG_INVALID—The logging of invalid references.

static java.lang.String--RUNTIME_LOG_WARN_STACKTRACE—Stack trace output for warning messages.

static java.lang.String--UNKNOWN_PREFIX—Unknown message prefixes.

static java.lang.String--VM_CONTEXT_LOCALSCOPE—A switch for local context in VM; the default is false.

static java.lang.String--VM_LIBRARY—The name of the local Velocimacro library template.

static java.lang.String--VM_LIBRARY_AUTORELOAD—A switch for autoloading library-sourced VMs (for development).

static java.lang.String--VM_MESSAGES_ON—A switch for VM messages; the default is true.

static java.lang.String--VM_PERM_ALLOW_INLINE—boolean (true/false); the default is true; allows inline (in-template) macro definitions.

static java.lang.String--VM_PERM_ALLOW_INLINE_REPLACE_GLOBAL—boolean (true/false); the default is false; allows inline (in-template) macro definitions to replace existing ones.

static java.lang.String--VM_PERM_INLINE_LOCAL—Switch for forcing inline macros to be local : default false.

static java.lang.String--WARN_PREFIX—Warning message prefixes.

- Context createContext(HttpServletRequest, HttpServletResponse)—The createContext() method allows developers to create their own Context objects, which can be used for a private merge().
- void setContentType(HttpServletRequest,HttpServletResponse)--By default, handleRequest() will output in text/HTML format, but you can change to another format, such as XML or even an image file.
- void mergeTemplate(Template, Context, HttpServletResponse)—If you want to control the output yourself instead of relying on the handleRequest() method, then you can get your own context using the createContext() method listed earlier and merge it with a template and output to the response object passed to the handleRequest() method. The mergeTemplate() method takes all three objects and produces the output.
- void requestCleanup(HttpServletRequest, HttpServletResponse, Context)—If you handle the output yourself, you should override the requestCleanup() method to handle any last-minute issues. By default, this method has no implementation.
- protected void error(HttpServletRequest, HttpServletResponse, Exception)—The error() method is called when an exception occurs in the processing of a user's request. You can override this method to provide more advanced error handling. The default implementation sends an error message and a stack trace back to the user.

Adding Reports

Our application to this point has focused on generating output in the form of HTML. But what if you don't want any fancy HTML tables and just want to run a text-based report of all the CDs in the database? Well, consider the Velocity template in Listing 12.12.

```
CD Database ID                    Artist                   Title<BR>
--------------------------------------------------------------<BR>
#set ($counter = 0)
#foreach($value in $cds)
  #if ($counter == 50)
    #set ($counter = 0)
CD Database ID                    Artist                   Title<BR>
--------------------------------------------------------------<BR>
  #else
```

Listing 12.12 A Velocity template that produces a text report. (continues)

```
    #set ($counter = $counter + 1)
  #end
$value.id                                   $value.artist    $value.title<BR>
#end
```

Listing 12.12 A Velocity template that produces a text report. (continued)

The Velocity template in Listing 12.12 is designed to output a heading to a page, list 50 CDs in the database, and then produce another heading. The number of CDs between headings can be changed to accommodate various outputs. To produce the full report of CDs in the database, you need to add a button to the primary CD index.html page. Here's the code for the new button:

```
<h3>Reports</h3>
<form action="http://localhost:8080/cd/cdVelocityHandler" method="post">
<input type="submit" name="submit" value="fullreport"> -
download 'report.txt' to your local system
</form>
```

This new form displays a button called FullReport on the index page. When the user clicks the button, control is passed to the cdVelocityHandler servlet defined in Listing 12.11. The code that handles the new button appears in Listing 12.13.

```
else if (req.getParameter("submit").equals("fullreport")) {
      try {
        if (cdHome == null) {
          context.put("message", "Sorry we had an error");
        } else {
          Collection cds = cdHome.findAllCDs();
          context.put ("cds", cds);
          try {
            template = getTemplate("fullreport.vm");
          } catch( Exception e ) {
            e.printStackTrace();
          }
        }
      } catch(Exception e) {
        e.printStackTrace();
      }
    }
```

Listing 12.13 The control servlet report task.

There isn't anything special about the new code--except the findAllCDs query associated with the CDRecordBean entity bean. Listing 12.14 shows the query for the new report.

```
<query>
  <query-method>
    <method-name>findAllCDs</method-name>
  </query-method>
  <ejb-ql>SELECT o FROM CDTable o</ejb-ql>
</query>
```

Listing 12.14 The bean query.

The new query pulls all of the rows from the CDTable database table. Once all of the rows are pulled, the resulting Collection object is placed in the context. Finally, the fullreport.vm Velocity template is called to output the results of the query. The results of this process are shown in Figure 12.5.

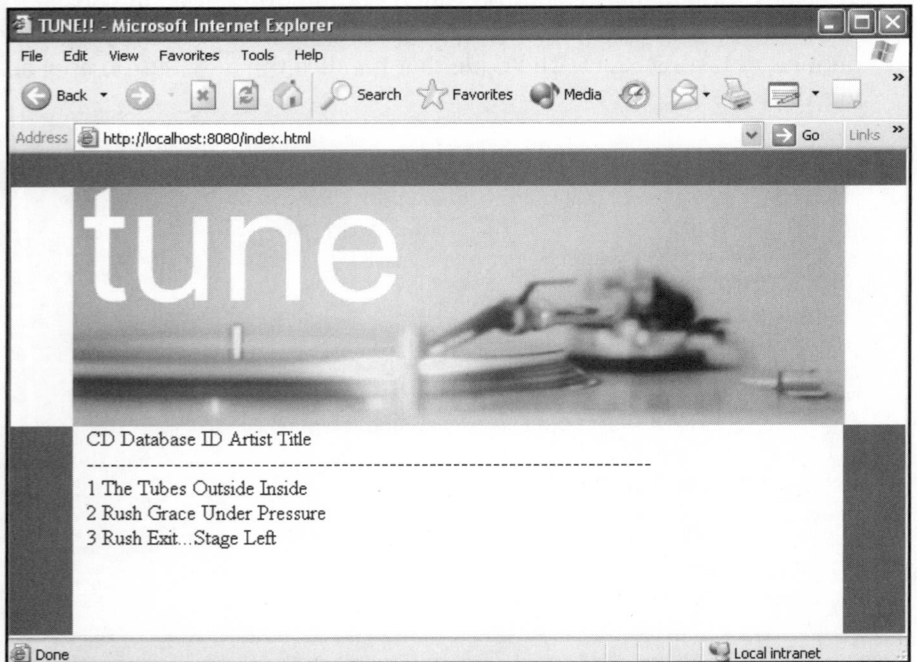

Figure 12.5 The report output in a browser.

As you can see, the output isn't all you might have hoped for--the text output didn't render well in the HTML of the Web browser. What if you could produce a properly formatted text file and offer the option for the user to download the file? Consider the new Velocity template in Listing 12.15.

```
CD Database ID                                        Artist              Title
-----------------------------------------------------------------

#set ($counter = 0)
#foreach($value in $cds)
  #if ($counter == 50)
    #set ($counter = 0)
CD Database ID                                        Artist              Title
-----------------------------------------------------------------
  #else
    #set ($counter = $counter + 1)
  #end
$value.id
$value.artist$stringlength.tabs($value.artist)$value.title
#end
```

Listing 12.15 The Velocity template for text only.

The purpose of the Velocity template in Listing 12.15 is to properly format the report using tabs the data produced from the database. What this means is that the strings under the Artist and Title headings will be properly formatted and aligned with each other regardless of their length. You won't see any jagged rows. To accomplish this, you have to produce the right number of tabs after the Artist value is displayed in the template but before the Title value. If you look in the template code, you will see a line like the following:

```
$value.artist$stringlength.tabs($value.artist)$value.title
```

This line isn't one command but three:

```
$value.artist
$stringlength.tabs($value.artist)
$value.title
```

The $value.artist and $value.title commands simply produce the artist and title for the current row being displayed. The interesting part of the command is $stringlength..tabs($value.artist). The $stringlength reference relates to an object placed in the context using the StringLength class, as shown in Listing 12.16.

```
public class StringLength {
  public StringLength(){}

  public String tabs(String st) {
    String s = new String();
```

Listing 12.16 The StringLength class. (continues)

```
      for (int i=3;i>st.length()/5;i--)
        s = s + "\t";

      return s;
    }
  }
```

Listing 12.16 The StringLength class. (continued)

The StringLength class has a single job: to expose a method called tabs(). The method calculates and returns a string with the total number of tabs necessary to line up the artist and title values in our report. The name of the artist is passed to the tabs() method and tabs are returned.

Now that you have a Velocity template that will produce the right output, you have to determine how the control servlet will produce a file for the user to download. The code in Listing 12.17 shows the control servlet code for the Full-Report button.

```
else if (req.getParameter("submit").equals("fullreport")) {
      try {
        if (cdHome == null) {
          context.put("message", "Sorry we had an error");
        } else {
          Collection cds = cdHome.findAllCDs();
          context.put ("cds", cds);
          try {
            res.setContentType("APPLICATION/OCTET-STREAM");
            res.setHeader("Content-Disposition","attachment;
filename=report.txt");
            template = getTemplate("fullreport.vm");
          } catch( Exception e ) {
            e.printStackTrace();
          }
        }
      } catch(Exception e) {
        e.printStackTrace();
      }
    }
```

Listing 12.17 The servlet code for downloading the report.

As you can see, the findAllCDs query is used to pull all of the CD information from the database and the fullreport.vm Velocity template is used for the output. Two additional commands are included:

```
res.setContentType("APPLICATION/OCTET-STREAM");
res.setHeader("Content-Disposition","attachment; filename=report.txt");
```

These two commands tell the user's browser that the return information from the <form> interaction is a file called report.txt, which will be presented to the user as a download dialog box. Figure 12.6 shows an example of the file downloaded using this application.

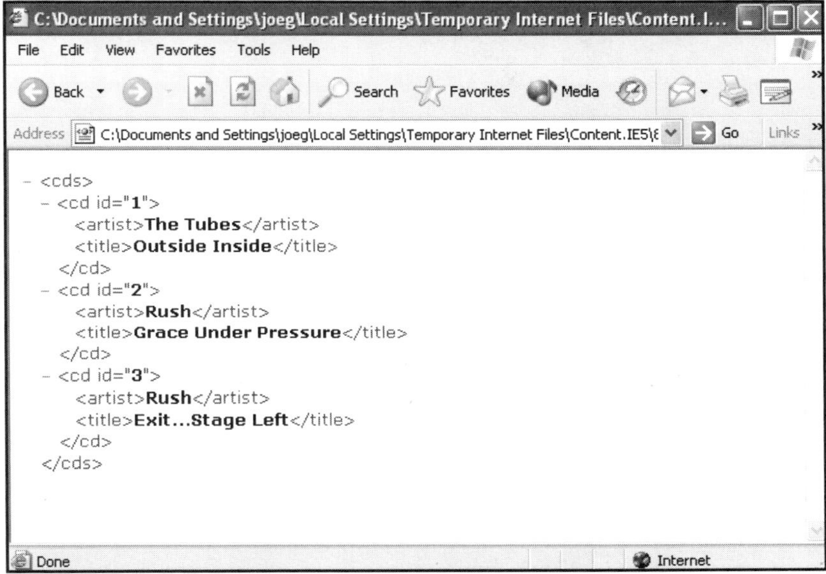

Figure 12.6 The report output.

What's Next

In this chapter, we introduced the possibilities available to the developer when mixing Velocity and servlets. In the next chapter, we show how to expand Velocity driven sites to be usable from around the world using internationalization techniques.

CHAPTER 13

Velocity and Internationalization

If you are building a world-class Web site, would you want to code just to an American, or even just an English-speaking, audience? Of course not. Numerous Web sites around the world provide the user with a list of target countries, a map, or links that display content in a language appropriate for the selected country and language. Fortunately, some of the components within Java itself offer a solid way to internationalize applications and Web sites. You can use Velocity to highlight these components and develop an easy methodology for internationalization. In this chapter, we briefly cover those Java components and then introduce a Velocity application based on the CD collection Web application found in Chapter 12, "Using Velocity with Servlets."

Java Internationalization Components

In this section, we examine the Java components that you can use to internationalize your Web applications. For a complete understanding of this process, see the Java Tutorial Trailhead at http://java.sun.com/docs/books/tutorial/i18n/. Before we start, let's narrow our focus a little to building a Web application that can be read in both English and German.

Probably one of the easiest ways to present a Web application in two languages is to build two pages. Suppose you have an original Web page called index.html. For the English page, you might use the name /en/index.html and call the German page indexgerman.html. Or you could build directories for the files, such as /en/index.html and /de/index.html.

Of course, building two or 20 pages for the same content in different languages is a waste of time. If you have the opportunity to build your Web application using Java and servlets as well as Velocity, that's a much better solution.

The Java Locale Class

The Java Locale class is designed to be a catchall object for other Java classes. The Locale object is passed to a class that knows how to deal with various locations in the world. You create a Locale object by passing two parameters: the language you want to use and the country. Both the language and country are identified by two-character abbreviations. For example, the English language is represented by *en* and the German language by *de*. The countries are represented by *US* and *DE*, respectively.

So, you can create a Locale object using the following code:

```
Locale location = new Locale('en', 'US');
```

You can view a full list of language codes at www.ics.uci.edu/pub/ietf/http/related/iso639.txt. The country codes can be found at /www.chemie.fu-berlin.de/diverse/doc/ISO_3166.html.

Resource Bundles

For Java internationalization, most of the work is accomplished in the ResourceBundle object. This object acts like a large multidimensional map that lets you supply a key string and return a value based on the Locale object provided to the bundle. The ResourceBundle object relies on *properties files*, which are just text files with key value relationships defined within them. There will always be a default properties file called MessagesBundle.properties. This bundle is used if the ResourceBundle object cannot find another properties file that matches the provided locale. Let's first look at how you create a ResourceBundle object:

```
message = ResourceBundle.getBundle("MessagesBundle", location);
```

The statement instantiates a ResourceBundle object based on the property filename of MessagesBundle and the provided Locale object. If you are planning to code a Web application for English/U.S. and German/Germany locations, you need two additional properties files:

- MessagesBundle_en_US.properties
- MessagesBundle_de_DE.properties

The ResourceBundle object is responsible for choosing the proper properties file. As we mentioned, each properties file contains key value pairs. For example, to display a greeting to your user, you include an entry like this one in the properties file:

```
Greet = Hello
```

Of course, you have to include the appropriate entry in the default, the U.S., and the German files. You then ask the ResourceBundle object to return the value for the key "Greet' based on the current Locale object. For example:

```
String hello  = messages.getString("Greet");
```

With this code, the proper greeting is presented to the user. Now let's see how you can use this knowledge to build an international Web site.

An International CD Web Application

In the previous chapter, you created an application that allowed you to store and retrieve CDs and their tracks in a database. As you'll recall, the application displayed a primary Web page with options to enter CDs and tracks, as well as options for viewing that information. The application presented this page in English, but there might be times when you want to either provide the application to another country or post it on the Internet for all to use. This means you have to *internationalize* the application, which you can accomplish by creating a template from the primary display page.

Let's begin by prompting users to select the language and country in which they would like the Web page to be displayed. Listing 13.1 shows the HTML code you need, and Figure 13.1 shows the output from the HTML page.

```
<HTML>
<BODY>
<form action="http://localhost:8080/cd/cdIndex">
<select name="country">
<option value="US">US</option>
<option value="DE">DE</option>
</select>
<BR>
<select name="language">
<option value="en">us</option>
<option value="de">de</option>
</select>
<input type="submit" value="submit">
</form>
</BODY>
</HTML>
```

Listing 13.1 The international.html file.

Figure 13.1 The language/country select page.

There are two important things to glean from the code in Listing 13.1. The first is the action in the <form> tag. When users click the submit button, they are sent to a new servlet called cdIindex. This servlet is responsible for obtaining the text for the display screen in the requested language. Also note the country and language selection boxes. The inputs in the form are passed to the cdIndex servlet so that it knows the correct properties file to use for displaying text.

The output from the cdIndex servlet is a Velocity template displaying information for entering and viewing CDs. Listing 13.2 shows this template.

```
<HTML>
<HEAD>
    <TITLE></TITLE>
    <link rel="stylesheet" type="text/css" href="default.css">
</HEAD>
<BODY BGCOLOR="#3A6BA5" link="ffffff" alink="999999" vlink="ffffff">

<table border="1" >
<tr><td>
$createstring<BR>
<form action="http://localhost:8080/cd/cdVelocityHandler"
method="post">
<table>
<tr><td>$title</td><td><input name="title"></td></tr>
<tr><td>$artist</td><td><input name="artist"></td></tr>
<tr><td>$tracks</td><td><input name="tracks"></td></tr>
</table>
  <input type="submit" name="submit" value="new">
</form>
</td>
<td valign="top">
$displaystring<BR>
<form action="http://localhost:8080/cd/cdVelocityHandler"
```

Listing 13.2 The index.vm Velocity template. (continues)

```
method="post">
<table>
<tr><td>$artist</td><td><input name="artist"></td></tr>
</table>
  <input type="submit" name="submit" value="obtain">
</form>
</td>
</tr>
<tr>
<td valign="top">
$viewstring<BR>
<form action="http://localhost:8080/cd/cdVelocityHandler" method="post">
<table>
<tr><td>$ID</td><td><input name="id"></td></tr>
</table>
  <input type="submit" name="submit" value="tracks">
</form>
</td>
<td valign="top">
$addstring<BR>
<form action="http://localhost:8080/cd/cdVelocityHandler"
method="post">
<table>
<tr><td>$ID</td><td><input name="id"></td></tr>
<tr><td>$name</td><td><input name="name"></td></tr>
<tr><td>$length</td><td><input name="length"></td></tr>
</table>
  <input type="submit" name="submit" value="addtrack">
</form>
</td>
</tr>
</table>
</BODY>
</HTML>
```

Listing 13.2 The index.vm Velocity template. (continued)

The display page is broken up into four tasks. Each of the tasks displays an instruction and several form fields to be filled in by the user. All of the text displayed on the page has been converted to Velocity references. The Velocity references are filled by the cdIndex servlet, shown in Listing 13.3.

```
import java.io.*;
import java.util.*;
import javax.servlet.*;
import javax.servlet.http.*;
import org.apache.velocity.Template;
```

Listing 13.3 cdIndex.java. (continues)

```
import org.apache.velocity.context.Context;
import org.apache.velocity.servlet.VelocityServlet;
import org.apache.velocity.exception.*;
import javax.naming.*;
import javax.ejb.*;
import cd.*;

import org.apache.velocity.app.Velocity;

public class cdIndex extends VelocityServlet {

    protected Properties loadConfiguration(ServletConfig config )
        throws IOException, FileNotFoundException
    {
        Properties p = new Properties();

        String path = config.getServletContext().getRealPath("/");
        if (path == null) {
            System.out.println(
              " SampleServlet.loadConfiguration() : unable to "
              + "get the current webapp root.  Using '/'. Please fix.");
            path = "/";
        }

        p.setProperty( Velocity.FILE_RESOURCE_LOADER_PATH,  path );
        return p;
    }

  public Template handleRequest( HttpServletRequest req,
   HttpServletResponse res, Context context ) {
    Template template = null;

    String country = req.getParameter("country");
    String language = req.getParameter("language");

    Locale currentLocale = new Locale(language, country);
    ResourceBundle messages =
      ResourceBundle.getBundle("MessagesBundle", currentLocale);

    context.put("title", messages.getString("title"));
    context.put("artist", messages.getString("artist"));
    context.put("ID", messages.getString("ID"));
    context.put("name", messages.getString("name"));
    context.put("length", messages.getString("length"));
    context.put("tracks", messages.getString("tracks"));
    context.put("createstring", messages.getString("createstring"));
    context.put("displaystring", messages.getString("displaystring"));
    context.put("viewstring", messages.getString("viewstring"));
    context.put("addstring", messages.getString("addstring"));
```

Listing 13.3 cdIndex.java. (continues)

```
        try {
          template = getTemplate("index.vm");
        } catch( Exception e ) {
          e.printStackTrace();
        }

        return template;
      }
    }
```

Listing 13.3 cdIndex.java. (continued)

The cdIndex servlet has two jobs. First, it obtains the language and country information from the <form> that called it and uses the information to build a Locale object. The Locale object is used to obtain a ResourceBundle object. Depending on the language and country selected, the ResourceBundle chooses either the default properties file, the U.S. file, or the German file (shown in Listings 13.4 through 13.6, respectively). These files all reside in the same directory as the cdIndex servlet class file.

The second and probably most important task is for the servlet to fill the context with the appropriate references and their values. As you can see in the code, each of the references are added along with a value selected using the messages.getString(String) method call. The result is a context filled with the references needed by the cdIndex Velocity template.

When users select the US option, they see the screen shown in Figure 13.2. If they select German, they see the page shown in Figure 13.3. As you can see, adding internationalization to your application is a piece of cake. To add Spanish, for example, just include the appropriate identifiers in the HTML selections and build the appropriate properties file.

```
title = Title:
artist = Artist:
ID = ID:
name = Name:
length = Length:
tracks = Tracks:
createstring = To Create a New CD:
displaystring = To display CDs for an Artist
viewstring = To see all Tracks for a CD
addstring = To add a new track
```

Listing 13.4 MessagesBundle.properties.

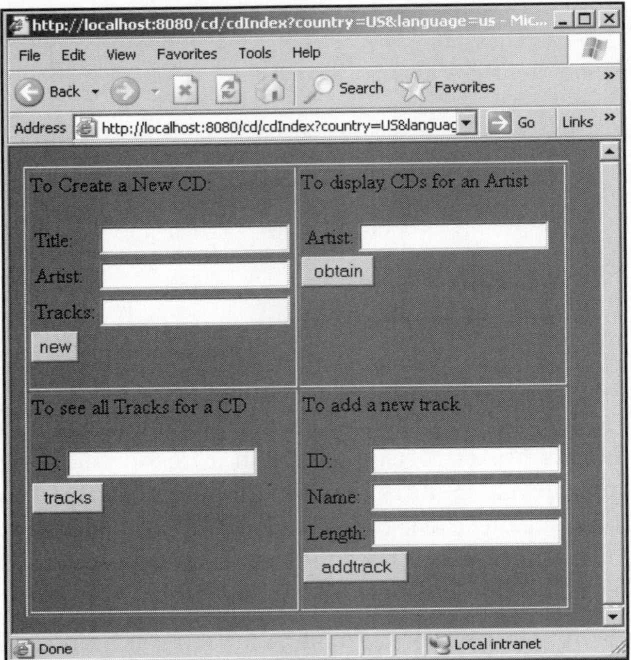

Figure 13.2 The U.S. display page.

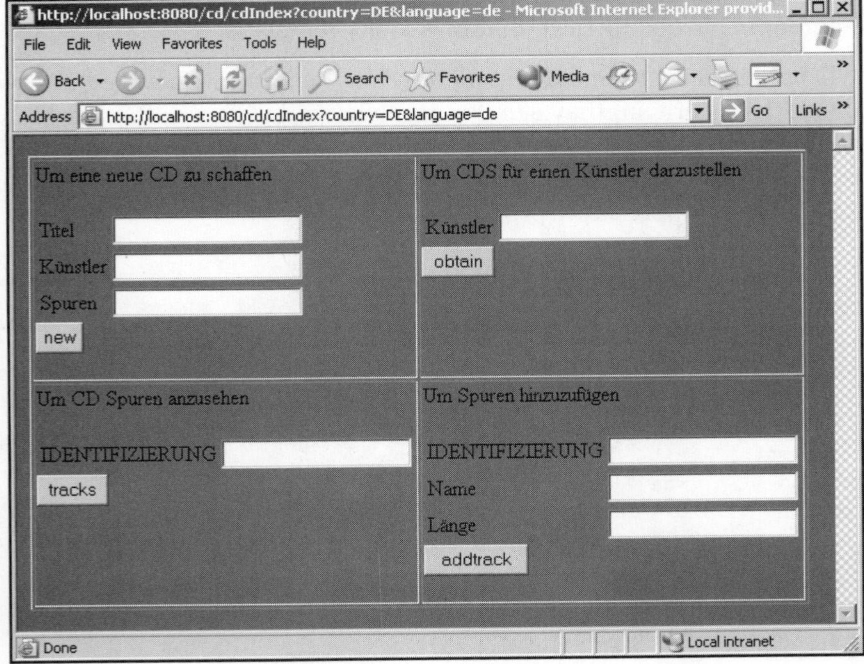

Figure 13.3 The German display page.

```
title = Title:
artist = Artist:
ID = ID:
name = Name:
length = Length:
tracks = Tracks:
createstring = To Create a New CD:
displaystring = To display CDs for an Artist
viewstring = To see all Tracks for a CD
addstring = To add a new track
```

Listing 13.5 MessagesBundle_en_US.properties.

```
title = Titel
artist = Kônstler
ID = IDENTIFIZIERUNG
name = Name
length = L?nge
tracks = Spuren
createstring = Um eine neue CD zu schaffen
displaystring = Um CDS fôr einen Kônstler darzustellen
viewstring = Um CD Spuren anzusehen
addstring = Um Spuren hinzuzufôgen
```

Listing 13.6 MessagesBundle_de_DE.properties.

What's Next

In this chapter, we showed you how to combine Java's internationalization features with Velocity to build world-class Web sites that your users can view in a variety of languages. In the next chapter, we look at using Velocity with Turbine, an application framework that provides the tools you need to build enterprise-level applications.

CHAPTER 14

Using Velocity and Turbine

If you have been developing Web applications for very long, you probably realize that you spend a good amount of your time reinventing the wheel. Typical tasks include database connection pooling, building control servlets, writing navigation menus, and designing a wide variety of pages. Where is the reuse, the components, the frameworks? Fortunately, many people have thought about such problems and created the tools Web developers need. In this chapter, we introduce Turbine, a framework that attempts to bring Web development into the same arena as traditional software development. What makes this framework so important is that it relies on Velocity for the view component of the MVC paradigm.

What Is Turbine?

Turbine, another of the Apache Software Foundation's Jakarta projects is one of the most visible frameworks for Web development using Velocity. Some of its features include:

- It is based on servlets for the controller component.
- It emphasizes security inherent in applications like shopping carts.
- You can use it independently of the Web.

Turbine isn't just another application server; it is an *application framework* that provides developers with the tools they need to build enterprise-level applications without having to duplicate the work of others. This isn't to say that you can toss your application server. The framework has to be hosted and executed by the appropriate environment, such as Tomcat or Resin. Turbine provides services that you would typically have to build for a specific Web application. In addition, Turbine is designed to work in the MVC arena with EJBs, controller servlets, and screens written using Velocity.

As we begin our quest into understanding what Turbine is and how it relates to Velocity, it will become very clear that Turbine is designed for the Web developer. If you're a Web designer who isn't familiar with code, specifically Java, you may have a tough time with the material initially, but you can certainly work through the detailed steps we provide. Of particular importance to Web designers, though, is Velocity's role in building the screens used in Turbine to display results to the user. Note that Velocity isn't the only template language that you can use with Turbine; it also supports WebMacro, JSP, Cocoon, and Freemarker.

With all of this in mind, bucket your seat belt and get ready to learn about a framework designed by developers for developers!

The Turbine Architecture

First you need a clear picture of the architecture around which Turbine was designed. Figure 14.1 illustrates the various modules in the framework.

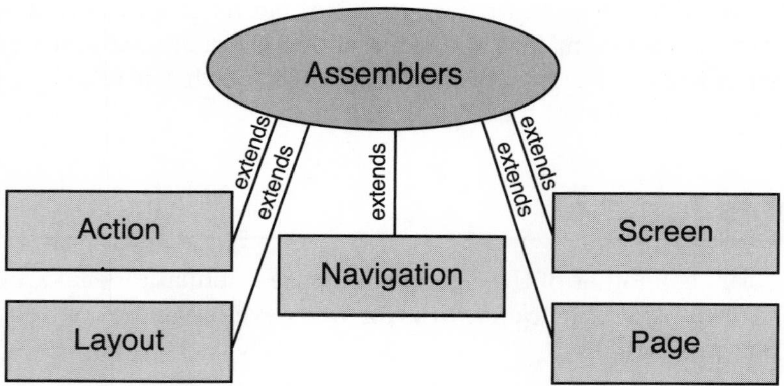

Figure 14.1 The Turbine architecture.

As you can see, the framework includes five major modules, all under the direction of assemblers:

Action—Code that performs a specific task

Navigation—Velocity templates that display navigational links and controls

Screen—Typically a combination of a Velocity template and a Java class for displaying key information in the body of a Layout module

Layout—A Velocity template describing how the page will look

Page—A conceptual object that contains all of the above modules

Let's explore each of these modules in order.

The Action Module

As you might expect, the Action module is a snippet of Java code that performs a specific task. One of the most important tasks this module performs is the processing of information passed to the user in an HTML <form>. The code in an Action module that processes this information is specific to the form to which it is attached, but in general you know that the information will have to be validated, processed, and possibly persisted. Figure 14.2 shows the flow perspective between the Action and other modules.

As you can see in Figure 14.2, the Page module executes an Action module in response to a POST or GET request. The Action module "communicates" with the Page module to determine the proper screen to return to the user.

If you think about the paradigm being created here, you can easily create a library of Action modules that can be reused throughout your Web application without creating new code for each page. Consider a shopping site where you want the user to be able to add items to the shopping cart regardless of where those items appear in the application. By writing the processing code for the form in an Action module, you ensure that the same module can be used throughout your site without any code change.

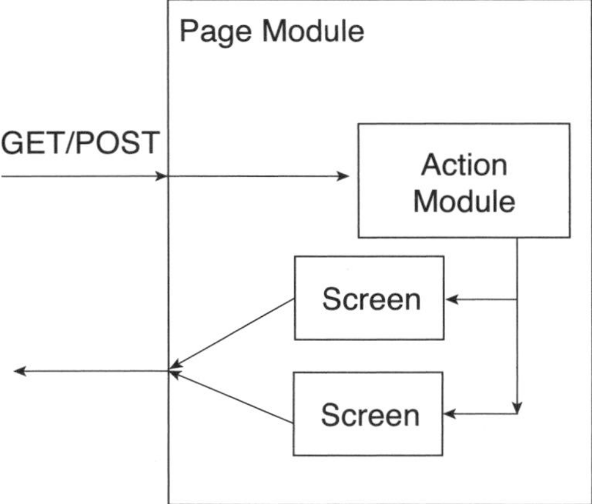

Figure 14.2 The Action module flow.

In our traditional Web development model, the code for handling the form processing would be found in the servlet called by the form. However, with Action modules, you can keep the business logic and the interface to the database separate from the controller. You can even use EJBs if you so desire.

The Navigation Module

When you visit a Web site, you are presented with a navigation scheme on the page. The scheme might be at the top of the page, or at the bottom, or on the left side of the page. Turbine supports navigation schemes with the Navigation module. A Web application might have many different navigation schemes, including, but not limited to, the location: the top, bottom, or side of the page. The Navigation module is used to handle the schemes, and the schemes change based on the particular page presented to the user. The modules have the ability to communicate with the database to obtain information through mechanisms like EJBs. As we discuss a bit later, Navigation modules are executed by the Layout module.

The Screen Module

A Web page includes navigation information as well as information pertinent to that page. The "important" page content is typically placed in the body of the page. The body is handled in Turbine using a Screen module. This module is responsible for rendering HTML tags that are passed back to the user. It would not be uncommon for the Screen module to access the database to pull information specific to the user.

The Layout Module

All Web pages have a physical layout or template they follow when presenting information to the user. In some cases, the same template may be used throughout the application or site, but in other cases—like a bookstore, for example—the template changes based on the page presented to the user. Layouts in Turbine are defined in the Layout module. This module provides placeholders for Navigation modules as well as the body or screen of the page defined by the Screen module. The Layout module is responsible for executing both the Navigation and Screen modules depending on the layout of the page.

The Page Module

For the most part, a Page module is a container for the other modules and is the first module to receive a request from a user's browser. If the request contains an action defined within the Page module, it will be executed. After the action has been performed, the Page module communicates with the Screen module to determine the layout that will be executed.

Module Object Encapsulation

Figure 14.3 shows how all of the modules are encapsulated within one another. When a Page module is called, it executes an enclosed Action module if requested by the call from the user's browser. Next, it calls the Layout module to determine how the screen should appear to the user. The Layout module calls the Navigation modules to display the navigation information for this page. Finally, the Screen module is executed to place the requested information in HTML format on the page.

As you can see, the Turbine framework views a Web page as a collection of objects. Each of the objects in the page is responsible for specifying how it is presented to the user in the form of HTML tags.

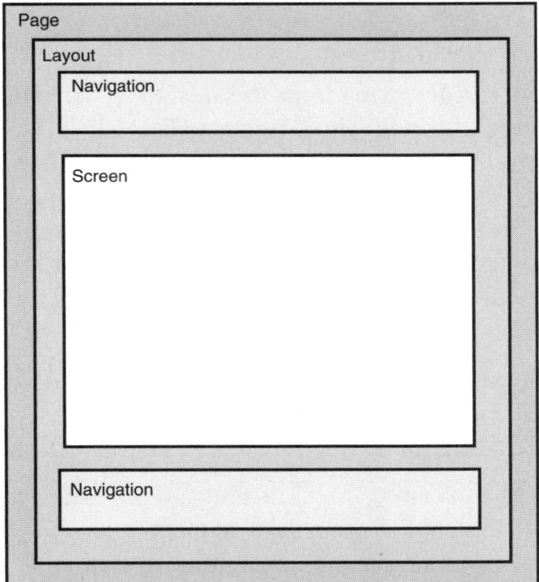

Figure 14.3 The Turbine modules.

Loaders

For each of the five modules we just discussed, Turbine defines five classes, called *loaders*, with one loader being responsible for knowing how to load a particular module. Figure 14.4 shows the hierarchical layout of loaders used in Turbine. As you can see, loaders are available for each of the five modules discussed in the previous section.

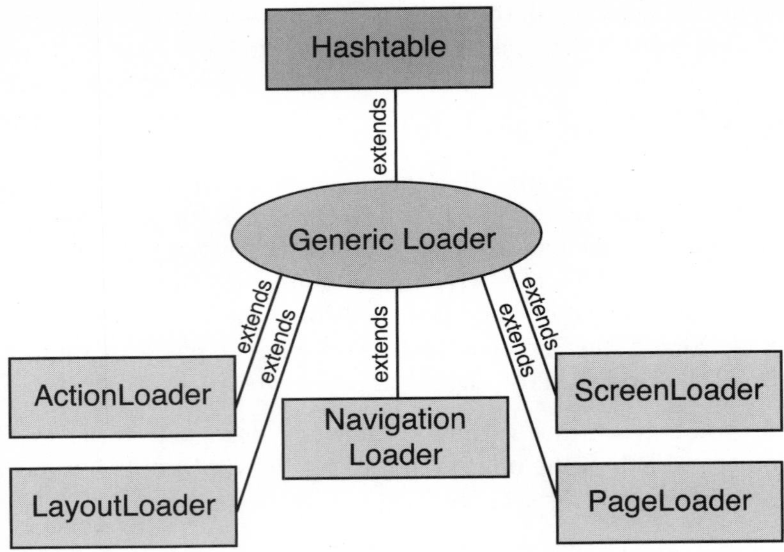

Figure 14.4 Loader modules.

Every effort has been made in the design of Turbine and the loaders to give them a degree of intelligence. Using a CLASSPATH variable defined as a property in TurbineResources.properties, you can define a specific path or set of paths where the loaders attempt to locate a resource. Once a loader has pulled a resource into memory from the hard drive, it has the option to cache the module for use again at a later time. As you might expect, multiple loaders can attempt to load a single module, and therefore all modules have to be written in a thread-safe manner.

How Does It Work?

Before we dive into installing Turbine and building a few applications, let's take a moment to look at the process of requesting a Web page using the Turbine system. First, we outline the layout of a test system.

The user makes a request using a Web browser. The request is then dispatched to a URL corresponding to a Turbine controller servlet. The request is made using HTTP—thus the need for a traditional Web server on the server machine. The Web server might be Apache or Resin's built-in HTTP server. The servlet request is then transferred to the application server as specified in a configuration file.

When the Turbine servlet receives the request from the user, it checks to see whether an HttpSession object exists for the current user. Since one of the foundations of the Turbine system is security, all users have to be logged into the application. The HttpSession object is a result of the login. Turbine uses either cookies or extended URLs with session information in them. If no HttpSession object exists, the system automatically redirects the user to a login page, which you configure through the TurbineResources.properties file.

One of the more important jobs of the Turbine servlet is the creation of a RunData object. This object is a non-thread-safe object designed to carry information such as Action, Screen, and Document objects, as well as any information passed to the servlet through the Request object.

The Turbine servlet attempts to determine if the user is logging into the application by examining the currently defined action for the user. If the action's value is *LoginUser*, the corresponding action is executed. Ultimately, a method called validateUser() is executed, within which the developer writes code to validate the user's username and password against some store, like a database. Upon validation, the user is either directed back to the Login screen or the DefaultPage. All of this work is performed by the SessionValidator action, which can be overridden to provide other functionality.

When the DefaultPage executes, it checks for an action and executes it. After the action, the DefaultPage queries the Screen module associated with the DefaultPage for its layout, which is then executed. The Layout module executes the Navigation and Screen modules, and finally, control returns to the Turbine servlet and a new HTML page is delivered to the user.

Obtaining and Installing TDK

The first step in our quest for using Velocity and Turbine is obtaining the Turbine system and installing it. The Turbine system is broken into several downloads. While it is possible to use Turbine in a stand-alone situation, the most powerful configuration is a combination of Turbine and an application server like Tomcat and Velocity. You can download a preconfigured environment in the form of a Turbine Development Kit (TDK) from http://jakarta.apache.org/builds/jakarta-turbine/release/.

Within this directory, you can find all of the released versions of TDK. At the time of this writing, the most current release version is 2.1. Click on the directory of the most recent release to find the various downloads for Turbine. You'll see TAR.GZ and zip files for TDK, Turbine, and Torque. You want to download the TDK, so click on the zip or TAR.GZ most appropriate for your environment (Windows users need the zip, and Unix/Linux users need the TAR.GZ).

Once you've downloaded the file to your system, unzip or tar/ungzip the file to an appropriate directory. In both cases, the install creates a /tdk directory with numerous subdirectories.

Before you test the installation, you must install two additional systems on your system:

Ant—Available at jakarta.apache.org/ant (this needs to be in your path so it can be executed in any directory)

JDK—Available at sun.java.com

Testing the TDK Installation

Testing the TDK installation involves two steps. First you have to compile the sample applications that accompany the TDK. You execute the compile by changing to the /tdk directory and executing Ant (simply type *ant*). The Ant application executes based on the build.xml file contained in the /tdk directory. After several seconds, the build completes. In most cases, the build is successful. If you experience problems, check the mailing lists for Turbine located on the Turbine Web site.

Once the build has completed, it's time to test the system. Change to the /bin directory of the /TDK root directory. Part of the TDK installation is a fully functional and preconfigured Tomcat application server. Although Turbine and Velocity can be used with Resin (as discussed later in this chapter), Tomcat is the recommended application server.

If you are executing on Windows, you execute the Tomcat server by issuing the command

```
catalina.bat run
```

If you are executing on Unix/Linux, execute Tomcat with the command

```
catalina.sh start
```

If the execution is successful, you see output like this:

```
Using CLASSPATH:  ..\bin\bootstrap.jar;c:\j2sdk1.4.1_01\lib\tools.jar
Starting service Tomcat-Standalone
Apache Tomcat/4.0-b6-dev
Starting service Tomcat-Apache
Apache Tomcat/4.0-b6-dev
```

With Tomcat executing, browse to the following URL to see the sample application that ships with the TDK:

```
http://localhost:8080/newapp/servlet/newapp
```

If the browse is successful, you see a display like the one shown in Figure 14.5.

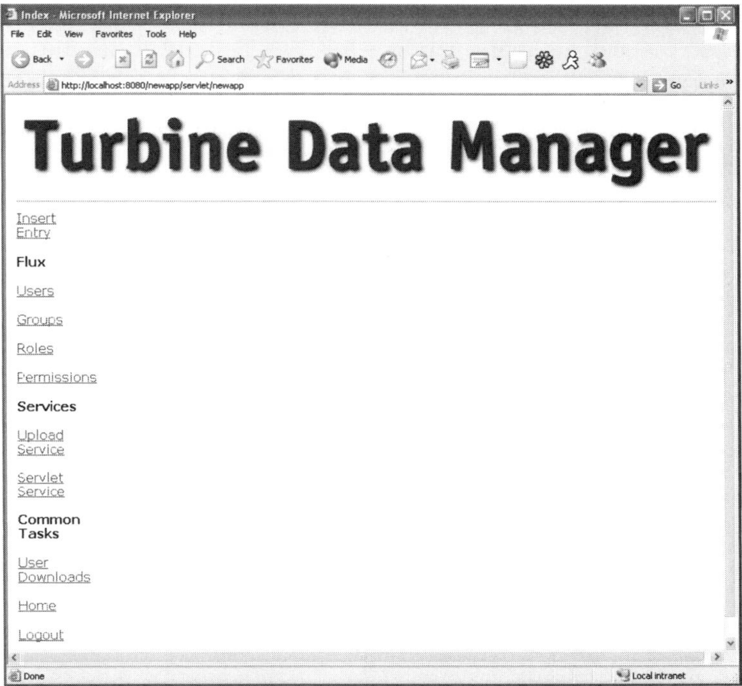

Figure 14.5 TDK sample application.

At this point, you know that your installation of the TDK has been successful. If you are interested in learning more about the TDK sample application, check the documentation that ships with the TDK using the URL

```
http://localhost:8080
```

Your First Turbine Application

Now that you've installed the TDK, you can begin the process of building your own application that uses Turbine as an MVC framework and Velocity as the view component. The first step is to add a task to the Ant build file, as well as an appropriate directory structure in build.properties. Open the build.properties file located in the /tdk root directory. Modify the first three variables in this file:

turbine.app—The name of your application (testApplication, in our example)

target.package—The name of the package for your application (com.company.testApplication, in our example)

target.directory—The directory where your package will be built (usually the same name as target.package—com/company/testApplication, in our example)

Next, execute Ant to build your new application. Remember that Turbine is a framework, so you will get many services for free. The Ant script moves various files into your specified application directories. In the next section of this chapter, we explore the files placed in the directories.

Turbine (and probably your application) will be using a database. When building a new Turbine application, change to the /tdk/webapps/*<your application name>*/WEB-INF/build directory and open the build.properties file. Make these changes:

- Locate the database entry that defaults to mysql and change to the appropriate value. The value you specify is used when Turbine creates SQL statements.
- Locate the databaseUrl entry and add the appropriate JDBC connection string. Place the appropriate JDBC drivers in the /WEB-INF/lib directory.
- Change the databaseDriver entry to the JDBC driver class.
- Change the databaseUser to the login user for the database.
- Change the databasePassword to the login user for the database.
- Change the databaseHost to the IP for the server.

At this point, the system must create a database table for Turbine. So, change to the directory /tdk/webapps/*<your application name>*/WEB-INF/build directory and execute *ant init*. The Ant build script connects to the database you specified in the build.properties file and creates the necessary tables. When the any init command executes, a number of errors can occur. For example, the build.xml file looks only for Windows 98, Windows NT, and Windows 2000, and if you are running Windows XP, just change all of the 98 monikers to XP or include an additional <target> element for XP. Another error that may arise is the build script's attempt to access the command-line administration tool for your database. Ensure that the /bin directory of your database server is in the system path.

Once the ant init command is successful, it's time to try out your new application. (Keep in mind that we will add look and feel with Velocity shortly!) To see your application, start Tomcat and then browse to

```
http://localhost:8080/testApplication/servlet/testApplication
```

You will see a Turbine login, as shown in Figure 14.6.

To access your new application, type *turbine* as both the username and password. After entering this information, you see the screen shown in Figure 14.7.

Let's now move ahead and look at the application you just built and how to expand to a new application that does something you need.

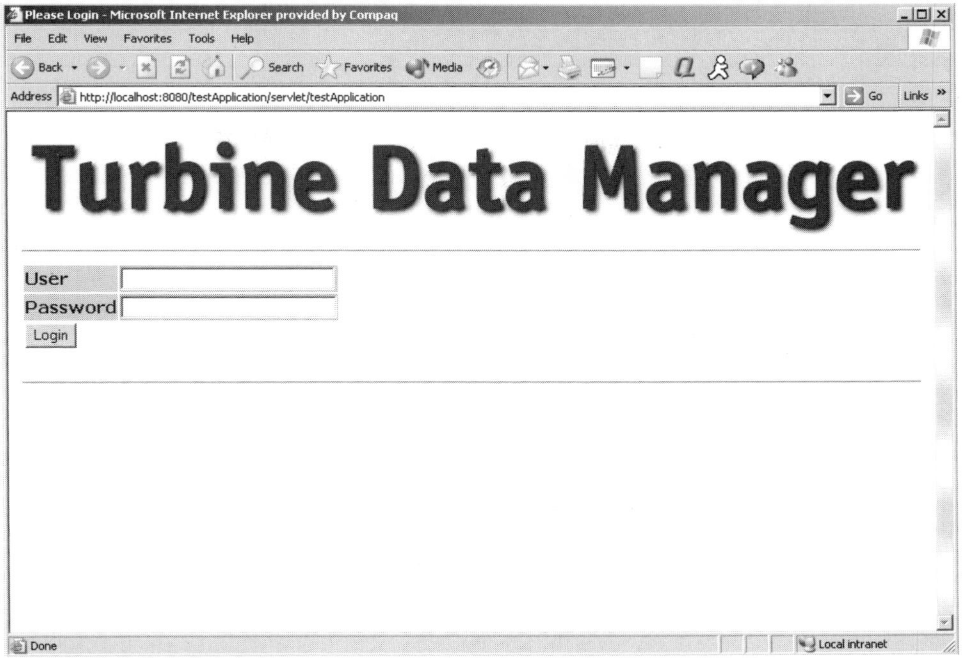

Figure 14.6 The Turbine login.

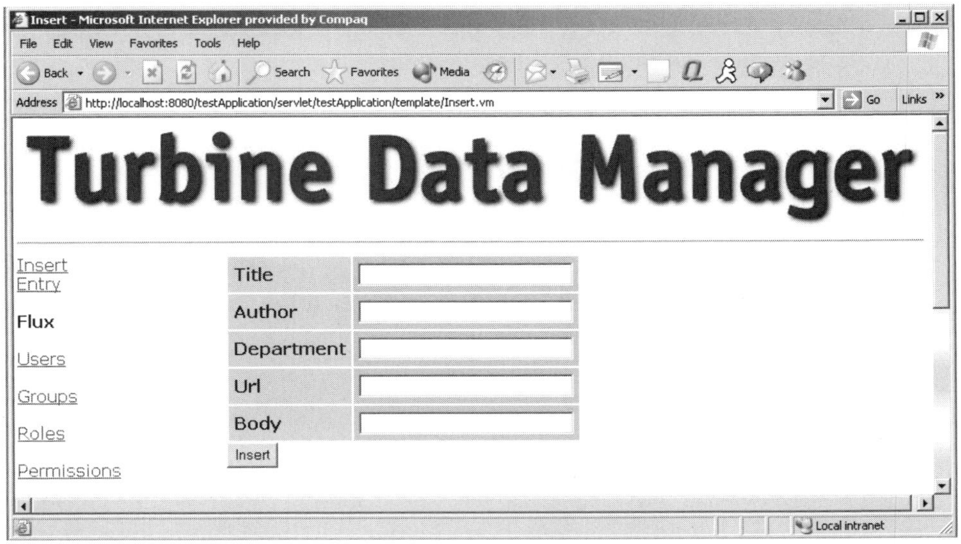

Figure 14.7 The Turbine main page.

Dissecting the Application

Okay, you've installed Turbine and seen the output produced from the sample application—but what does it all mean? Well, let's look at the application and see how you could use what you've learned about Velocity to make appropriate changes to it. Let's go through the application click by click and discuss the various base classes, methods, and functions involved in making a Turbine application.

When you browse to your sample application's URL as shown earlier, control is given to a universal servlet called the Turbine servlet. Regardless of what occurs within this servlet, you need some kind of HTML output to be produced for the client. As you will see in the course of this discussion, there are only a couple ways that you might have contacted the server—through a link or a form. In the first case, you are calling the server through the primary application URL.

The URL to your application is first handled by a Web server, either internal or external to the application server. When the URL is finally passed to the application server, it checks its list of hosted applications to determine if the URL matches one of them. In this case, Tomcat finds that the application testApplication is hosted and a directory structure exists for it. One of the first things Tomcat and Resin will do is open the web.xml file located in the /WEB-INF directory of the application. This is a configuration file that tells the server what class to execute when a particular URL pattern is found. The web.xm file of your application includes these elements:

- <servlet-name>testApplication</servlet-name>
- <servlet-class>org.apache.turbine.Turbine</servlet-class>

These elements tell the application server to execute the code found in the Turbine class. It just so happens that the Turbine servlet is found in the Turbine class. When the Turbine servlet executes, it immediately attempts to execute a default page. The default page for an application is defined in the file /WEB-INF/conf/TurbineResource.properties. About 25 percent into the file is the following setting:

```
services.VelocityService/default.layout.template = /Default.vm
```

Thus, because no layout or action is associated with the call to your application (we show you how to add that a bit later), the Turbine servlet uses the default.vm layout. The default.vm layout (Listing 14.1) is located in the /templates/app/layouts directory.

```
<table width="100%">
  <tr>
    <td colspan="2">
      $navigation.setTemplate("/DefaultTop.vm")
    </td>
  </tr>
  <tr>
    <td width="20" align="left" valign="top">
      $navigation.setTemplate("/Menu.vm")
    </td>
    <td align="left" valign="top">
      $screen_placeholder
    </td>
  </tr>
  <tr>
    <td colspan="2">
      $navigation.setTemplate("/DefaultBottom.vm")
    </td>
  </tr>
</table>
```

Listing 14.1 The default.vm Velocity template.

The default.vm file is a Layout module for a page in your application. The code in the file represents how the page will appear in the user's browser. There isn't much on the page, but you could easily add various look-and-feel components, such as a colored background and illustrations (like the CD application in Chapter 12, "Using Velocity with Servlets"). The default.vm file contains four Velocity references:

- The first defines a navigation component for the top of the page.
- The second defines another navigation component representing a nav bar on the left part of the Web page.
- The third is the screen component, where you define the body of the page.
- The fourth is another navigation component at the bottom of the screen.

Any changes you make to this template are reflected in the page the user receives.

At this point, you might be asking what the $navigation.setTemplate(String) method does. Remember that Velocity provides the ability to make method calls against objects in the context. The $navigation.setTemplate(String) makes a method call, setTemplate(String), against the $navigation object found in the context. The result of the method call is placed in the default.vm template to be returned to the user. Now, the change to the default.vm template is taking place in memory, so it isn't permanent. In the case of the $screen_placeholder reference, the Velocity parser attempts to replace the reference with whatever is associated with the $screen_placeholder reference. As you know from our discussion of the Turbine process flow, the Layout module calls appropriate Screen modules and automatically replaces the code returned from a particular Screen module into $screen_placeholder. All of this is done without any work on your part. Some of this gets a little deep, so hold on as we trace what is occurring.

You might be asking where the $navigation and $screen_placeholder references are placed. Both of these references use objects placed in a context supplied by the Turbine servlet itself and really aren't something we access ourselves. We let Turbine handle these references. So, Turbine takes the Layout file and attempts to resolve each of the references. The easiest to consider are the $navigation ones. Let's look at one of the navigation component template files. The code in Listing 14.2 represents the menu.vm template.

```
<font face="$ui.sansSerifFonts">
<a href="$link.setPage("Insert.vm")">Insert Entry</a>
<p>
<b>Flux</b>
<br>
<a href="$link.setPage("user,FluxUserList.vm")">Users</a>
<br>
<a href="$link.setPage("group,FluxGroupList.vm")">Groups</a>
<br>
<a href="$link.setPage("role,FluxRoleList.vm")">Roles</a>
<br>
<a href="$link.setPage("permission,FluxPermissionList.
  vm")">Permissions</a>
<p>
<b>Services</b>
##<br>
##<a href="">Intake Service</a>
##<br>
##<a href="">Localization Service</a>
##<br>
##<a href="">Pull Service</a>
##<br>
##<a href="">Scheduler Service</a>
<br>
<a href="$link.setPage("Upload.vm")">Upload Service</a>
<br>
<a href="$link.setPage("ServletInfo.vm")">Servlet Service</a>
```

Listing 14.2 The menu.vm Velocity template. (continues)

```
<br>
##<a href="">Unique Id Service</a>
##<br>
##<a href="">XML-RPC Service</a>
##<br>
##<a href="">XSLT Service</a>
<p>
<b>Common Tasks</b>
<br>
<a href="">User Downloads</a>
<p>
<a href="$link.setPage("Index.vm")">Home</a>
<p>
<a href="$link.setAction("LogoutUser")">Logout</a>
</font>
```

Listing 14.2 The menu.vm Velocity template. (continued)

The menu.vm template includes quite a bit of Velocity code. Two different calls to the context take place. The first is the $link.setPage(String) method call. This code accesses the "link" object found in the context and passes in the name of the Velocity template that should be used when a user clicks on a link. The system adds the appropriate path information and possibly modifies the URL for those users who don't allow cookies. For example, the $link.setPage("Upload.vm") call produces a link like the following:

```
http://localhost:8080/TestApplication/servlet/TestApplication/
template/Upload.vm
```

Next is setAction(String), another method call to the link object in the context. This method is also associated with a link on a page, but instead of just putting in a link, you get a link with an associated action attached to it. The $link.set Action("LogoutUser") produces the link

```
http://localhost:8080/TestApplication/servlet/TestApplication/
action/LogoutUser
```

As you might expect, the logoutuser action is a Java class that extends an Action base class in some form. As you look through the code for the sample application, you see code like

```
$link.setPage("UploadComplete.vm").setAction("Upload")
```

This type of call creates a link to a template and denotes an action that must occur. As we discussed earlier, the action is executed before the page is built.

Now you might be wondering where the code comes from that fills the $screen_placeholder. This is where things start to get a little tricky. The information for the $screen_placeholder is generated through a Screen module. A Screen module is created using two components: a Velocity template and a Java class. The template provides the look and feel, and the Java class adds references to the context for the template to use. Later in this chapter, we explain why both of these components are necessary. For the system to work correctly, the template is given the same name as the Java class.

So when the default.vm layout is used, where does it get a Screen module since a screen isn't specified in the URL? The answer: back in the Turbine-Resources.properties file. Within this file are two entries:

```
template.homepage=/Index.vm
template.login=/Login.vm
```

Because no screen is specified in the URL, Turbine automatically uses the index.vm screen. The code for this screen is found in the directory webapps/TestApplication/templates/app/screens, and we've shown it in Listing 14.3. Your system uses the Velocity template to substitute for the placeholder, depending on the screen you want to display.

```
$page.setTitle("Index")
$page.setBgColor("#ffffff")

#set ( $headings = ["Title", "Dept", "Author", "Url","Body"," "] )

#if ($entries)
<table>
  <tr>
    <td>
      <table cellspacing="1" cellpadding="1">
        <tr>
          #foreach ($heading in $headings)
          #headerCell ($heading)
          #end
        </tr>

        #foreach ($entry in $entries)
        <tr>
          #entryCell ($entry.Title)
          #entryCell ($entry.Dept)
          #entryCell ($entry.Author)
          #entryCell ($entry.Url)
          #entryCell ($entry.Body)
          <td><a href="$link.setPage("Form.vm").addPathInfo("rdfid",
  $entry.RdfId)">Edit</a></td>
        </tr>
        #end
      </table>
    </td>
```

Listing 14.3 The index.vm code. (continues)

```
    </tr>
  </table>
#end
```

Listing 14.3 The index.vm code. (continud)

The code in Listing 14.3 is one of many screens that you can use as a replacement for the $screen_placeholder reference in the default.vm page. We'd like to point out a couple of things in this listing. First, note that this page is designed to show dynamic data produced from the database through the $entries reference. The $entries reference is filled and added to the context in a page called index.java, as shown in Listing 14.4. Because the name of the Java class is the same as that of a template, the Turbine system automatically uses the index.vm page when the index.java class is called by the user's Web browser. It is the responsibility of the index.java class to put the appropriate values in the $entries reference. Second, note that the index.vm Velocity template takes advantage of Velocimacros. The #entryCell() is a macro that provides formatting within the display table.

```
package org.mycompany.newapp.modules.screens;

import java.util.Vector;
import org.apache.turbine.modules.screens.VelocityScreen;
import org.apache.turbine.util.RunData;
import org.apache.turbine.util.db.Criteria;
import org.mycompany.newapp.om.RdfPeer;
import org.apache.velocity.context.Context;

public class Index extends SecureScreen  {
  public void doBuildTemplate(RunData data, Context context) {
    context.put("entries", getEntries());
  }

  private Vector getEntries() {
    try {
      Criteria criteria = new Criteria();
      return RdfPeer.doSelect(criteria);
    } catch (Exception e) {
      return null;
    }
  }
}
```

Listing 14.4 Java code for the index.vm template.

As you can see, the index.java class extends the SecureScreen class, which means the Index class is a screen and requires the user to log into the system to be displayed. Okay, let's stop here for a moment. The SecureScreen class is derived from a Turbine base class called VelocityScreen. All Screen modules inherit from VelocityScreen (if no validation is required) or SecureScreen (if validation is required). However, all of this hinges on the template.login property we listed earlier. If there is a proper template and associated Java class for the listed login property, the user is required to log into the system to use it. (You actually saw this when you executed the testApplication code and had to enter Turbine/Turbine as a username/password combination.) If you remove the /login.vm from the template.login property, the system won't prompt for a login because it doesn't know which default screen to use for logging into the system.

Let's return to the index.java file. The purpose of the Index class is to build the $entries reference so that the index.vm template will have data to present to the user. Within the VelocityScreen base class from which SecureScreen is derived is a method called doBuildTemplate(). This method is automatically called by the Turbine system when a Screen module needs to render its template. Thus, Turbine calls doBuildTemplate(), the Screen modules put all of the required Velocity references into the context, and the associated template picks up the references to ultimately return HTML that Turbine places in the $screen_placeholder reference—all nice and clean.

Before you run the code to see if all of this actually pans out, let's take a moment to explore the doBuildTemplate() method as well as some of the references on the index.vm Velocity template. Although you cannot see it, the index.vm and index.java files query the database and display any results. You need to understand this so you can use the same technique in your own code.

From a high level, the code in the index.java file puts a reference in the context called $entries and associates it with the values returned by the getEntries() method. The getEntries() method uses a Peer object, which is a helper object for performing a select on the database. The resulting rows are placed in the context.

Okay, what does all of that mean? When the Layout module calls the index Screen module, the doBuildTemplate() method executes, which adds a reference called $entries to the supplied Context object. The value associated with the $entries reference is obtained from the getEntries() method within the Index class. Although this method contains only two lines of code, a lot of work is being performed.

The first line of code obtains an object of type Criteria. The Criteria class is a helper for obtaining information from a database managed by Turbine and an associated package called Torque. Using the Criteria class, you can place filters or limits on a SELECT SQL command executed against a database. When instantiated without parameters or additional methods used against it, the object tells a SELECT to pull all rows and columns from a database. The full list of methods for the Criteria object are found here http://jakarta.apache.org/turbine/torque-3.0.0/apidocs/org/apache/torque/util/Criteria.html

Now, the last line of code in the getEntries() method returns

```
RdfPeer.doSelect(criteria);
```

A lot occurs with this statement, and we will need to take a database detour to explain it all.

Handling Databases in Turbine

All of the databases for a Turbine application are defined in a configuration file found at /webapps/testApplication/WEB-INF/conf/testapplication-schema.xml. Listing 14.5 shows what is currently in this file.

```
<database>
  <table name="RDF">
    <column name="RDF_ID" required="true" autoIncrement="true"
primaryKey="true" type="INTEGER"/>
    <column name="TITLE" size="255" type="VARCHAR"/>
    <column name="BODY" size="255" type="VARCHAR"/>
    <column name="URL" size="255" type="VARCHAR"/>
    <column name="AUTHOR" size="255" type="VARCHAR"/>
    <column name="DEPT" size="255" type="VARCHAR"/>
  </table>
</database>
```

Listing 14.5 The database schema XML.

From the listing, you see that defining a database in Turbine is very easy. Just provide the columns, size, type, and other attributes for a particular column. You add the table to your database store by executing the command

```
ant init
```

from the /webapps/testApplication/WEB-INF/build directory. When you do, Ant executes a task that builds all of the databases found in the schema XML file. If you take a close look at the Ant build XML file, you see that the first operation is to DROP any table with the table name found in the schema XML file. Thus, all data is lost from existing tables. You can either modify the Ant task or make sure you define all of your tables up-front.

Figure 14.8 shows a listing of the tables produced for the testApplication.

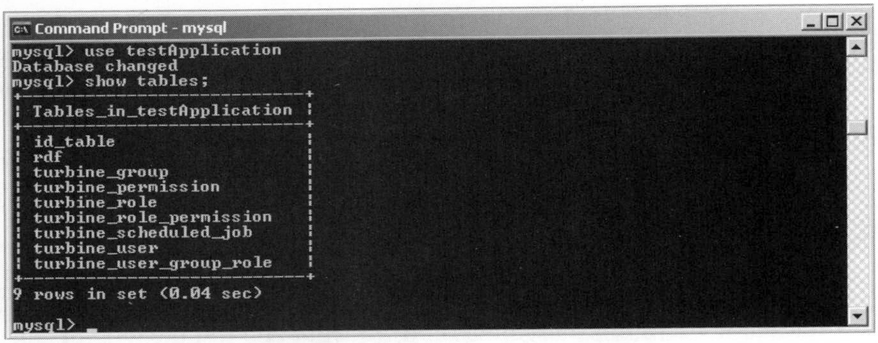

```
Command Prompt - mysql
mysql> use testApplication
Database changed
mysql> show tables;
+--------------------------+
| Tables_in_testApplication |
+--------------------------+
| id_table                 |
| rdf                      |
| turbine_group            |
| turbine_permission       |
| turbine_role             |
| turbine_role_permission  |
| turbine_scheduled_job    |
| turbine_user             |
| turbine_user_group_role  |
+--------------------------+
9 rows in set (0.04 sec)

mysql> _
```

Figure 14.8 Tables for testApplication in MySQL.

Two primary operations take place when the new table is created. First, the schema is written to the database specified in the database configuration (completed as part of the Turbine configuration). The second operation is the creation of the code that handles SELECT, INSERT, DELETE, UPDATE, and other database tasks. All of this code is placed in the directory /webapps/testApplication/WEB-INF/src/java/*com/company/testApplication*/om. The path *com/company/testApplication* is dependent on the name of your application.

In this directory, you find four files that include the name of your table. In the case of the RDF table created by Turbine using the Torque system, these files are:

- BaseRdf.java
- BaseRdfPeer.java
- Rdf.java
- PdfPeer.java

The BaseRdf.java file contains all of the setter/getter methods for a row in the database. Make no changes to this file. Rdf.java is a derived class from BaseRdf.java, where specific application logic could reside if needed. BaseRdfPeer.java is a helper class that uses BaseRdf.java to do the low-level database work. The object contains methods for doing all of the normal operations on a database. RdfPeer.java is a derived class from BaseRdfPeer.java, where application logic can be placed. This is the object used in the code to obtain or place data in the appropriate table.

Executing the Select

Based on the information we've presented, the getEntries() method creates a Criteria object with no limits on the table or results returned. Next, the Criteria object is provided to the doSelect() method of the RdfPeer class. This method isn't overridden in the RdfPeer class, so a call is made to the doSelect() method of the BaseRdfPeer class. This method retrieves rows from the database based on the Criteria object passed in.

Displaying the Result

Once getEntries() returns, the rows from the RDF table are provided as a value to the $entries reference placed in the Context object. After the Index object has done its work, the Turbine servlet merges the context with the index.vm template to provide the code for the $screen_placeholder reference. The final step is returning an HTML page to the user.

Adding a User with testApplication

On the page returned to the user from the default.vm layout and index.vm/java Screen module are numerous links on the left navigation bar. The first link is called Insert Entry. The underlying link placed on the page by the Velocity code

```
<a href="$link.setPage("Insert.vm")">Insert Entry</a>
```

is

```
http://localhost:8080/testApplication/servlet/testApplication/
template/Insert.vm
```

As you can see, this resembles our original URL to the application—except we now have new path information: /template/Insert.vm. When you click this link, the default.vm layout is used, but instead of the default index.vm, you have told the Turbine servlet to use the Screen module defined by the insert.vm and insert.java combination. Let's take a moment and look at insert.vm, as shown in Listing 14.6.

```
$page.setTitle("Insert")

<meta http-equiv="Content-Type" content="text/html; charset=iso-
8859-1">
</head>

<body bgcolor="#ffffff" leftmargin="0" topmargin="0"
marginwidth="0" marginheight="0">
<form
  method="post"
  action="$link.setPage("Index.vm").setAction("SQL")">
  <div align="left">
    <table bgcolor="#ffffff" cellpadding="5">
      <tr>
        #formCell ("Title" "title" "")
      </tr>
      <tr>
        #formCell ("Author" "author" "")
```

Listing 14.6 The insert.vm Velocity template. (continues)

```
      </tr>
      <tr>
        #formCell ("Department" "dept" "")
      </tr>
      <tr>
        #formCell ("Url" "url" "")
      </tr>
      <tr>
        #formCell ("Body" "body" "")
      </tr>
    </table>
    <input type="submit" name="eventSubmit_doInsert" value="Insert"/>
  </div>
</form>
```

Listing 14.6 The insert.vm Velocity template. (continued)

We've covered almost everything in the insert.vm Velocity template; however, this time the code includes a <form> tag. This tag is used to pull information from the user and supply it to the server for storage in the database. The form action includes a Turbine Action module reference:

```
<form action="$link.setPage("Index.vm").setAction("SQL")">
```

The Turbine action is found as a call to the SQL action. To tell the SQL action what to do, the input button has the name eventSubmit_doInsert. This is quite a bit to remember, but let's think about what the code is doing. First, the user clicks the Insert Entry link. The Turbine servlet pulls the default layout, default.vm, which renders the appropriate Navigation modules in addition to calling the doBuildTemplate() method on the insert.java class. However, if you look in the /src/com/mycompany/testApplication/modules/screens/ directory, you won't find an insert.java source file. This brings up a good point. Screen modules don't need to consist of both VM and Java class files. If a Screen module has only a VM template, the Turbine server simply renders the Velocity template without any changes to the context. If only a Screen module class is included, the class is responsible for providing all of the output because there will be no Velocity template to render for HTML output.

In our case, the insert.vm Velocity template is rendered to the $screen_placeholder reference based on the current Context object. At this point, the user enters data into the <form> input fields and clicks the submit button. The click causes the Turbine servlet to execute an Action module called SQL. Remember all actions are executed before the Layout object.

The SQL action is found in the modules/actions directory. The source for the action (Listing 14.7) is found in the directory /src/com/mycompany/testApplication/modules/actions under the SQL.java file.

```
import org.apache.velocity.context.Context;
import org.apache.turbine.util.RunData;
import org.apache.turbine.util.db.Criteria;
import org.apache.turbine.modules.actions.VelocityAction;
import com.company.testApplication.om.Rdf;
import com.company.testApplication.om.RdfPeer;

public class SQL extends SecureAction {
    public void doInsert(RunData data, Context context)
        throws Exception {
        Rdf entry = new Rdf();
        data.getParameters().setProperties(entry);
        entry.save();
    }

    public void doUpdate(RunData data, Context context)
      throws Exception {
        Rdf entry = new Rdf();
        data.getParameters().setProperties(entry);
        entry.setModified(true);
        entry.setNew(false);
        entry.save();
    }

    public void doDelete(RunData data, Context context)
        throws Exception {
        Criteria criteria = new Criteria();
        criteria.add(RdfPeer.RDF_ID, data.getParameters().getInt("rdfid"));
        RdfPeer.doDelete(criteria);
    }

    public void doPerform(RunData data, Context context)
        throws Exception {
        data.setMessage("Can't find the button!");
    }
}
```

Listing 14.7 The SQL Action class.

The SQL Action is derived from SecureAction. By using the SecureAction base class, the action is executed *only* when a user is logged into the system. The submit button uses a value of doInsert. Within the doInsert() method, the system makes use of the global runData object, where the parameters from the <form> are located. In this case, you aren't using a Peer object for the RDF table but are using the RDF class itself. The values from the <form> are placed in the RDF object and saved to the database.

Once the SQL Action has stored the new information in the appropriate database, the default layout is executed using its Navigation modules as well as the index.vm screen as specified in the <form action>. Figure 14.9 shows the database after we've added a new entry, and Figure 14.10 shows the testApplication page.

```
Command Prompt - mysql
mysql> select * from rdf;
+--------+---------------+------+----------------------+--------------------+------+
| RDF_ID | TITLE         | BODY | URL                  | AUTHOR             | DEPT |
+--------+---------------+------+----------------------+--------------------+------+
|      1 | Mastering JXTA | none | http://www.amazon.com | Joseph D. Gradecki | CS   |
+--------+---------------+------+----------------------+--------------------+------+
1 row in set (0.00 sec)

mysql>
```

Figure 14.9 A database entry in MySQL.

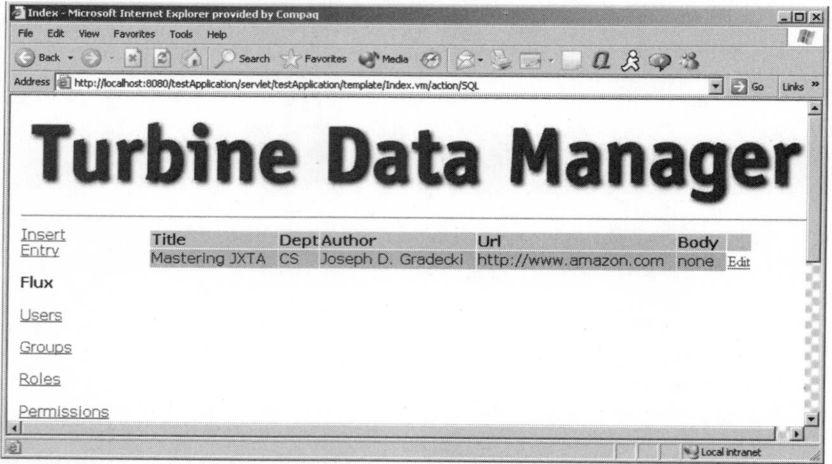

Figure 14.10 The testApplication page after the insert.

Notice the edit link to the right of the entry on the screen in Figure 14.10. If you hover your mouse over the link, you see that the link looks like the following

```
http://localhost:8080/testApplication/servet/testApplication/
tempalte/Form.vm/rdfid/1
```

At this point, you should have a good idea of what the code is going to do when you click the link. The form.vm and form.java Screen module files are invoked. This time, you have a form.java file. As you might expect, the rdfid/1 information on the end of the URL is used to pull the row from the database and display it, as shown in Figure 14.11. The code for the Form class appears in Listing 14.8.

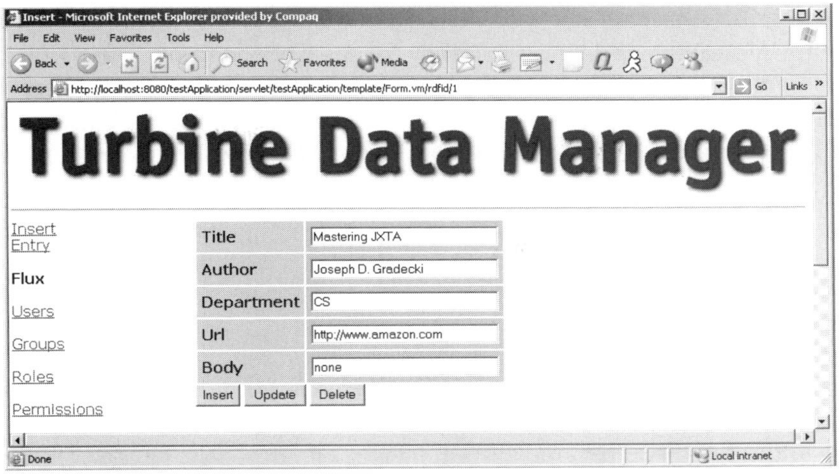

Figure 14.11 An edit on the database row.

```
public class Form extends SecureScreen {
  public void doBuildTemplate( RunData data, Context context {
    try {
      int entry_id = data.getParameters().getInt("rdfid");
      Criteria criteria = new Criteria();
      criteria.add(RdfPeer.RDF_ID, entry_id);
      Rdf rdf = (Rdf) RdfPeer.doSelect(criteria).elementAt(0);
      context.put("entry", rdf);
    } catch (Exception e){
    }
  }
}
```

Listing 14.8 The form.java code.

As you know, the code for the Screen module executes before the Velocity template. So the doBuildTemplate() code in Listing 14.8 takes the primary key supplied on the link, pulls the database row, and places it in the context for the form.vm Velocity template to display to the user. The rdfid at the end of the link is translated into a parameter and placed in the RunData object. then it is pulled out and used with a Criteria object to locate just the one database row. The elementAt(0) is used to pull the one row and place it in the context under the "entry" reference.

Note that actions don't return results. When you need to get information from the database, use a class for a Screen module. If there is something you need to convey from the action, you can set a message variable in the RunData object by using the command data.setMessage(String).

When writing your actions, you derive a new class from either VelocityAction or Secure Action depending on whether the user needs to be logged into the system for the action to take place. In either case, the action contains one or more ActionEvents. As you saw in the SQL Action, there are events for submit button values as well as a method called doPerform(RunData, Context). The doPerform() method is a default method for the action. If no other methods are available or the button click on a form doesn't match any of the ActionEvents in the class, the doPerform() method is executed.

Rebuilding and Deployment

Once you modify your application, you have to rebuild it. This is easy with the current TDK. Just move to the /webapps/testApplication/WEB-INF/build directory and issue the command

```
ant compile
```

Finally, it isn't a requirement that Turbine execute on Tomcat. If you want to move to Resin, BOSS, or another application server, just package up your testApplication or other application name directory structure and deploy it elsewhere. You might need to remove or adjust the DTD in the web.xml file.

Advanced Velocity in Turbine

The last section was quite a mouthful, and we covered most of the primary features of using Velocity with Turbine. However, we want to cover a few additional advanced features. Of course, you can check the Turbine documentation for more information.

The RunData Object

Throughout our discussion of the sample application, we referred to the RunData object and obtained a reference to the object using the data keyword. The RunData object has many methods and fields that can be useful to a developer when producing a Web application. Since the RunData object is available in both templates and most of the Module Java classes, a developer should take advantage of the object. Some of its methods are:

void setMessage(String msg)—Sets a message in the RunData object. This is useful for error handling and other information passed from, say, an Action module.

string getMessage()—Returns the RunData message.

parameter Parser getParameters()—Returns parameters passed from an HTML <form> or on the URL of a link.

void setTitle(String)—Specifies the title for the page often seen as the first statement in a Velocity Screen module template.

user getUser()—Gets the current user in the session.

boolean userExists()—Checks if the current user exists in the session.

boolean removeUserFromSession()—Invalidates the current user from the session.

void setRedirectUri(String ruri)—Sets the URI for a redirection.

If you are processing information in a Screen module Java class and you want to change the Screen module template, you can use the getTemplateInfo() method to obtain a TemplateInfo object and use setScreenTemplate(String) to set a new template dynamically.

The TemplateLink Object

In all of the Velocity templates, you create new links to other templates using the TemplateLink object, which is derived from DynamicURI. The new link is added with the code

```
$link.setPage(String);
```

The $link reference is a TemplateLink object, which along with DynamicURI has an extensive list of methods and fields for aiding in the building of dynamic links. All of the links in our example are to dynamic pages. We can also link to static HTML pages with the same command:

```
$link.setPage("/docs/static/privacy.html")
```

The new static page is the primary page of the user's Web browser without any navigation or layout controls. A better option is to use the static page within a Velocity template and maintain the look and feel of the Web application.

The TemplatePageAttributes Object

When the $page reference is used in a Velocity template, a TemplatePageAttributes object is obtained. This object allows elements of the current page to be changed, such as the title and background color. For example:

```
$page.setBgColor("#FF0000")
```

This command produces a red background. You allow access to the <body> tag with the addAttribute(string, int) command. Other useful commands include:

addAttribute(String name, String value)—Adds the attribute "name" and "value" to the body tag.

setBackground(String url)—Sets the background URL.

setDescription(String description)—Sets a description tag.

setKeywords(String description)—Sets a keyword tag.

setLinkColor(String color)—Specifies the link color.

setStyleSheet(String url)—Sets a stylesheet.

setTextColor(String color)—Specifies the text color.

setVLinkColor(String color)—Specifies the vlink color.

What's Next

As you learned in this chapter, Velocity is a major component in the development of Turbine-driven Web applications. In the next chapter, we explore another framework, called Maverick.

CHAPTER 15

Using Velocity and Maverick

Maverick is a Model-View-Controller (MVC) framework designed to be used with Java and Java 2 Enterprise Edition (J2EE). In true developer fashion, Maverick is open source and works with a variety of templating solutions, among them Velocity and JSP. In addition, Maverick enables you to perform transformations of templates using Extensible Stylesheet Language (XSL) as well as Declarative Velocity Style Language (DVSL), a transformation language designed for Velocity templates.

When designing a framework, you typically have to make a tradeoff between creating a minimalist framework and providing a rich set of services. Maverick takes the view that many good components have already been written to handle connection pools and other such services; therefore, its goal is to provide a skeleton for pulling all of the pieces together.

Although Java and servlets serve as the foundation on which Maverick is written, it doesn't try to force a specific solution for the model and view components of the paradigm. The system includes two examples (which we cover later in this chapter) written in Velocity and JSP with the JavaServer Pages Standard Tag Library (JSTL). Another templating solution known to work is Domify/XSLT. At the other end of the paradigm is the model, and Maverick allows you to pull data straight from the database using JDBC or to rely on entity EJBs.

The framework adds the ability to further simplify the view component by applying transformations on the view output before it is sent back to the user. You can perform transformations using XSLT, DVSL, FOP (Formatting Objects Processor), or Perl. All of the transformations can be chained together to form a large variety of output options. For the look and feel of an application, you can apply a wrapping transformation to a view that embeds one view within another.

By far one of the most important features of Maverick is the maverick.xml file contained within each Web application. This file acts as a roadmap for the components of an application. Tasks within the application are considered *commands*, which in turn may have controller and view components. View components are chosen based on the outcome of a controller class and its internal operations. The configuration file is written in XML and provides an easy way to configure a Web application.

How Maverick Works

As we mentioned, you confirgure a Web application in Maverick through an XML file called maverick.xml. Listing 15.1 shows an example.

```
<?xml version="1.0"?>

<maverick version="2.0" default-view-type="document">
  <commands>
    <command name="HelloWorld">
      <controller class="HelloWorld"/>
      <view name="success" path="HelloWorld.vm"/>
      <view name="error" path="error.vm" />
    </command>

    <command name="displayAll">
      <view name="all" path="all.vm"/>
    </command>
  </commands>
</maverick>
```

Listing 15.1 An example maverick.xml file.

In a Maverick Web application, much of the work is accomplished in a servlet called the *dispatcher*. The dispatcher, as you will see shortly, works with a map of workflow objects created from the maverick.xml file. The map is created during the load phase of the Maverick-hosted application. This phase is designed to handle all of the initialization tasks so the exection phase can be as clean as possible. With a preconfigured Map object, Velocity's execution phase consists of simple method calls and lookups against the Map object.

The Load Process

To get an idea of the load phase and the objects within the workflow tree, let's walk through the processing of the configuration file in Listing 15.1. For the Maverick framework, the <command> element represents a Command object and is the top-level object within the map. From an implementation perspective, two interfaces are available to the framework: CommandSingleView and CommandMultipleViews.

To build the proper Command object, you use a CommandFactory. It creates an object based on the number of <view> elements found within a particular <command> element. When a command is being processed by Maverick, the framework uses the Command object to determine whether it needs to look up a View object based on the interface type used. In the case of CommandSingleView, the framework can bypass any lookup and just use the single view associated with the command.

Each command contains a single Controller object (whether or not one is specified in the maverick.xml file). The ControllerFactory builds a Controller object using the supplied <controller> element defined in the <command> element, or it creates a null controller if a <controller> element is not found.

For all of the possible views in a command, the ViewFactory is used to build View objects. If multiple <view> elements are found in a command, a Map is created to hold key/value pairs based on the name of the view and its pathname. If any transform elements are found in the <command> element, a TransformStep object is used to render the transformation. Otherwise, if no transformations are found, the template passes through to a response output stream.

The Execution Process

Before you start using Maverick, let's take a moment to see how the system processes an HTTP request from a user's Web browser. Figure 15.1 shows an example of the process.

Here are the steps in this process:

1. The user makes a request of a Maverick command. The command is usually a request like localhost:8080/maverick/Signup.m.
2. The application server where Maverick is hosted processes the .m extension on the request and forwards the URL to a class called dispatcher.
3. The dispatcher class looks in its previously built Web application Map for the command. The command is determined by stripping off the .m and matching the name against the <command> elements that are defined in the maverick.xml file.

4. When a command object is found, the go() method is called for the controller class associated with the command.
5. The controller class, if not null, processes its statements, and optionally sets the Model object for the command. Based on its processing, a String is returned indicating the view used as a response to the command.
6. The command object checks a Map object to determine which template corresponds to the String returned by the controller. A View object is returned from the search.
7. The go() method of the View object is executed and passed the Model object from the controller.
8. The View's go() method processes the current template and possibly sends the output to another step based on the getNextStep() method. Otherwise, the output is copied to an output stream and displayed to the user.

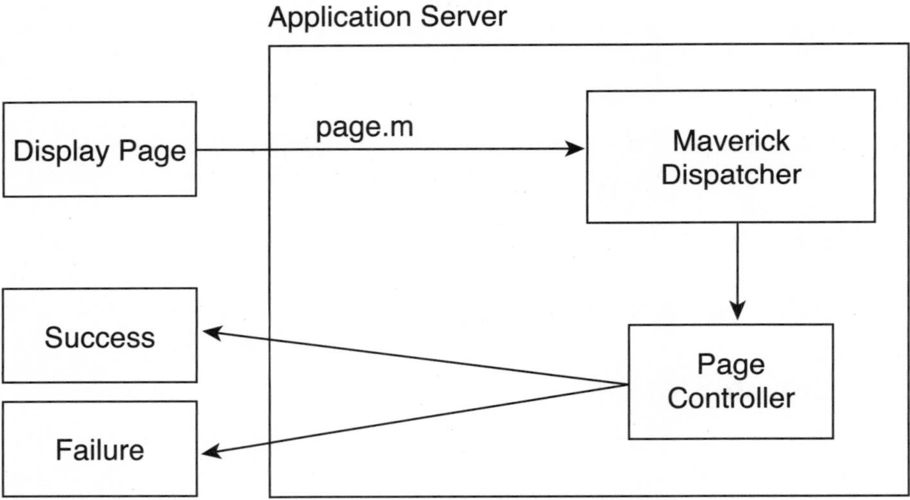

Figure 15.1 Maverick's execution process.

Downloading and Installing Maverick

The Maverick project is hosted on SourceForge and is available at http://mav.sourceforge.net/. Click on the Downloads link on the left navigation screen to bring up the download page for the project. The page is divided into many different sections--including the primary Maverick download as well as optional components. Let's download two files.

First you need the Maverick system file. As of this writing, the most current version of Maverick is 2.1.2, and it is the topmost file on the download page. The files are supported only in zip format. Click on the file and save it to a temporary page on your system. Then, move to the bottom of the download page, download the latest optional Velocity version file, and save it to a temporary location.

Requirements

The current Maverick system has the following prerequisites:

- **An application server**—The Maverick system requires an application server--such as Tomcat 4, Jetty 4, Resin, or Orion--that supports Servlet API 2.3.
- **J2SDK 1.2+**—We developed the examples in this chapter using version 1.4.1.
- **JAXP 1.1**—Use the stand-alone or the version used in the current J2SDK release.

Installing Maverick

Technically there isn't anything to install on the Maverick system because it ultimately consists of a primary JAR along with several support JARs. Figure 15.2 shows the directories associated with the distribution.

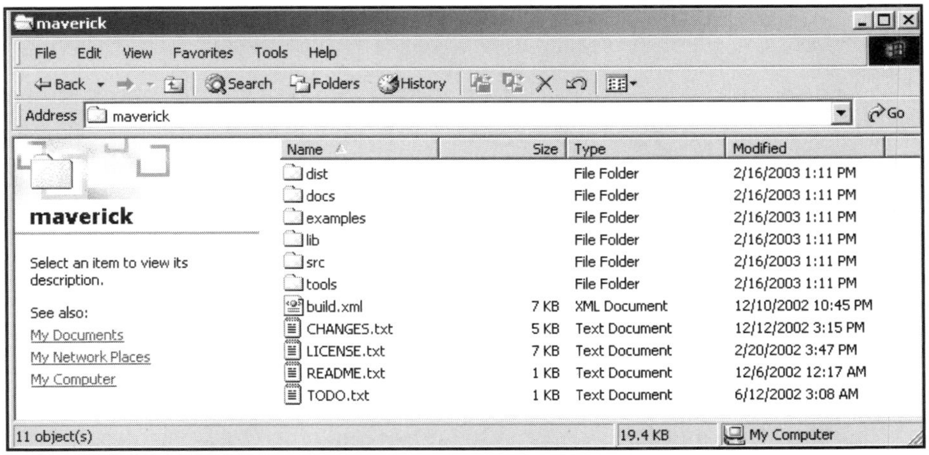

Figure 15.2 Maverick installation directories.

The directories are:

- **/dist**—Includes the example Web archive (WAR) files as well as the primary Maverick JAR
- **/docs**—Contains the manual as well as the JavaDoc
- **/examples**—Contains the source code for the Friendship and Shunting examples
- **/lib**—Includes all support JAR files
- **/src**—Includes the source code for Maverick
- **/tools**—Contains properties and XSL stylesheets

Testing the Installation with the FriendBook Application

Within the /dist directory is a WAR file for the FriendBook application called friendbook-jsp.war. This WAR files consists of the files found in the /examples/friendship-jsp directory along with the necessary Maverick files that execute the application. Let's install this sample application to make sure you have an operating system.

For this example, we assume that you have an appropriate application server installed on your machine. In the test environment, we installed Tomcat. Start by copying the JAR file log4j.jar from the maverick/lib directory to the Tomcat /lib directory. Next, move the friendbook-jsp.war file to the /webapps directory. Now start Tomcat and browse to the URL

```
http://localhost:8080/friendbook-jsp
```

You should see a page prompting you to either log into the application or create a new login. At this point, you know that your system is ready for development. If you don't get the login screen, make sure you have the log4j.jar in the /lib directory. You can check the Maverick mailing list archive for additional help.

Installing the Optional Velocity Module

If you were able to get the FriendBook application up and running, let's switch to the optional Velocity module. Earlier we went through the process of downloading the optional Velocity file and saving it. Using your favorite unzip package, extract the contents of opt-velocity-2.0.zip.

The result of the extraction is a directory structure like the Maverick one shown earlier. Within the /dist directory is a WAR file called friendbook-velocity.war, which is the FriendBook application written with Velocity templates instead of JSP templates. You can use this application as a template for your own applications, as you see in a moment.

Use the same steps as we described for the JSP version and place the files in the /webapps directory of Tomcat. Move the log4j.jar file and browse to the URL

```
http://localhost:8080/friendbook-velocity
```

After several seconds, you see the same login page that you did for the JSP version. The key to the Velocity application and its templates is that the view type used doesn't change. The "normal" document view is used along with a servlet called VelocityViewServlet. This servlet was designed to be used with Struts (as you learn in Chapter 17, "Using Velocity and Struts"). The Maverick team was able to reuse the servlet and provide Velocity templates with Maverick. In addition to the FriendBook application, a transformation type called DVSL is included with the optional Velocity package. DVSL is a transformation language (like XSLT) designed specifically to be used with Velocity.

The Maverick Hello World

Now it's time to look at how you can use Maverick to write a simple application. Let's follow the Hello World example here with two additional applications using Velocity. The development of a Maverick application consists of five primary steps:

- Writing the web.xml file
- Writing the maverick.xml file
- Building controller classes
- Building view files
- Building the model

Writing the web.xml File

When you write a new application for Maverick, you have to first build the application framework. You need the following directory structure:

- **/webapps/<*application name*>**--Contains the view files
- **/webapps/<*application name*>/WEB-INF**--Holds the web.xml and maverick.xml files
- **/webapps/<*application name*>/classes**--Contains the source and class files
- **/webapps/<*application name*>/lib**--Holds the library files

Next you build the web.xml file (see Listing 15.2).

```
<?xml version="1.0"?>
<!DOCTYPE web-app PUBLIC
  "-//Sun Microsystems, Inc.//DTD Web Application 2.2//EN"
  "http://java.sun.com/j2ee/dtds/web-app_2_2.dtd">

<web-app>
  <servlet>
    <servlet-name>dispatcher</servlet-name>
    <display-name>Maverick Dispatcher</display-name>
    <servlet-class>org.infohazard.maverick.Dispatcher</servlet-class>
    <load-on-startup>2</load-on-startup>
  </servlet>

     <servlet>
          <servlet-name>velocity</servlet-name>
          <servlet-class>
      org.apache.velocity.tools.view.servlet.VelocityViewServlet
          </servlet-class>

          <load-on-startup>2</load-on-startup>
     </servlet>

  <servlet-mapping>
    <servlet-name>dispatcher</servlet-name>
    <url-pattern>*.m</url-pattern>
  </servlet-mapping>

     <servlet-mapping>
          <servlet-name>velocity</servlet-name>
          <url-pattern>*.vm</url-pattern>
     </servlet-mapping>
</web-app>
```

Listing 15.2 The HelloWorld web.xml file.

The web.xml file consists of two primary tasks that evaluate URLs for the Web application. The first task directs any URL ending with .m (which is assumed to be a Maverick class) to the Maverick dispatcher defined in the org.infohazard.maverick.Dispatcher class. The dispatcher then executes the appropriate class. The second task directs any URL ending with .vm to the VelocityViewServlet class, which makes the appropriate reference substitutions. Without both of these servlet mappings, the Web application wouldn't be able to operate correctly.

The dispatcher servlet class includes several init-parameters that you can use to configure the dispatcher:

configFile—Defines the path to the maverick.xml configuration file. The default path is /WEB-INF/maverick.xml.

configTransform—Defines the path to an XSL file that you can use to transform the maverick.xml configuration file. You can use this file to change the loaded maverick.xml file as needed for your Web application. The default is no transformation.

currentConfigCommand—Outputs the current maverick.xml file.

reloadCommand—If defined, instructs Maverick to reload its configuration file and all cached data.

defaultRequestCharset—Allows the default charset to be overridden. The default is ISO-8859-1.

Writing the maverick.xml File

The web.xml file is responsible for determining how URLs are handled. The maverick.xml configuration file defines the Maverick application, including the commands that will be directed from the dispatcher, the controller you want to use for a command, and any possible views. For the HelloWorld application, use the configuration file shown in Listing 15.3.

```
<?xml version="1.0"?>

<maverick version="2.0" default-view-type="document">
  <commands>
    <command name="HelloWorld">
      <controller class="HelloWorld"/>
      <view name="success" path="HelloWorld.vm"/>
      <view name="error" path="error.vm" />
    </command>
  </commands>
</maverick>
```

Listing 15.3 The HelloWorld application maverick.xml file.

You have to define all of your Maverick commands in the configuration file. Commands may have a controller associated with them, or they may include a redirect. For your HelloWorld application, you have a single command called HelloWorld. Associated with this command is a controller, also called HelloWorld, which corresponds to a class defined in the next section. The result of the controller is a string that must match one of the name attributes of a <view> element.

The elements that may appear in a maverick.xml configuration file are:

<maverick>—Contains the root element for the configuration file

<commands>—Contains <command> elements

<command>—Defines the behavior and components of a single command

<controller>—Contains a controller for a command; requires a corresponding Java class

<views>—Includes the views that may be used with an associated controller of a command

<view>—Contains a view that is part of a command or a globally referenced view

<transform>—Defines a transformation file that can be used on a view

<modules>—Contains elements for pluggable modules

<view-factory>—Defines a pluggable view type

<transform-factory>--Defines a pluggable transform type

<**shunt-factory>**—Defines a shunt factory

Building Controller Classes

Your HelloWorld command has a single controller as defined in the maverick.xml file. The controller is called HelloWorld—the name of the class that implements the controller, as shown in Listing 15.4.

```
import org.infohazard.maverick.ctl.Throwaway2;

public class HelloWorld extends Throwaway2{

  public String go() throws Exception {
    this.getCtx().setModel(new Model());

    return SUCCESS;
  }


  public class Model {
    protected String message = "Hello World!";

    public String getMessage() {
      return message;
    }
  }
}
```

Listing 15.4 The HelloWorld controller class.

The Maverick system includes quite a number of base classes for building controller classes, all defined in the org.infohazard.maverick.ctl package. Some of the classes populate a bean from the parameters of a <form>, and others do not. In either case, the base classes define either a go() or a perform() method, which will be called automatically by the Maverick dispatcher. Our example uses a couple of different base classes.

In the HelloWorld example, you don't have parameters to deal with from a <form>. This means you can take advantage of a controller base class called Throwaway2. This base class doesn't worry about parameters and has a go() method that must be overridden in order to handle the functionality of the controller.

Your controller will be very simple. You place a message in the model, or context in terms of Velocity, and return the "success" string. The string is then matched with one of the views defined in the maverick.xml file.

The model for your controller is a public class called Model. You instantiate an object of the class and assign its attribute, message, as "Hello World!". Next, you assign the Model object to the controller using the command

```
this.getCtx().setModel(new Model());
```

Finally, the go() method returns a "success" string. You compile the HelloWorld class and place it in the /WEB-INF/classes directory by using the command

```
javac -classpath -..\lib\maverick.jar" HelloWorld.jar
```

Building View Files

The HelloWorld application uses two primary view files. The first one is the welcome screen presented to the user. The code for this Velocity template is shown in Listing 15.5.

```
<p>Say Hello:</p>

<form action="HelloWorld.m" method="post">
  <input type="submit" value="Hello"/>
</form>
```

Listing 15.5 The welcome.vm file.

The primary functionality in the welcome template is a form that exposes a button called Hello. When a user clicks the button, a POST request is made to the server using the URL in HelloWorld.m. The Tomcat application server processes the URL and sends the request to the Maverick dispatcher (because of the .m extension). The dispatcher then calls the go() method of the controller.

Once the “success” string is returned from the controller, the HelloWorld.vm Velocity template is processed and returned to the user. Listing 15.6 shows the HelloWorld.vm template.

```
$request.setAttribute("title", "Success")

<html>
     <head>
          <META http-equiv="Content-Type" content="text/html;
charset=ISO-8859-1">
          <title>$title </title>
     </head>
<body>
Success - $model.Message
</body>
</html>
```

Listing 15.6 The HelloWorld.vm file.

Probably the most important part of the HelloWorld.vm Velocity template is the line

```
Success - $model.Message
```

As you learned in previous chapters, the reference $model.message accesses the Model object from the context, which relates directly to the model used in Maverick.

Velocity and Maverick

With that introduction of Maverick and Velocity behind us, let’s look at using the two technologies to build a sample Web application that will handle storing and retrieving news items from a database. This Web application consists of a database (MySQL in the test environment) having a table with the following schema:

```
id int auto_increment not null primary key
headline varchar(128)
date varchar(32)
textfield text
```

The Web application itself consists of four Maverick commands, two controllers, and five Velocity templates.

Commands

The commands for your application all relate to operations that a user will need to perform. The commands are:

News—The controller for putting new articles into the database

NewsSearch—The controller for searching on the database

NewsSearchEntry—The page that displays the search output

welcome—The page that displays fields for entering a new article

All of the commands are defined in the maverick.xml file, shown in Listing 15.7.

```
<?xml version="1.0"?>

<maverick version="2.0" default-view-type="document"
 default-transform-type="document">
  <commands>
    <command name="News">
      <controller class="NewsEntry"/>
      <view name="success" path="NewsEntry.vm">
       <transform path="frame.vm"/>
      </view>

      <view name="error" path="error.vm">
       <transform path="frame.vm"/>
      </view>
    </command>

    <command name="NewsSearch">
      <controller class="NewsSearch"/>
      <view name="success" path="NewsResults.vm">
          <transform path="frame.vm"/>
      </view>

      <view name="error" path="error.vm">
        <transform path="frame.vm"/>
      </view>
    </command>

    <command name="NewsSearchEntry">
      <view path="NewsSearch.vm">
      <transform path="frame.vm"/>
      </view>
    </command>
```

Listing 15.7 The News Web application maverick.xml file. (continues)

```
    <command name="welcome">
      <view path="NewsEntry.vm">
      <transform path="frame.vm"/>
      </view>
    </command>
  </commands>
</maverick>
```

Listing 15.7 The News Web application maverick.xml file. (continued)

Let's take a closer look at each of the commands and what they are designed to do when called.

welcome

The welcome command is triggered by a URL with a value of welcome.m. The purpose of this command is to display the NewEntry.vm template, which allows the user to enter a new article. The <view> NewsEntry.vm is transformed with the Frame.vm template, and no controller is associated with the command.

NewsEntry

After a user has entered information on the NewsEntry.vm template page, that data needs to be placed in the database. The <form> action on the NewsEntry page is a URL to the Maverick command NewsEntry.m. This command includes a <controller> element for the NewsEntry controller class. A successful update of the database results in the display of the NewsEntry.vm page. Otherwise, an error page lets the user know there was a problem.

NewsSearchEntry

On the menu part of the display is a link called Search. When the user clicks on this link, a Maverick URL is used via the command NewsSearchEntry. No controller is associated with this command–only a view. The NewsSearchEntry.vm template displays another form that allows the user to enter a keyword for searching the database. When the user clicks the form's submit button, the NewsSearch command is sent to Maverick.

NewsSearch

The NewsSearch command has a controller called NewsSearch, which searches the database for the supplied keyword and returns the results to the Velocity template NewsResults.vm.

Controllers

The primary functionality for the news application is contained in two controllers. The NewsEntry controller is designed to take the values submitted by the user and place them in a news table based on the schema discussed earlier. The code is shown in Listing 15.8.

```
import java.sql.*;
import org.infohazard.maverick.ctl.Throwaway2;
import org.infohazard.maverick.flow.*;
import javax.servlet.http.*;

public class NewsEntry extends Throwaway2{

  public String go() throws Exception {
    String returnValue = "";
    Model m = new Model();
    ControllerContext cxt = this.getCtx();

    cxt.setModel(m);

    try {
      Class.forName("com.mysql.jdbc.Driver");

      Connection connection = DriverManager.getConnection(
        "jdbc:mysql://localhost/velocity");
      Statement statement = connection.createStatement();

      int i = statement.executeUpdate(
        "INSERT INTO news VALUES(null, '" +
        cxt.getRequest().getParameter("headline") + "','" +
        cxt.getRequest().getParameter("date") + "','" +
        cxt.getRequest().getParameter("text") +"')");

      statement.close();
      connection.close();

      if (i == 1) {
        returnValue = SUCCESS;
      } else {
        returnValue = ERROR;
      }
    } catch(SQLException e) {
      m.setMessage("SQLException: " + e.getMessage());
      returnValue = ERROR;
    }
```

Listing 15.8 The NewsEntry command controller. (continues)

```
    return returnValue;
  }


  public class Model {
    protected String message;

    public String getMessage() {
      return message;
    }

    public void setMessage(String m) {
      message = m;
    }
  }
}
```

Listing 15.8 The NewsEntry command controller. (continued)

As you can see, there really isn't much to the NewsEntry controller. If the insert to the database is successful, a SUCCESS value is returned to Maverick; otherwise, ERROR is returned. The other controller in the system is called NewsSearch (Listing 15.9).

```
import java.util.*;
import java.sql.*;
import org.infohazard.maverick.ctl.Throwaway2;
import org.infohazard.maverick.flow.*;
import javax.servlet.http.*;

public class NewsSearch extends Throwaway2{

  public String go() throws Exception {
    String returnValue = ERROR;
    Vector v = new Vector();
    Model m = new Model();
    ControllerContext cxt = this.getCtx();
    cxt.setModel(m);

    try {
      Class.forName("com.mysql.jdbc.Driver");

      Connection connection = DriverManager.getConnection(
        "jdbc:mysql://localhost/velocity");
      Statement statement = connection.createStatement();
```

Listing 15.9 The NewsSearch command controller. (continues)

```
      ResultSet rs = statement.executeQuery(
        "SELECT * FROM news WHERE textfield like '%" +
        cxt.getRequest().getParameter("keyword") + "%'");

      while (rs.next()) {
        v.add(new Result(rs.getString("headline"),
         rs.getString("date"), rs.getString("textfield")));
      }
      statement.close();
      connection.close();
      returnValue = SUCCESS;

    } catch(Exception e) {
e.printStackTrace();
      returnValue = ERROR;
    }
    m.setResults(v);

    return returnValue;
  }


  public class Model {
    protected Vector results;

    public Vector getResults() {
      return results;
    }

    public void setResults(Vector r) {
      results = r;
    }
  }
}
```

Listing 15.9 The NewsSearch command controller. (continued)

The NewsSearch controller has a little more work to do. It uses the keyword supplied by the user in a query to find articles in the database. The result this search is a ResultSet. The values in the ResultSet are stored in individual Result classes (defined in Listing 15.10). All of the Result classes are put in a Vector and placed in the Model object. The results are displayed in the SearchResult.vm Velocity template.

```
public class Result {

  String headline;
  String date;
  String text;

  public Result(String h, String d, String t) {
    headline = h;
    date = d;
    text = t;
  }

    public String getHeadline() {
      return headline;
    }

    public String getDate() {
      return date;
    }

    public String getText() {
      return text;
    }
}
```

Listing 15.10 The result helper class.

Velocity Templates

To provide a good look and feel to your site, you can employ a number of Velocity templates:

Frame—Provides a common look and feel to the site

NewsEntry—Displays a form for article entry

NewsSearchEntry—Displays a form for keyword entry

SearchResults—Displays the results from a search

Error.vm—Displays errors from the news entry

The code for the Frame.vm Velocity template is shown in Listing 15.11. The HTML provides a nice frame for all of the other templates in the system. At the top of the frame are two links for the NewsEntry and NewsSearch commands. These links allow a user to access this functionality from anywhere in the Web application.

```
<html>
<head>
<title>$title</title>
</head>
<body bgcolor="#ffffff">
<STYLE>A:link {
     COLOR: #ffffff; TEXT-DECORATION: none
}
A:visited {
     COLOR: #ffffff; TEXT-DECORATION: none
}
A:hover {
     COLOR: #ffff80; TEXT-DECORATION: underline
}
</STYLE>
<table border="0" cellpadding="0" cellspacing="0" width="711">
<!-- fwtable fwsrc="logoxp.png" fwbase="logoxp.gif"
  fwstyle="Dreamweaver" fwdocid = "742308039" fwnested="0" -->
  <tr>
    <td><img src="images/spacer.gif" width="116" height="1"
      border="0"></td>
    <td><img src="images/spacer.gif" width="102" height="1"
      border="0"></td>
    <td><img src="images/spacer.gif" width="274" height="1"
      border="0"></td>
    <td><img src="images/spacer.gif" width="104" height="1"
      border="0"></td>
    <td><img src="images/spacer.gif" width="115" height="1"
      border="0"></td>
    <td><img src="images/spacer.gif" width="1" height="1"
      border="0"></td>
  </tr>

  <tr>
    <td colspan="5"><img name="logoxp_r1_c1"
      src="images/logoxp_r1_c1.gif" width="711" height="29"
      border="0"></td>
    <td><img src="images/spacer.gif" width="1" height="29"
border="0"></td>
  </tr>
  <tr>
    <td rowspan="4"><img name="logoxp_r2_c1"
      src="images/logoxp_r2_c1.gif" width="116" height="114"
      border="0"></td>
    <td colspan="3" background="images/logoxp_r2_c2.gif">
      <div align="center">
```

Listing 15.11 The Frame.vm Velocity template. (continues)

```
<a class="nav" href="News.m">Entry</a>      
<a class="nav" href="NewsSearchEntry.m">Search</a>
      </div>
    </td>
    <td rowspan="4"><img name="logoxp_r2_c5"
      src="images/logoxp_r2_c5.gif" width="115" height="114"
      border="0"></td>
    <td><img src="images/spacer.gif" width="1" height="26"
border="0"></td>
  </tr>
  <tr>
    <td colspan="3"><img name="logoxp_r3_c2"
      src="images/logoxp_r3_c2.gif" width="480" height="23"
      border="0"></td>
    <td><img src="images/spacer.gif" width="1" height="23"
border="0"></td>
  </tr>
  <tr>
    <td rowspan="2"><img name="logoxp_r4_c2"
      src="images/logoxp_r4_c2.gif" width="102" height="65"
      border="0"></td>
    <td background="images/logoxp_r4_c3.gif">
      <div align="center"><b><font size="3">News
        Achive</a></font></b></div>
    </td>
    <td rowspan="2"><img name="logoxp_r4_c4"
      src="images/logoxp_r4_c4.gif" width="104" height="65"
      border="0"></td>
    <td><img src="images/spacer.gif" width="1" height="36" border="0"></td>
  </tr>
  <tr>
    <td><img name="logoxp_r5_c3" src="images/logoxp_r5_c3.gif"
      width="274" height="29" border="0"></td>
    <td><img src="images/spacer.gif" width="1" height="29" border="0"></td>
  </tr>
  <tr>
    <td colspan="5" valign="top"> 
<BR><BR>
$wrapped

    </td>
    <td><img src="images/spacer.gif" width="1" height="304"
      border="0"></td>
  </tr>
</table>
</body>
</html>
```

Listing 15.11 The Frame.vm Velocity template. (continued)

The code for the NewsEntry.vm Velocity template is shown in Listing 15.12. The most important part of this template is the <form>. Users are allowed to enter information about a news article they want to place in the database. When they click submit, the form sends a Maverick command back to the server so the NewsEntry controller can insert the information into the database. The action for the <form> specifies the NewsEntry.m URL, which is processed by the Maverick dispatcher. Figure 15.3 shows how the NewsEntry page appears to a user.

```
$request.setAttribute("title", "News Entry")
<BR>
#if ($model.message)
  <HR>
  $model.message
  <HR>
#end


Welcome to News R US.<BR>
<BR>
Please enter a new items or click on the search button above.<BR>
<BR>
<form action="News.m" method="post">
Headline: <input type="text" name="headline"><BR>
Date: <input type="text" name="date"><BR>
Text: <input type="text" name="text"><BR>
<input type="submit" value="submit">
</form>
```

Listing 15.12 The NewsEntry.vm Velocity template.

The Velocity template that displays a form for searching the database appears in Listing 15.13. Called NewsSearch.vm, this template works in much the same way as the NewsEntry.vm template; it contains a form that includes an action with a NewsSearch.m URL. The Maverick dispatcher processes the URL and activates the NewsSearch controller, as specified in the maverick.xml file. Figure 15.4 shows how the page appears to the user.

```
$request.setAttribute("title", "News Search")

Enter text for search on:<BR>
<BR>
<form action="NewsSearch.m" method="post">
Search keyword: <input type="text" name="keyword">
<input type="submit" value="submit">
</form>
```

Listing 15.13 The NewsSearch.vm Velocity template.

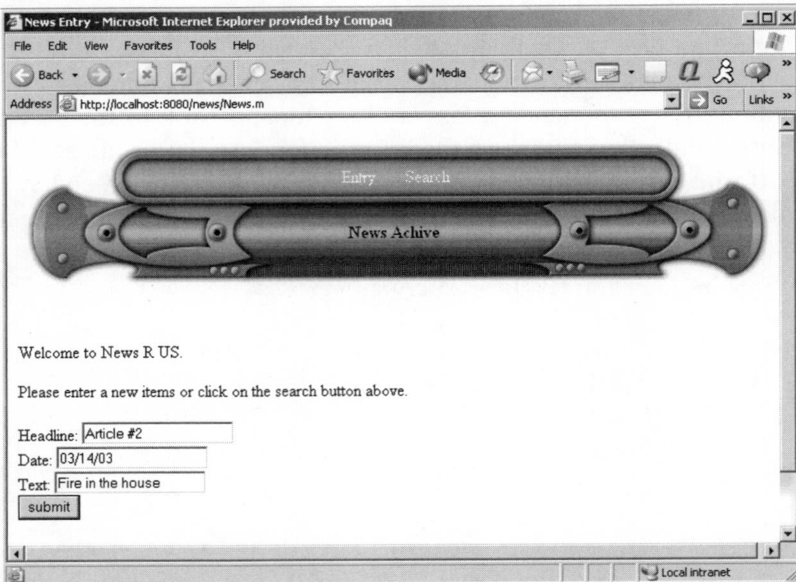

Figure 15.3 The NewsEntry page.

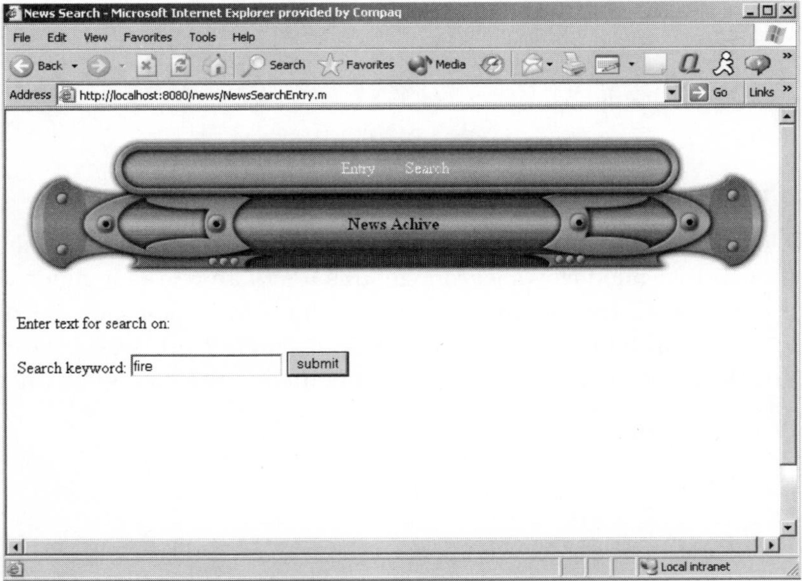

Figure 15.4 The NewsSearch page.

After a search is performed on the database, the results are displayed using the NewsResults.vm Velocity template, shown in Listing 15.14. The real work in the template is accomplished by the #foreach directive, which pulls Result objects from the vector in the model (or context). Each of the news articles found is displayed to the user. Figure 15.5 shows an example results page.

```
$request.setAttribute("title", "News Results")


The results of your search are:<BR>
<BR>
#foreach($value in $model.results)
  Headline: $value.headline<BR>
  Date:     $value.date<BR>
  Text:     $value.text<BR>
<HR>
#end
```

Listing 15.14 The NewsResults.vm Velocity template.

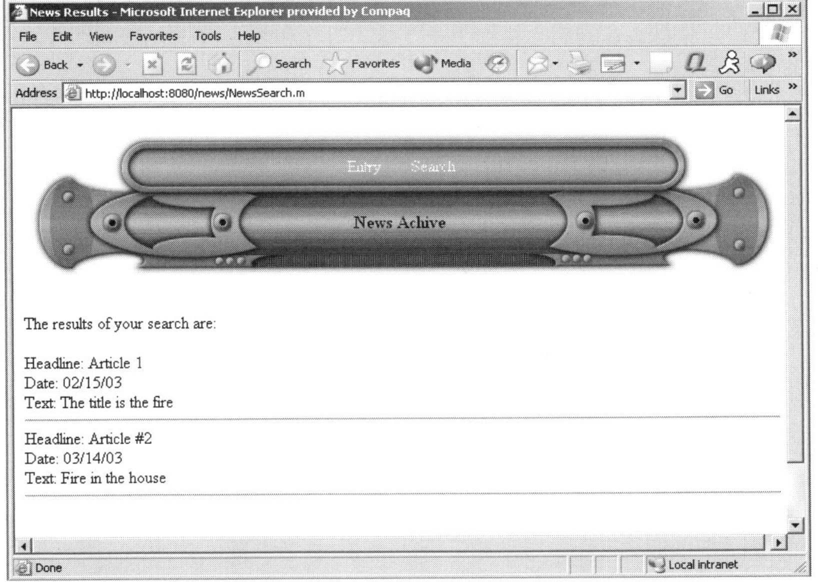

Figure 15.5 The NewsResults page.

Of course, our system wouldn't be complete without an error template (Listing 15.15).

```
$request.setAttribute("title", "News Error")

There has been an error
```

Listing 15.15 The Error.vm Velocity template.

What's Next

In this chapter, you learned how Velocity can be incorporated into the Maverick MVC framework to provide the functionality in the view component. In the next chapter, we explore Velocity integrated development environments (IDEs).

CHAPTER 16

Velocity IDEs

Integrated development environments (IDEs) can be a heated topic of discussion. Some people insist on using WordPad or VI, while others take advantage of the features a good IDE provides. Regardless of which camp you're in, using an IDE has become more popular especially when the IDE supports a WYSIWYG visualizer.

Tools that make the development process with Velocity easier include the following:

- A template for the IntelliJ IDEA IDE
- An addition for UltraEdit
- A Velocity mode for JEdit
- A syntax definition for TextPad
- A minor mode addition to Emacs that color-codes all view template library (VTL) constructs

In this chapter, we discuss these extensions and how to use them.

IntelliJ's IDEA

IntelliJ's IDEA IDE isn't just an editor for handling source code; it's a full-fledged development environment. It includes support for XML, EJB, JSP, and refactoring. You can download an evaluation copy at http://intellij.com/idea/download.jsp. You'll find versions for Windows, Linux, general Unix, and Mac. (You have to obtain an evaluation key via email.)

To install on Windows, just download the installer, which walks you through a series of wizard windows. Once you've completed the installation, obtain the Velocity template at http://cvs.apache.org/viewcvs/jakarta-velocity/contrib/tools/intellij/IntelliJ-Live-Template.xml by right-clicking on the download link, as shown in Figure 16.1, and selecting Save As.

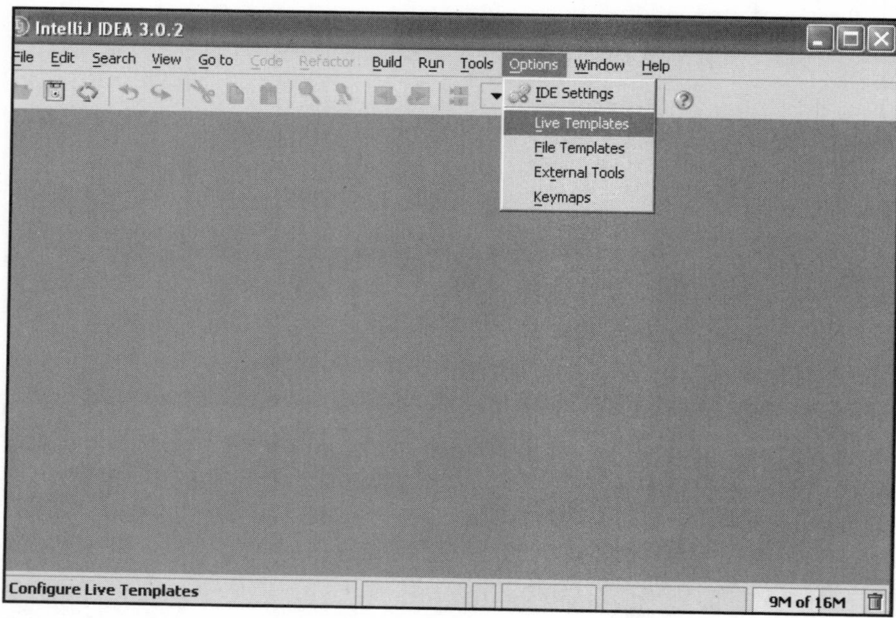

Figure 16.1 Downloading the IntelliJ IDEA template.

The template XML is really just a bunch of "templates" that open up into the full VTL syntax. To install the live templates found in the XML file, copy the file to the directory *<installation drive>*/Documents and Settings/*<install user>*/.IntelliJIdea\config\templates, as shown in Figure 16.2.

Once you place the file in the /config/templates directory, restart IDEA, click Options, and then click Live Templates. You will see the dialog box shown in Figure 16.3; at the top of the live templates list are the various entries for Velocity.

To see how these live templates work, simply start a new project and add a class. Within the new file, type one of the live templates. The test automatically fills in the entire structure so you don't have to worry about missing a closing #end, for example.

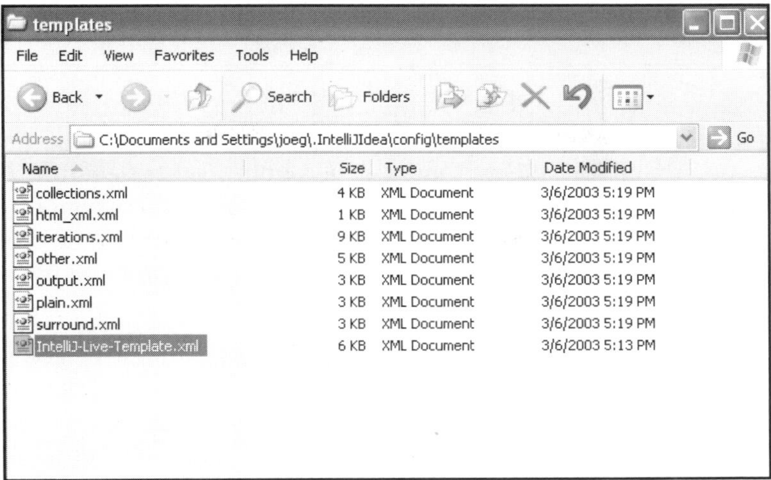

Figure 16.2 The templates directory.

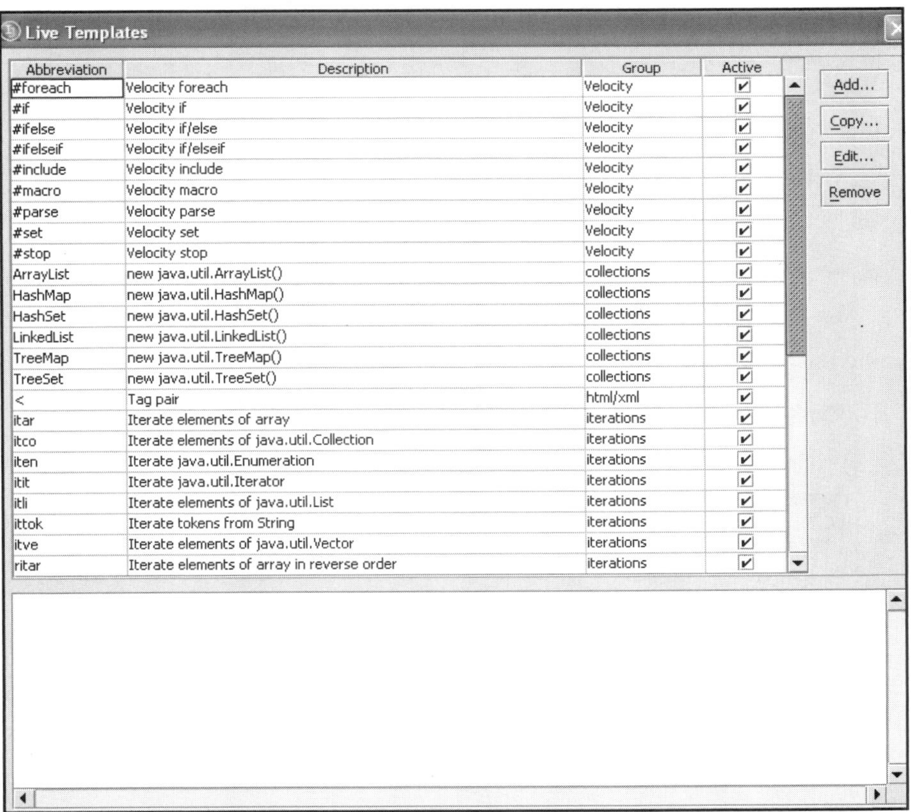

Figure 16.3 The Live Templates dialog box.

UltraEdit

You can download the UltraEdit editor at http://www.ultraedit.com. This product is available in a number of languages and is generally considered a "programmer's editor" rather than a general-purpose text editor. UltraEdit is a Windows-based product, so no Linux/Unix version is available. You can obtain a 45-day evaluation copy from http://www.ultraedit.com/downloads/index.html. The installation is easy; just execute the downloaded file and click through the windows.

Before launching the editor, you must make an adjustment to your support files. First, download the UltraEdit addition from http://cvs.apache.org/viewcvs/jakarta-velocity/contrib/tools/ultraedit/ultraedit.txt, as shown in Figure 16.4. Click on either the download or view links to see the information you need.

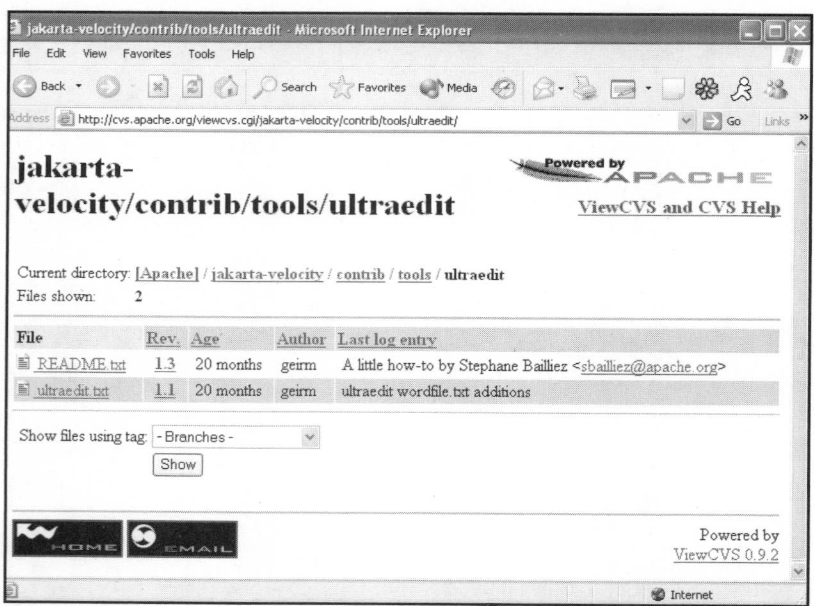

Figure 16.4 The UltraEdit additional CVS download.

Copy all of the information from the browser. Now, open *<ultraedit installation directory>*/word.txt and paste the information at the end of the file. Notice that the file contains a line that begins with

```
/L9"Velocity"
```

The *L9* is an increment value used by UltraEdit to determine additions. The most recent version of UltraEdit already includes the L9 in the word.txt file, so change it to *L10* and save the word.txt file. Be sure there is a blank line between the column above the L10 and the previous information in the file.

Now start UltraEdit and either create a new Velocity template or open a defined one. Figure 16.5 shows the template.

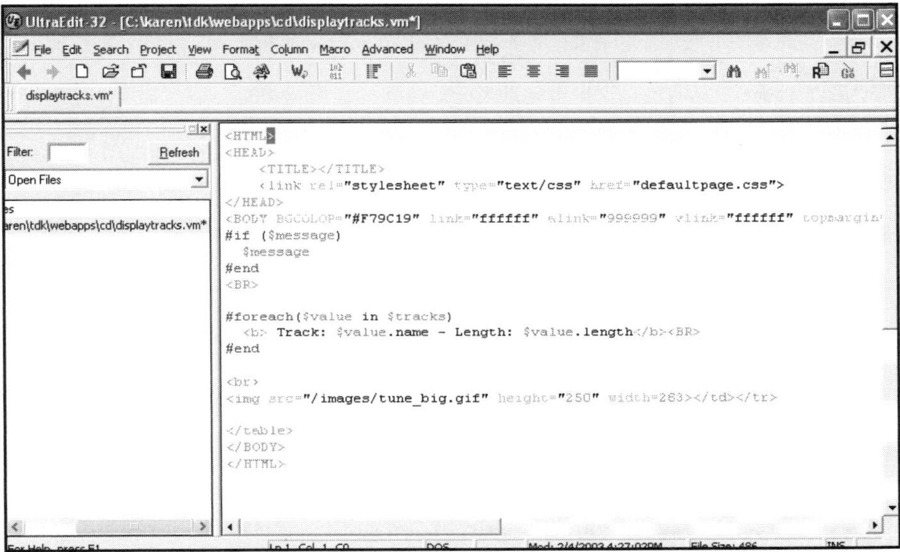

Figure 16.5 The UltraEdit Velocity template.

Although you can't see this in Figure 16.5, the Velocity references are highlighted in green and the directives in blue.

JEdit

JEdit is another "programmer's editor' but it happens to be open source. The editor is very powerful, and with the addition of plug-ins, it can become an IDE as well. Plug-ins are available for a wide range of formats. To download JEdit, browse to http://www.jedit.org. Once you've downloaded it, install the editor with the command

```
java -jar JEdit41installer.jar
```

The installation process consists of a straightforward set of wizards. With the editor installed, download the velocity.xml from http://cvs.apache.org/viewcvs.cgi/jakarta-velocity/contrib/tools/jedit/. Save the velocity.xml file to a mode directory of your installation.

Now open the catalog file of that mode directory and add the following:

```
<MODE NAME="velocity"  FILE="velocity.xml"
  FILE_NAME_GLOB="*.vw" />
```

If you currently have JEdit running, stop and restart it; otherwise, start JEdt. You will now see the syntax of your file's contents color-coded.

TextPad

TextPad is simply an editor for text files. You can download the application from www.textpad.com; it is available for Windows only. Several plug-ins exist for handling technologies like Velocity.

To install TextPad, just download the EXE file and double-click on it to launch the installation wizard. Click Next a few times to install the editor. You can obtain the Velocity plug-in at http://textpad.com/add-ons/synu2z.html (under the Velocity heading).

Download the plug-in, then unzip and extract the velocity.syn file to the <*installation*>/Program Files/Textpad4/system directory. The following steps should guide you through installing the plug-in:

Open TextPad and click Configure, then choose New Document Class.

1. Enter the class name *Velocity* in the dialog box that appears and click Next.
2. In the next dialog box, enter the names of your Velocity files. (I used *.vm.) Click Next.
3. In the next dialog box, enable the option Syntax Highlighting. Now click on the combo box arrow and select Velocity.syn. Click Next to continue.
4. Finally, click Finish.

Open a Velocity file with the extension VM and notice how the syntax for the Velocity commands are highlighted in various colors.

Emacs

If you use Emacs on either a Windows or a Unix flavor machine, you can obtain font locking or syntax coloring for the Velocity language. Download the EL file from http://cvs.apache.org/viewcvs/jakarta-velocity/contrib/tools/emacs/vtl.el and be sure to place the downloaded file in the appropriate directory of your Emacs installation.

Note that this EL file uses minor mode, so if you are currently uisng a major mode plug-in, the Velocity EL will not override it. To use the syntax coloring, load the file you want to edit and type

```
M-x vtl-mode
```

Your document will be highlighted based on the current VTL constructs in use.

What's Next

In this chapter, we described how you can add support for Velocity to various editors and IDEs. While the additions aren't earth-shattering, they provide more convenience for both the designer and the developer. In the next chapter, we discuss how to use Velocity with Struts.

CHAPTER 17

Using Velocity and Struts

This chapter introduces the last of three frameworks that enables you to create dynamic Web sites using the MVC paradigm and Velocity. Struts, produced under Apache's Jakarta project, is probably the most well-known of the Web frameworks available today; entire books have been written about Struts. Our goal in this chapter is to explain how to use Struts with Velocity (just as we did for Turbine and Maverick). We introduce an example registration system for illustration purposes.

Introducing Struts

As we mentioned earlier, entire books on the topic of Struts are available. This section serves as a short introduction to the major components of the system. Figure 17.1 shows a flow diagram of what occurs within the Struts framework.

As you can see in Figure 17.1, the entire process starts with a home page that presents the user with links or HTML forms. In the example we introduce later in this chapter, you present the user with a registration form. When the user clicks a link or submit button, the Struts ActionServlet is invoked. This servlet is designed to take the URL specified in the action attribute of the HTML form or the link URL and determine the "action" it should perform. You define the action in a configuration file along with the Action class and action JavaBean, as well as the response HTML pages.

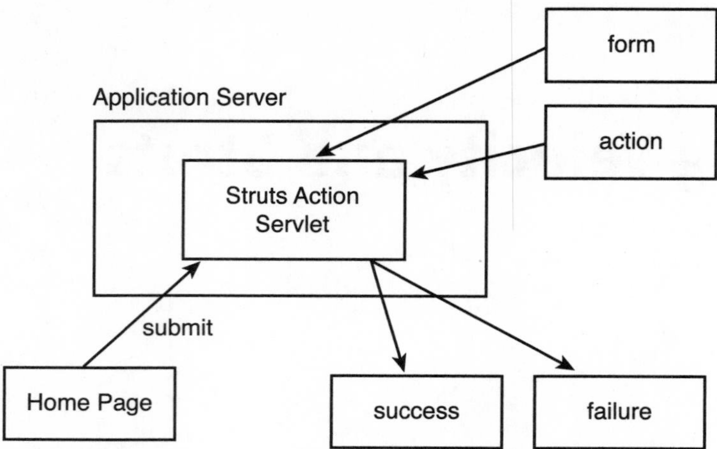

Figure 17.1 Struts flow diagram.

The Action class is defined around the Action base class, and the form data is defined around ActionForm. You can write the HTML response pages in JSP or Velocity (we use Velocity for our example). In the remainder of this chapter, we discuss the prerequisites necessary for Struts and provide an example using both Struts and Velocity.

Installing Struts

Struts is a framework and, as such, it relies on a few "friends" to accomplish its tasks. They include:

- An application server like Tomcat or Resin (we use Tomcat here)
- Ant, which is required to compile the source code for Struts or examples (but not for the example in this chapter)
- JDK
- Velocity, of course (you need the Velocity JAR, Struts library, Struts view, and associated dependencies)

To make the download easy, we've included all of the necessary libraries in the source code download for this chapter on the book's Web site at http://www.wiley.com/compbooks/gradecki.

A Sample Application

To see how simple it is to use Struts with a Velocity templating solution, let's build a Web application that allows a user to register using a username and password. The system displays a registration page with a form for gathering the username, password, and a copy of the password (which verifies that the user typed in the correct combination of characters).

Creating the registration system involves the following six steps:

1. Create an ActionForm.
2. Build the action.
3. Modify the struts-config.xml file.
4. Create an appropriate web.xml file.
5. Creating success and failure pages.
6. Create the register page.

Building the ActionForm

As you might expect, you use an HTML form to gather the username, password, and verification password. You need a method of getting the data entered by the user into the system so it can be processed. In the "old" way, you'd obtain the HttpServletRequest object and use the getParameter() method to get the values. Under Struts, you can use a JavaBean for the transport object. As you learned earlier, when a user clicks a submit button in a form, the action attribute of the <form> tag specifies a Struts action defined in the struts-config.xml file. Associated with the Struts action is an ActionForm. For our registration example, use the class defined in Listing 17.1.

```
import org.apache.struts.action.*;

public class RegisterForm extends ActionForm {
  protected String username;
  protected String password;
  protected String password2;

  public String getUsername() { return this.username; }
  public String getPassword() { return this.password; }
  public String getPassword2() { return this.password2; }
```

Listing 17.1 The RegisterForm code. (continues)

```
  public void setUsername(String username) { this.username =
username; };
  public void setPassword(String password) { this.password =
password; };
  public void setPassword2(String password) { this.password2 =
password; };

}
```

Listing 17.1 The RegisterForm code. (continued)

The RegisterForm class is designed to handle all of the data that is sent from your form. The class must inherit from ActionForm, which is a Struts base class. As you can see, the code in the class is what you would expect from a JavaBean. It includes protected attributes and getter/setter methods for each of them. Both the system and the developer use this Form class. The developer accesses it from the Velocity templates as well as in the Action object (which we discuss next).

Creating an Action

The Action object is where all of business work occurs, usually as a result of a user clicking on a link or a submit button. Based on the Struts configuration file, an Action object is put into play. Listing 17.2 shows the code for the RegisterAction class.

```
import org.apache.struts.action.*;
import javax.servlet.http.*;
import java.io.*;

public class RegisterAction extends Action {
  public ActionForward perform(ActionMapping mapping,
    ActionForm form, HttpServletRequest request,
    HttpServletResponse response) {
    RegisterForm rf = (RegisterForm) form;

    String username = rf.getUsername();
    String password = rf.getPassword();
    String password2 = rf.getPassword2();
    if (password.equals(password2)) {
      try {
        return mapping.findForward("success");
      } catch(Exception e) {
        return mapping.findForward("failure");
```

Listing 17.2 The RegisterAction code. (continues)

```
        }
      }
      return mapping.findForward("failure");
    }
  }
```

Listing 17.2 The RegisterAction code. (continued)

As you might expect, the RegisterAction class extends the Struts Action base class. The Struts system calls the perform() method, providing a Form object if appropriate, as well as the HttpServletRequest and Response objects. In this case, you immediately cast the Form class into RegisterForm and pull the values for the username, password, and verification password.

The code checks to see if the two passwords match. If they do, the code tells Struts to return a value of *success*, which is matched against the configuration file and the success.vm template. Otherwise, a value of failure is returned (and the failure.vm template is displayed).

Configuring Struts

Most of the structure for a Struts Web application is defined in the configuration file struts-conf.xml, as shown in Listing 17.3.

```
<?xml version="1.0" encoding="ISO-8859-1" ?>

<!DOCTYPE struts-config PUBLIC
          "-//Apache Software Foundation//DTD Struts Configuration 1.0//EN"
          "http://jakarta.apache.org/struts/dtds/struts-
config_1_0.dtd">

<struts-config>

  <form-beans>
    <form-bean name="registerForm" type="RegisterForm"/>
  </form-beans>

  <action-mappings>
    <action     path="/struts"
                type="RegisterAction"
                name="registerForm">
      <forward name="success" path="/success.vm"/>
      <forward name="failure" path="/failure.vm"/>
    </action>
  </action-mappings>
</struts-config>
```

Listing 17.3 The Struts configuration file.

In the configuration file, you define the Form JavaBeans, including their name, which is also a reference for the <action> element and the class name. Next, you define all of the actions that can occur in the application. In this example you have only one, named struts. When the struts action is called from a <form> or link, the framework activates the RegisterAction action and uses the RegisterForm form to pull the data from the <form> data. Also defined in the <action> element are the forwards, which represent the pages where results are provided to the user.

The web.xml File

In addition to the Struts configuration file, you need to create a web.xml file so the application server knows how to handle requests from the user. Listing 17.4 shows this file.

```
<?xml version="1.0" encoding="ISO-8859-1"?>

<!DOCTYPE web-app
  PUBLIC "-//Sun Microsystems, Inc.//DTD Web Application 2.2//EN"
  "http://java.sun.com/j2ee/dtds/web-app_2_2.dtd">

<web-app>

  <!-- Action Servlet Configuration -->
  <servlet>
    <servlet-name>action</servlet-name>
    <servlet-class>org.apache.struts.action.ActionServlet</servlet-class>
    <init-param>
      <param-name>config</param-name>
      <param-value>/WEB-INF/struts-config.xml</param-value>
    </init-param>
    <init-param>
      <param-name>debug</param-name>
      <param-value>2</param-value>
    </init-param>
    <init-param>
      <param-name>detail</param-name>
      <param-value>2</param-value>
    </init-param>
    <init-param>
      <param-name>validate</param-name>
      <param-value>true</param-value>
    </init-param>
    <load-on-startup>2</load-on-startup>
  </servlet>
```

Listing 17.4 The web.xml file. (continues)

```
  <servlet>
    <servlet-name>velocity</servlet-name>
    <servlet-class>org.apache.velocity.tools.view.servlet.
VelocityViewServlet</servlet-class>
    <init-param>
     <param-name>toolbox</param-name>
     <param-value>/WEB-INF/toolbox.xml</param-value>
   </init-param>
   <load-on-startup>10</load-on-startup>
  </servlet>

   <!-- Action Servlet Mapping -->

  <servlet-mapping>
    <servlet-name>velocity</servlet-name>
    <url-pattern>*.vm</url-pattern>
  </servlet-mapping>

  <servlet-mapping>
    <servlet-name>action</servlet-name>
    <url-pattern>*.do</url-pattern>
  </servlet-mapping>


  <!-- Struts Tag Library Descriptors -->
  <taglib>
    <taglib-uri>/WEB-INF/struts-bean.tld</taglib-uri>
    <taglib-location>/WEB-INF/struts-bean.tld</taglib-location>
  </taglib>

  <taglib>
    <taglib-uri>/WEB-INF/struts-html.tld</taglib-uri>
    <taglib-location>/WEB-INF/struts-html.tld</taglib-location>
  </taglib>

  <taglib>
    <taglib-uri>/WEB-INF/struts-logic.tld</taglib-uri>
    <taglib-location>/WEB-INF/struts-logic.tld</taglib-location>
  </taglib>
</web-app>
```

Listing 17.4 The web.xml file. (continued)

The web.xml file consists of two important parts. The first is a definition of <servlet-mapping> and <servlet> elements for Struts. The configuration says that any URL that ends in .do will be redirected to the ActionServlet servlet provided with Struts. The second important part is the configuration section for Velocity, which specifies that all .vm URLs are to be directed to VelocityViewServlet. Notice the parameter to the Velocity <servlet> for a toolbox.xml file. This file is shown in Listing 17.5.

```
<?xml version="1.0"?>

<toolbox>
  <tool>
  <key>toolLoader</key>
  <class>org.apache.velocity.tools.tools.ToolLoader</class>
  </tool>

<tool>
  <key>link</key>
  <class>org.apache.velocity.tools.struts.LinkTool</class>
</tool>

<tool>
  <key>msg</key>
  <class>org.apache.velocity.tools.struts.MessageTool</class>
</tool>

<tool>
  <key>errors</key>
  <class>org.apache.velocity.tools.struts.ErrorsTool</class>
</tool>

<tool>
  <key>form</key>
  <class>org.apache.velocity.tools.struts.FormTool</class>
</tool>
</toolbox>
```

Listing 17.5 The toolbox.xml file.

The toolbox.xml file defines several classes that the Struts ActionServlet can use to provide a bridge between Struts, its Form JavaBeans, and Velocity templates. You can find all of the code in the Velocity Struts plug-in.

The Success Page

When a user provides a username and two passwords that match, the Register-Action class instructs the Struts ActionServlet to use the success forward. The success forward, defined in the Struts configuration file, tells the system to use the success.vm Velocity template to display output to the user. The code for the template is shown in Listing 17.6.

```
<HTML>
<HEAD>
  <TITLE>Success</TITLE>
</HEAD>
<BODY>
  Registration Success!
  Thanks for logging in $!registerForm.username
  <P><A href="register.vm">Try Another?</A></P>
</BODY>
</HTML>
```

Listing 17.6 The success.vm template.

The template is fairly basic, but you get the idea. If the user is successful in providing accurate information, you pull the username from the RegisterForm object created when the RegisterAction action was executed by Struts. Notice the use of the $! directive. This directive tells Velocity to search all available Context objects for the registerForm object and the username() method. Figure 17.2 shows the result of this page.

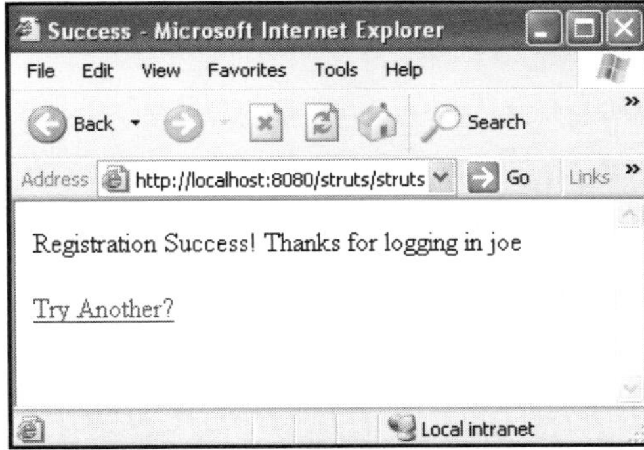

Figure 17.2 Success under Struts and Velocity.

The failure page looks like the success Velocity template but of course tells users that they must try again.

The Register Page

Throughout this discussion we have referenced the page where the user provides information and submits it to the server. Listing 17.7 shows the register Velocity template that provides this capability.

```
<html>
<head>
<title>Register</title>
<meta http-equiv="Content-Type" content="text/html; charset=iso-8859-1">
</head>

<body bgcolor="#CCCCCC" text="#006699" link="#006699"
  vlink="#006699" alink="#006699">
<table width="80%" border="1" cellspacing="0" cellpadding="0"
  bgcolor="#999999" bordercolor="#000000" align="center">
  <tr>
    <td>
      <table width="100%" border="0" cellspacing="0" cellpadding="0">
        <tr>
          <td>
            <div align="center"><font face="Verdana, Arial,
  Helvetica, sans-serif" size="-1"><a href="http://localhost:
  8080/register.vm">Home</a></font></div>
          </td>
        </tr>
      </table>
    </td>
  </tr>
</table>
<table width="80%" border="1" cellspacing="0" cellpadding="0"
bordercolor="#000000" align="center">
  <tr>
    <td width="22%" align="right"><img src="header2.gif"
width="200" height="75"></td>
  </tr>
</table>
<table width="80%" border="1" cellspacing="0" cellpadding="0"
bordercolor="#000000" align="center">
  <tr>
    <td align="left" valign="top" height="423">
      <table width="100%" border="0" cellspacing="0" cellpadding="0">
        <tr>
          <td width="20%" height="9"><font face="Verdana, Arial,

Helvetica, sans-serif" size="-2" color="#000000">$date</font></td>
          <td width="43%" height="9"> </td>
          <td width="37%" height="9" bgcolor="#000000">
            <table width="100%" border="0" cellspacing="0" cellpadding="0">
              <tr bgcolor="#000000">

              </tr>
            </table>
```

Listing 17.7 The register.vm template. (continues)

```
          </td>
        </tr>
      </table>
      <table width="69%" border="0" cellspacing="0"
cellpadding="0" align="center">
        <tr>
          <td width="71%" height="246" align="left" valign="top">
            <p> </p>

<form action="struts.do" method="post">
  username: <input type="text" name="username"/><BR>
  password: <input type="text" name="password"/><BR>
  again   : <input type="text" name="password2"/><BR>
<input type="submit" name="submit" value="Register"/>
</form>

          </td>
        </tr>
      </table>
    </td>
  </tr>
</table>
<p> </p>
<p> </p><p> </p>
<p> </p>
</body>
</html>
```

Listing 17.7 The register.vm template. (continued)

A good deal of the template consists of formatting information. At the end, however, the code creates an HTML form with an action attribute set equal to *struts.do*. As you'll recall, the name of your action in the Struts configuration file is also struts. When the struts.do URL is provided to the server, the .do is stripped and the "struts" string is matched against the <action> elements in the configuration.

Setup

The setup for the application is quite simple. The directory structure looks like this:

/webapps/struts

/webapps/struts/register.vm

/webapps/struts/success.vm

/webapps/struts/failure.vm

/webapps/struts/WEB-INF/web.xml

/webapps/struts/WEB-INF/struts-config.xml

/webapps/struts/WEB-INF/toolbar.xml

/webapps/struts/WEB-INF/classes/RegisterForm.java

/webapps/struts/WEB-INF/classes/RegisterAction.java

/webapps/struts/WEB-INF/lib/struts_1_0_2.jar

/webapps/struts/WEB-INF/lib/dom4j.jar

/webapps/struts/WEB-INF/lib/commons-collections.jar

/webapps/struts/WEB-INF/lib/velocity-1.3-dev.jar

/webapps/struts/WEB-INF/lib/velocity-tools-library-0.2.jar

/webapps/struts/WEB-INF/lib/velocity-tools-struts-0.8.jar

/webapps/struts/WEB-INF/lib/velocity-tools-view-0.7.jar

Compile

To compile the Action and Form classes, use the following command:

```
javac "../lib/struts_1_0_2.jar;./;" *.java
```

Once the Java source files have been compiled, restart the application server.

Run

Execute the application by browsing to this URL:

```
http://localhost:8080/struts/register.vm
```

You should see the screen shown in Figure 17.3. Enter a username and your password twice, then click submit.

What's Next

In this chapter, we explained how to use Velocity and Struts to provide a comprehensive MVC solution for developing dynamic Web pages. In the next chapter, we build a complete example using Velocity.

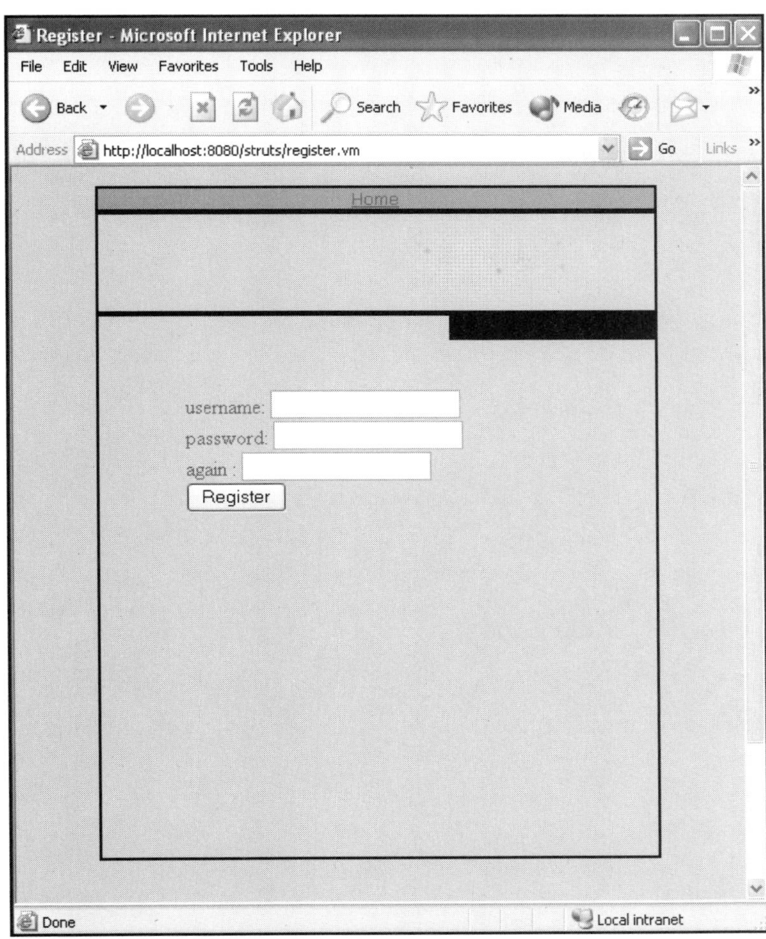

Figure 17.3 The register.vm template output.

The Hotel Reservation Velocity Application

Now that you're familiar with Velocity and you've seen how to use it in various examples, in this chapter we examine a fairly large Web application that uses Velocity to handle all its view components. We illustrate how to use Velocity in a situation that calls for a production system.

The Hotel Specifications

For this application, you'll construct a hotel reservation system (HRS) for Motel 37, a fictitious hotel that has just five rooms available. The Web application must allow users to perform three main functions:

- Search for a room to book
- Book a room
- Look up an existing reservation

In addition to these three tasks, the application should present a good Web site flow and include pages that help users move through the site. This means you need to have a home page that introduces the hotel and provides users with task options as well as navigation controls. If users want to book a new room in the hotel, they need to know what rooms are available for a given timeframe and the amenities the available rooms offer. When the results of the search are presented to users, they can either book one of the rooms or perform another search. Once they book a room, they should be provided with a reservation number, which they can use to look up the reservation at a later time. Of course, all of this functionality must be contained within a proper look and feel. Figure 18.1 shows the page map for the hotel reservation system.

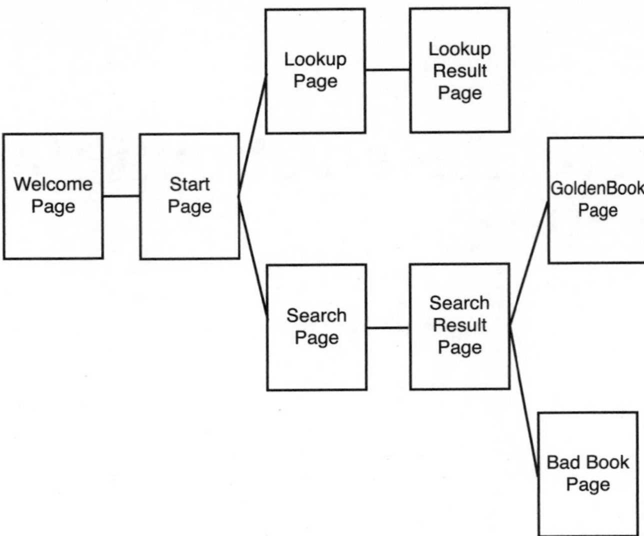

Figure 18.1 The Hotel 37 page map.

As you can see in the figure, the Velocity view templates are broken down into four major areas. The first is the frame template, which handles all of the common look-and-feel aspects of the site. All pages presented to the user are wrapped by the Velocity frame template, which is called frame.vm. Next, you have the introduction pages. These pages include home.vm (which handles all initial views of the Web application) and start.vm (which handles those users who need to use the Web application for searching or looking up a reservation).

Searching the database for an open room is accomplished by search.vm, and the results of the search are presented in the page bookIt.vm. The bookIt.vm template is also used to indicate the desire of the user to book an actual room. The results of a successful booking attempt are confirmed by the goodBook.vm template; badBook.vm indicates when the booking has failed.

In order to look up a previously successful reservation, the customer uses the reservation number provided on the goodBook.vm template page and enters it into the lookup.vm template page. If the application finds the reservation in the database, the displayReservation.vm template is displayed to the user. If no reservation is found using the supplied reservation number, the noReservation.vm template is displayed.

The Hotel Architecture

Of course, just providing the templates doesn't do much for the functionality that must appear behind the scenes. Figure 18.2 shows a sample architecture diagram for the HRS.

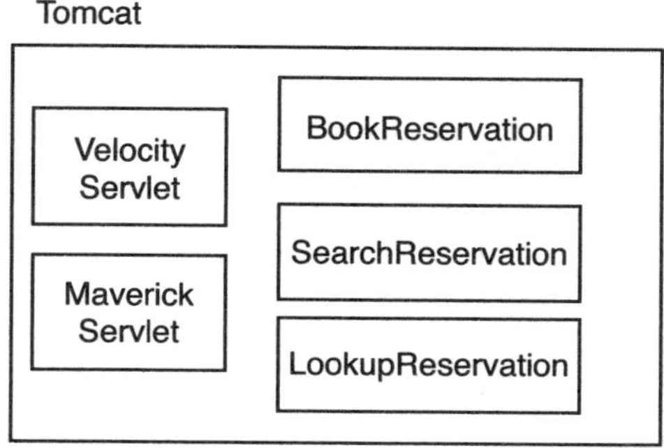

Figure 18.2 The HTS's architecture.

As Figure 18.2 shows, this solution uses Maverick as a framework for the MVC paradigm and MySQL as the underlying database. Seven commands are associated with the Maverick framework:

- doWelcome
- startReservation
- doSearch
- doLookup
- lookupReservation
- bookReservation
- searchReservation

Only three of the commands--lookupReservation, bookReservation, and searchReservation--have controller objects associated with them. The LookupReservation controller is responsible for looking up a supplied reservation number in the database and populating the model with appropriate information for display to the user. The BookReservation populates the database with a new reservation using the information supplied in the appropriate form. Finally, the SearchReservation controller uses information supplied by the user to determine whether any rooms are available based on the desired criteria.

The Hotel Database Schema

The HRS application requires two tables in its database. You can build the first table, called rooms, with the following MySQL SQL dump:

```
CREATE TABLE rooms (
  id int(11) NOT NULL default '0',
  beds varchar(16) default NULL,
  smoking int(11) default NULL,
  refrigerator int(11) default NULL,
```

```
  baserate double default NULL,
  PRIMARY KEY  (id)
) TYPE=MyISAM;


INSERT INTO rooms VALUES (1,'double',0,0,110);
INSERT INTO rooms VALUES (2,'king',0,1,140);
INSERT INTO rooms VALUES (3,'suite',1,1,190);
INSERT INTO rooms VALUES (4,'double',1,1,110);
INSERT INTO rooms VALUES (5,'king',1,1,140);
```

The rooms table is designed to hold information about all of the rooms in the hotel as well as the amenities provided by each. Another table, called reservations, holds all of the reservations currently attributed to the hotel. You can build this table with the following:

```
CREATE TABLE reservations (
  id int(11) NOT NULL auto_increment,
  room int(11) default NULL,
  indate date default NULL,
  outdate date default NULL,
  adults int(11) default NULL,
  children int(11) default NULL,
  cost double default NULL,
  PRIMARY KEY  (id)
) TYPE=MyISAM;
```

Configuring the Maverick XML

Because you are using Maverick as your control framework, you must build a maverick.xml file appropriate for your page map and controllers. Listing 18.1 shows the maverick.xml file for the HRS application.

```
<?xml version="1.0"?>

<maverick version="2.0" default-view-type="document"
 default-transform-type="document">
  <commands>
     <command name="doWelcome">
       <view path="home.vm">
         <transform path="frame.vm"/>
       </view>
     </command>

     <command name="startReservation">
       <view path="start.vm">
         <transform path="frame.vm"/>
```

Listing 18.1 The maverick.xml file. (continues)

```
      </view>
     </command>

     <command name="doSearch">
       <view path="search.vm">
         <transform path="frame.vm"/>
       </view>
     </command>

     <command name="doLookup">
       <view path="lookup.vm">
         <transform path="frame.vm"/>
       </view>
     </command>

          <command name="lookupReservation">
        <controller class="LookupReservation"/>
          <view name="success" path="displayReservation.vm">
             <transform path="frame.vm"/>
          </view>

          <view name="error" path="noReservation.vm">
             <transform path="frame.vm"/>
          </view>
         </command>

     <command name="bookReservation">
        <controller class="BookReservation"/>
          <view name="success" path="goodBook.vm">
          <transform path="frame.vm"/>
          </view>

          <view name="error" path="badBook.vm">
            <transform path="frame.vm"/>
          </view>
         </command>

     <command name="searchReservation">
        <controller class="SearchReservation"/>
          <view name="success" path="bookIt.vm">
          <transform path="frame.vm"/>
          </view>

          <view name="error" path="search.vm">
            <transform path="frame.vm"/>
          </view>
      </command>
   </commands>
 </maverick>
```

Listing 18.1 The maverick.xml file. (continued)

The maverick.xml file includes all seven of the commands you need to present the appropriate view pages to the user. Notice that all of the view elements include transform subelements for handling the addition of the velocity frame.vm template (which wraps each template for the site's look and feel).

The Look and Feel Frame

You know that one of the most important things a Web site can provide is a common look and feel. The navigation menus and logos should appear in the same place on every page of the site. This look-and-feel component makes users feel more comfortable with the flow from page to page. Listing 18.2 shows the frame.vm Velocity template used in the HRS Web application.

```
<html>
<head>
<title>$title</title>
</head>
<body bgcolor="#FFFFFF" text="#000000">
<table width="85%" border="0" cellspacing="0" cellpadding="5">
  <tr>
    <td width="25%">
      <img src="images/title1.jpg" width="200" height="100"
        alt="Your logo here" border="0">
    </td>
    <td width="75%"><img src="images/banner_space.jpg"
width="468" height="60" alt="Banner space here" border="0"></td>
  </tr>
  <tr>
    <td width="25%"><font size="-1"><i><font face="Verdana,
Arial, Helvetica, sans-serif">
Getting to know you in 37 different ways</font></i></font></td>
    <td width="75%"> </td>
  </tr>
</table>
<table width="85%" border="0" cellspacing="0" cellpadding="0">
  <tr>
    <td width="13%" bgcolor="#0033FF" align="left"><img
src="images/left_corner.gif" width="50" height="50"></td>
    <td width="55%" bgcolor="#0033FF" align="center"><b><font
color="#FFFFFF" face="Verdana, Arial, Helvetica, sans-serif">

</font></b></td>
    <td width="32%" align="left"><img src="images/
right_corner.gif" width="50" height="50"></td>
  </tr>
  <tr>
```

Listing 18.2 The frame Velocity template. (continues)

```
    <td width="5%" bgcolor="#0033FF" height="183" valign="top">
      <table width="100%" border="0" cellspacing="0" cellpadding="5">
        <tr>
          <td bgcolor="#0033FF"><a href="doWelcome.m"><font
color="#FFFFFF" face="Verdana, Arial, Helvetica,
sans-serif">Home</font></a></td>
        </tr>
        <tr>
          <td><a href="startReservation.m"><font color="#FFFFFF"
face="Verdana, Arial, Helvetica, sans-serif">Reservations</font>
</a></td>
        </tr>
      </table>
    </td>
    <td width="95%" height="183" align="center" valign="top">
      <p> </p>
      <table width="95%" border="1" cellspacing="0"
cellpadding="5" bordercolor="#0033FF">
        <tr>
          <td bgcolor="#0099FF" align="left"><b><font
face="Verdana, Arial, Helvetica, sans-serif" size="-1">
$wrapped
          </td>
        </tr>
      </table>
    </td>
  </tr>
  <tr>
    <td width="13%" bgcolor="#0033FF" height="189" valign="bottom">
<img src="images/bottom_left.gif" width="150" height="75"></td>
    <td width="55%" height="189">
      <table width="100%" border="0" cellspacing="0" cellpadding="0">
        <tr>
          <td> </td>
        </tr>
        <tr>
          <td align="center" height="65"><font face="Verdana,
Arial, Helvetica, sans-serif" size="1">&copy;
            Copyright 2003, Motel 37</font></td>
        </tr>
      </table>
    </td>
    <td width="32%" height="189"> </td>
  </tr>
</table>
<p> </p>

</body>
</html>
```

Listing 18.2 The frame Velocity template. (continued)

The look and feel for the application isn't complex, but it includes all of the major features a good Web site requires. Figure 18.3 shows how the frame appears to the user.

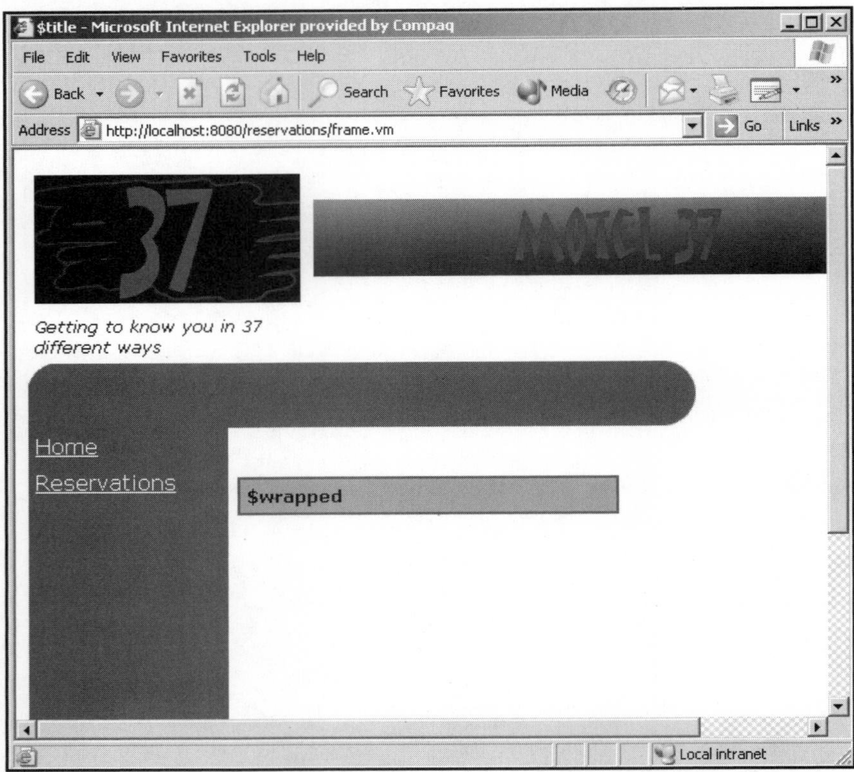

Figure 18.3 The look and feel frame.

There are a couple different areas where you have to change the frame depending on the functions provided by your Web application. The first area is the left navigation menu. The HTML tags for the menu are as follows:

```
<td bgcolor="#0033FF">
  <a href="doWelcome.m">
    <font color="#FFFFFF" sans-serif">
      Home
    </font>
  </a>
</td>

<td>
  <a href="startReservation.m">
    <font color="#FFFFFF" sans-serif">
      Reservations
    </font>
  </a>
</td>
```

In the HRS application, two links are available on all pages: Home and Reservations. If users click on the Home link, they should be sent back to the home page of the Web application. The Maverick command doWelcome causes the home.vm Velocity template to be presented to the user (after being transformed with the frame.vm Velocity template).

The Reservations link sends users to the page where they can either search for a new room or look up a current reservation. This process starts on the start.vm Velocity template and is activated through the startReservation Maverick command.

If you want to expand the application with additional tasks, you can place a link in the navigation menu code. By using the Maverick MVC framework and Velocity templates, you can expand the functionality of an application quite easily.

The second important area in the frame is where all of the primary pages are located when transformed by the frame.vm Velocity template. Toward the end of the frame.vm code, you see a Velocity reference named $wrapped. The Maverick system places all view Velocity templates here in the look-and-feel template.

Building the Welcome Pages

When users first arrive at the HRS Web application, they are greeted with information about the site. Listing 18.3 contains the code for the welcome page; Figure 18.4 shows what the user sees.

```
$request.setAttribute("title", "Welcome")

Welcome to Motel 37<BR>
<BR><BR>
If you are interested in a reservation, searching, booking or
displaying a current one, click on the button.
<BR>
<form action="startReservation.m" method="post">
<input type="submit" name="submit"  value="Goto Reservation">
</form>
```

Listing 18.3 The home Velocity template.

All view templates should set the $title Velocity reference to properly display the title of each page on the user's browser. If you don't assign a value to the title reference, the user's browser will display text like "$title" in the title bar when the page is rendered.

The home.vm Velocity template features a <form> HTML tag, which includes only a single button, which the user clicks to begin the process of working with a reservation. The action for the <form> tag is the Maverick command startReservation. Notice the .m extension is used so the application server will be able to properly handle the Maverick command.

When users click the Goto Reservation submit button, they are transferred to the Start reservation page, as shown in Figure 18.5. The purpose of this page (see Listing 18.4) is to give users a common place where they can decide what type of reservation function they wish to perform. In the HRS application, two task functions are available: Search For A Room and Look Up A Reservation. Each function is started by the user clicking on the appropriate button displayed on the page. The buttons are placed within two different forms. For the Search For A Room function, the form action triggers the use of the doSearch.m Maverick command. The Look Up A Reservation function triggers the doLookup.m Maverick command. Each of these commands activates controller classes, as we discussed earlier.

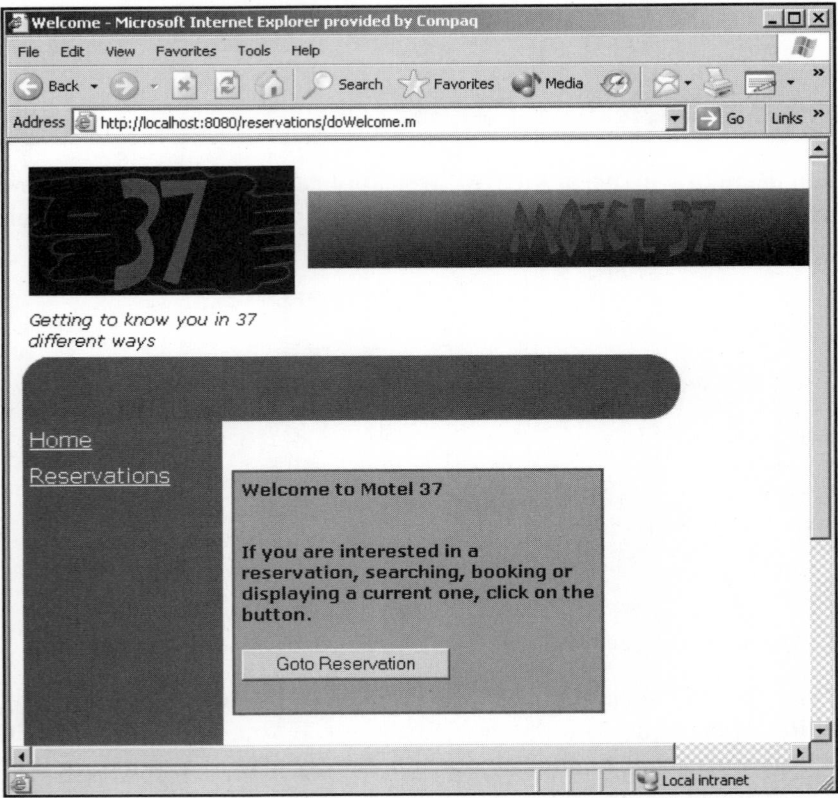

Figure 18.4 The welcome page.

```
$request.setAttribute("title", "Start")

Here are the operations available for a reservation:<br>
<BR>
Search for a room:
<form action="doSearch.m" method="post">
<input type="submit" name="submit"  value="Search for a Room">
</form>
<BR>
Look up a reservation:
<form action="doLookup.m" method="post">
<input type="submit" name="submit"  value="Lookup a Reservation">
</form>
```

Listing 18.4 The start Velocity template.

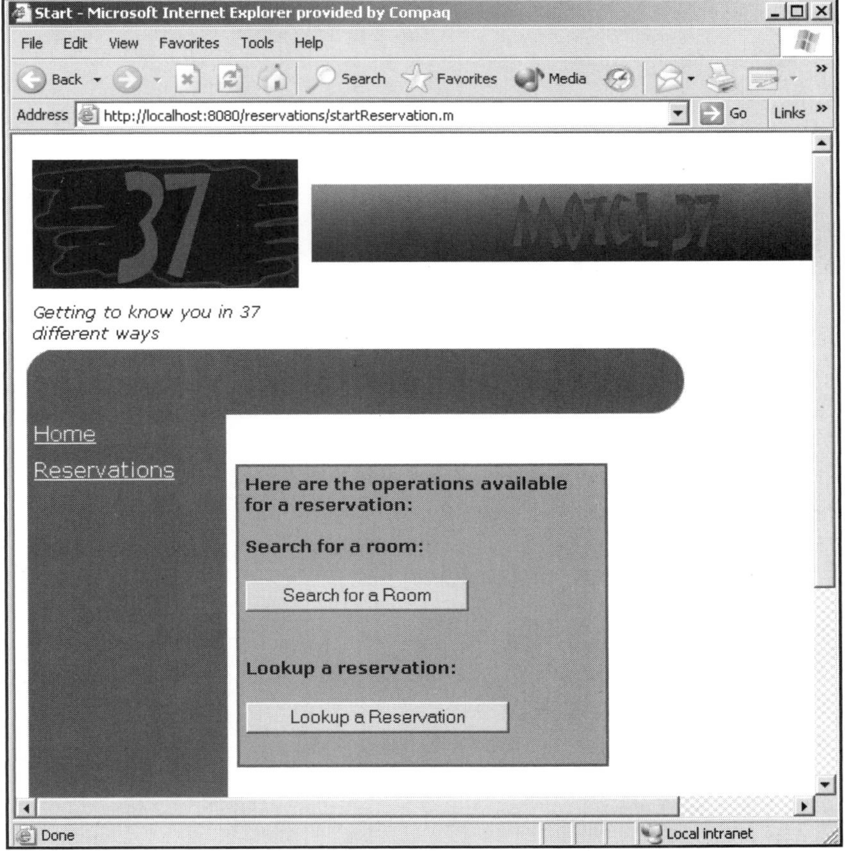

Figure 18.5 The start page.

Searching for a Room

When the doSearch.m Maverick command executes, the search.vm Velocity template is displayed to the user. This search page allows the system to gather all of the information necessary for the search controller to find an appropriate room for the user. The code for the search.vm Velocity template appears in Listing 18.5; Figure 18.6 shows the page within a browser window.

```
$request.setAttribute("title", "Reservation Search")

In order to find a room that is appropriate for your needs, we
need a little more information:<BR>
<BR>
<form action="searchReservation.m" method="post">
<table>
<tr>
<td>Enter date arriving:</td><td> <input type="text"
name="indate" value="yyyy-mm-dd"></td>
</tr>
<tr>
<td>Enter date departing:</td><td> <input type="text"
name="outdate" value="yyyy-mm-dd"></td>
</tr>
</table>
<BR>
<table>
<tr>
<td>Beds:</td>
<td>
<select name="beds" >
<option value="Any">Any</option>
<option value="double">Double</option>
<option value="king">King</option>
<option value="suite">Suite</option>
</select>
</td>
</tr>
<tr>
<td>Smoking:</td>
<td>
<select name="smoking" >
<option value="Any">Any</option>
<option value="0">No</option>
<option value="1">Yes</option>
</select>
</td>
</tr>
```

Listing 18.5 The search Velocity template. (continues)

```
<tr>
<td>Refrigerator:</td>
<td>
<select name="refrigerator" >
<option value="Any">Any</option>
<option value="0">No</option>
<option value="1">Yes</option>
</select>
</td>
</tr>
<tr>
<td>Cost:</td>
<td>
<select name="cost" >
<option value="Any">Any</option>
<option value="140.0">140.00</option>
<option value="170.0">170.00</option>
</select>
</td>
</tr>
</table>
<BR><BR>
<input type="submit" value="submit">
</form>
```

Listing 18.5 The search Velocity template. (continued)

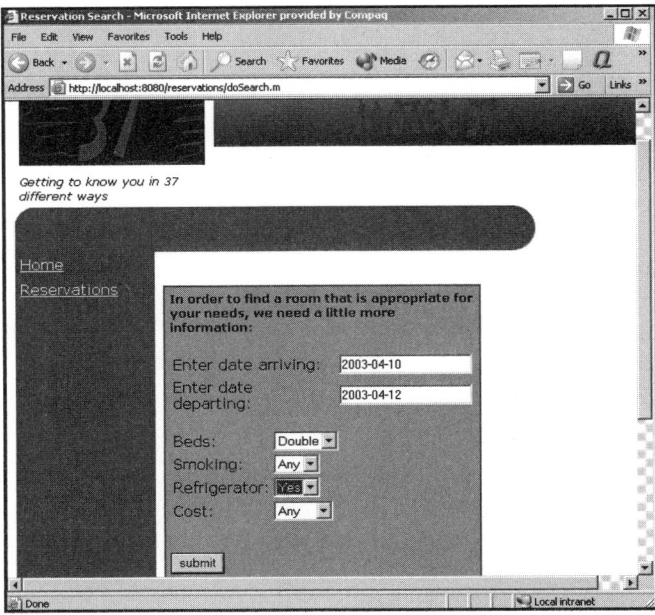

Figure 18.6 The search page.

For the search controller to be able to find a room for the user, the system must have the user's arrival and departure dates. Optionally, users can tell the system whether they want a refrigerator or a room in which smoking is permitted. They can also specify what type of bed they want and inquire about the cost of the room. Once all of this information is gathered, the user clicks the submit button to send the information to the server. The Maverick command searchReservation is the trigger for the server to put into play the SearchReservation controller class, which is shown in Listing 18.6.

```
import java.util.*;
import java.sql.*;
import org.infohazard.maverick.ctl.Throwaway2;
import org.infohazard.maverick.flow.*;
import javax.servlet.http.*;

public class SearchReservation extends Throwaway2 {
  Connection connection = null;
  Model m = null;
  ControllerContext cxt = null;
  HttpServletRequest request = null;

  private void setUpModel() {
    m = new Model();
    cxt = this.getCtx();
    request = cxt.getRequest();
    cxt.setModel(m);
  }

  private boolean loadDriver() {
    boolean ready = true;
    try {
      Class.forName("com.mysql.jdbc.Driver");
      connection =
DriverManager.getConnection("jdbc:mysql://localhost/products");
    } catch(Exception e) {
      ready = false;
    }
    return ready;
  }

  private ResultSet findInclusiveDates(String indate, String outdate) {
    ResultSet rs = null;
    try {
      Statement statement = null;
      String query = new String("SELECT DISTINCT room FROM
reservations WHERE ('" +
```

Listing 18.6 The SearchReservation class. (continues)

```
                     request.getParameter("indate") + "' >=
reservations.indate) and ('" +
                     request.getParameter("outdate") + "' <=
reservations.outdate)");

      statement = connection.createStatement();
      rs = statement.executeQuery(query);
    } catch(Exception e) {
      rs = null;
    }
    return rs;
  }


  private String buildReservationQuery(String indate, String
outdate, ResultSet rs) {
    String query = null;
    try {

      query = new String("SELECT DISTINCT rooms.id, rooms.beds,
rooms.refrigerator, rooms.smoking, rooms.baserate FROM rooms left
join reservations on (('" +
                      request.getParameter("outdate") +
                      "' <= reservations.indate) or ('" +
                      request.getParameter("indate") +
                      "' >= reservations.outdate)) ");

      boolean where = false;
      if (!request.getParameter("beds").equals("Any")) {
        query += " where beds = '" + request.getParameter("beds")
+ "'";
        where = true;
      }
      if (!request.getParameter("smoking").equals("Any")) {
        if (!where) {
          query += " where smoking = " + request.getParameter("smoking");
          where = true;
        } else {
          query += " and smoking = " + request.getParameter("smoking");
        }
      }
      if (!request.getParameter("cost").equals("Any")) {
        if (!where) {
          query += " where cost <= " + request.getParameter("cost");
          where = true;
        } else {
          query += " and cost <= " + request.getParameter("cost");
```

Listing 18.6 The SearchReservation class. (continues)

```
        }
      }
      if (!request.getParameter("refrigerator").equals("Any")) {
        if (!where) {
          query += " where refrigerator = " +
request.getParameter("refrigerator");
          where = true;
        } else {
          query += " and refrigerator = " +
request.getParameter("refrigerator");
        }
      }

      if (!where) {
        query += " where reservations.id IS NOT NULL";
      } else {
        query += " AND reservations.id IS NOT NULL";
      }

      if (rs.next()) {
        query += " and rooms.id NOT IN ("
              + rs.getString("room") + ",";
        while(rs.next()) {
          query += rs.getString("room") + ",";
        }
         query += "null)";
      }
    } catch(Exception e) {
     query = "";
    }

    return query;
  }

  private Vector executeReservationQuery(String query) {
    Vector v = null;
    try {
      Statement statement = connection.createStatement();
      ResultSet rs = statement.executeQuery(query);

      v = new Vector();
      while (rs.next()) {
        v.add(new Result(rs.getString("id"),
                         rs.getString("beds"),
                         rs.getString("smoking"),
                         rs.getString("refrigerator"),
                         rs.getString("baserate"), "", "", "", ""));
```

Listing 18.6 The SearchReservation class. (continues)

```
        }
      } catch(Exception e) {
        v = null;
      }
      return v;
    }

    public String go() throws Exception {
      String returnValue = ERROR;
      ResultSet rs = null;

      setUpModel();
      if (loadDriver()) {
        String indate = request.getParameter("indate");
        String outdate = request.getParameter("outdate");
        rs = findInclusiveDates(indate, outdate);
        String query = buildReservationQuery(indate, outdate, rs);
        Vector v = executeReservationQuery(query);
        m.setResult(v);
        returnValue = SUCCESS;
      } else {
        returnValue = ERROR;
      }

      m.setBeds(request.getParameter("beds"));
      m.setSmoking(request.getParameter("smoking"));
      m.setIndate(request.getParameter("indate"));
      m.setOutdate(request.getParameter("outdate"));
      m.setRefrigerator(request.getParameter("refrigerator"));
      m.setCost(request.getParameter("cost"));

      connection.close();
      return returnValue;
    }

    public class Model {
      protected Vector rs;
      String beds;
      String indate;
      String outdate;
      String smoking;
      String refrigerator;
      String cost;

      public Vector getResult() {
        return rs;
      }
```

Listing 18.6 The SearchReservation class. (continues)

```
public void setResult(Vector r) {
  rs = r;
}

public void setBeds(String b) {
  beds = b;
}

public String getBeds() {
  return beds;
}

public void setIndate(String i) {
  indate = i;
}

public String getIndate() {
  return indate;
}

public void setOutdate(String o) {
  outdate = o;
}

public String getOutdate() {
  return outdate;
}

public void setSmoking(String s) {
  smoking = s;
}

public String getSmoking() {
  return smoking;
}

public void setRefrigerator(String r) {
  refrigerator = r;
}

public String getRefrigerator() {
  return refrigerator;
}

public void setCost(String c) {
  cost = c;
}
```

Listing 18.6 The SearchReservation class. (continues)

```
        public String getCost() {
          return cost;
        }
    }
}
```

Listing 18.6 The SearchReservation class. (continued)

Handling a Reservation Search

The SearchReservation class in Listing 18.6 handles the process of finding a room based on the information provided by the user. The class is instantiated when the searchReservation Maverick command is encountered. Fundamentally, the controller takes the information from the user and adds data to the context or model so it can be displayed to the user.

The first thing the controller does is call a private method named setUpModel(). This method is responsible for obtaining the context from Maverick, instantiating a Model object, and adding the object to the context. The Model class is contained within the controller class as a private class and is designed to hold a Vector of Result objects. The model must include a vector of Result objects because the Velocity template cannot use a ResultSet object (which is obtained directly from a database call). Instead, you need to convert the information in the ResultSet and place it in a vector. In addition to the results from the database, the Model object includes attributes for the search information (such as bed types, smoking preference, and reservation dates).

Once the model is set up, the code attempts to load the MySQL database driver and build a connection to the remote database for the application. If the connection to the database is successful, the arrival and departure dates for a possible reservation are passed to the private findInclusiveDates() method.

Before going into the method itself, let's discuss how you determine if a room is available in the hotel. As you know, the application contains two tables. The first, room, is indexed on a room number. Each room number relates to a specific room with certain features (bed type, cost, availability of a refrigerator, and whether smoking is permitted). The reservation table holds all current reservations. For the reservation, you include the arrival and departure date as well as a link to the room number. To determine whether a particular room might be a match for a new arrival and departure date pair, you should consider three basic cases:

- The arrival and departure occur before any other reservation.
- The arrival and departure occur after any other reservation.
- The arrival and departure are the same as another reservation.

The application uses two different database calls to determine whether the reservation can be made. The first occurs in the findInclusiveDates() method. Here you execute a query that attempts to find all room numbers for which the requested arrival and departure occur during the same timeframe. The result of the method is either an empty result set (indicating no other reservations occur during the same time) or a set of rows with room numbers that cannot be used by the new reservation. This ResultSet object is passed to the method buildReservationQuery().

In buildReservationQuery(), a large query statement is created that joins the rooms and reservation tables and that includes any of the additional criteria that limits a reservation (such as smoking). The query string is passed to the executeReservationQuery() method, and the result is a Vector object that can be placed in the model to be used by the displayReservation Velocity template.

The model is also provided with the search criteria passed from the user. This data includes the arrival and departure dates as well as the cost, refrigerator request, bed type, and smoking toggles.

When SearchReservation locates any appropriate rooms for the user, the class returns either a SUCCESS or an ERROR value. The ERROR value doesn't indicate that no rooms were found; instead, it means that an error occurred during the search process. If the controller is able to successfully return results from the database, the SUCCESS value is returned. The Maverick XML file indicates that the bookIt.vm Velocity template should be returned to the user. The bookIt.vm template is shown in Listing 18.7; what the user sees appears in Figure 18.7.

```
$request.setAttribute("title", "Bookit")
<BR>
Based on the information provided by you:<BR>
<BR>
  In Date:      $model.indate<BR>
  Out Date:     $model.outdate<BR>
  Beds:         $model.beds<br>
  Smoking:      $model.smoking<br>
  Refrigerator: $model.refrigerator<br>
  Cost:          $model.cost<br>
<BR><BR>
We have come up with following rooms available:<BR>
<form action="bookReservation.m" method="Post">
Please enter the number of adults and children to be in the room:<br>
Adults: <input type="text" name="adults" value="1"><BR>
Children: <input type="text" name="children" value="0">
<BR>
<BR>
```

Listing 18.7 The bookIt Velocity template. (continues)

```
Here are the rooms available.  Click on the appropriate button to
book the room:<BR>
<BR>
#foreach($room in $model.result)
  <input type="hidden" value="$room.id" name="roomid">
  <input type="hidden" value="$model.indate" name="indate">
  <input type="hidden" value="$model.outdate" name="outdate">
  <input type="hidden" value="$room.cost" name="cost">
  Book this Room: <input type="submit" value="Book it"><BR>
  beds in room : $room.beds<br>
  cost: $$room.cost<BR>
<HR>
#end
</form>

To try another search:<BR>
<form action="doSearch.m" method="post">
<input type="submit" name="submit"  value="Search for a Room">
</form>
```

Listing 18.7 The bookIt Velocity template. (continued)

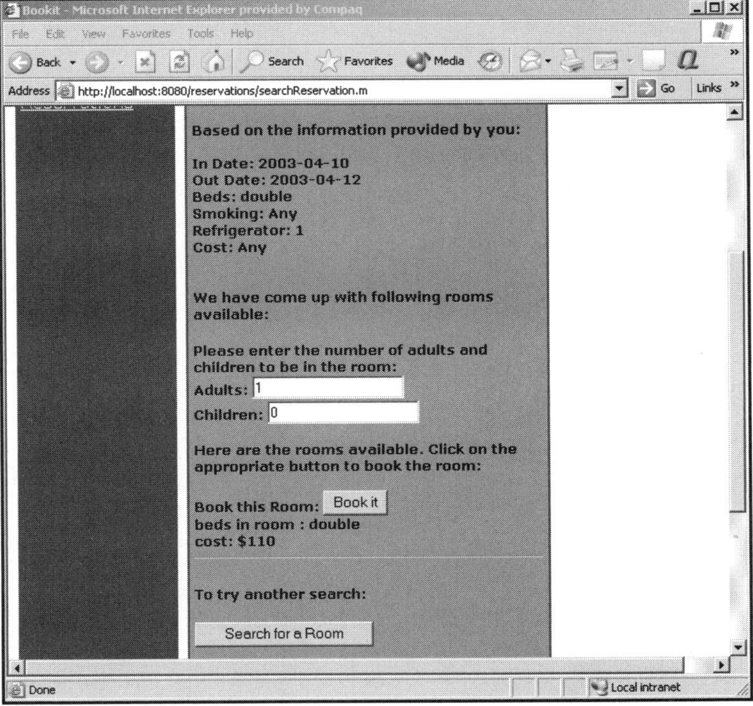

Figure 18.7 The search results page.

The results from the searching process have two purposes. The first is to display the original search criteria along with all of the rooms found that match the criteria. The second purpose is to display buttons the user can click to book an appropriate room. In order to book a room, the system needs to provide appropriate information to the booking controller. This information is supplied in the <form> tag using hidden fields. Of particular importance is the room ID, which acts as the relationship between the room and reservation tables.

Booking a Room

When the user clicks one of the buttons displayed by the bookIt.vm template, the bookReservation Maverick command is executed. This execution causes the BookReservation controller object to be instantiated and executed (Listing 18.8).

```
import java.sql.*;
import org.infohazard.maverick.ctl.Throwaway2;
import org.infohazard.maverick.flow.*;
import javax.servlet.http.*;

public class BookReservation extends Throwaway2{

  public String go() throws Exception {
    String returnValue = "";
    Model m = new Model();
    ControllerContext cxt = this.getCtx();
    HttpServletRequest request = cxt.getRequest();

    cxt.setModel(m);

    Connection connection = null;
    Statement statement = null;
    try {
      Class.forName("com.mysql.jdbc.Driver");

      connection = DriverManager.getConnection("jdbc:mysql://localhost/prod-
ucts");
      statement = connection.createStatement();

      String query = "INSERT INTO reservations VALUES(null, "
                   + request.getParameter("roomid") + ",'"
                   + request.getParameter("indate") + "','"
                   + request.getParameter("outdate") + "',"
                   + request.getParameter("adults") + ","
                   + request.getParameter("children") + ","
                   + request.getParameter("cost") +")";
```

Listing 18.8 The BookReservation class. (continues)

```
        int i = statement.executeUpdate(query);

        if (i == 1) {
          returnValue = SUCCESS;
         ResultSet rs = statement.executeQuery("SELECT LAST_INSERT_ID()");
         if (rs.next()) {
           m.setId(rs.getInt(1));
           } else {
           m.setId(0);
           returnValue = ERROR;
         }
        } else {
          returnValue = ERROR;
        }
      } catch(SQLException e) {
        System.out.println("SQLException: " + e.getMessage());
        returnValue = ERROR;
      } finally {
        statement.close();
        connection.close();
      }
      return returnValue;
    }


    public class Model {
      protected int id;

      public int getId() {
        return id;
      }

      public void setId(int i) {
        id = i;
      }
    }
  }
```

Listing 18.8 The BookReservation class. (continued)

Based on what we've discussed previously, you can probably guess that the BookReservation controller class inserts a new row into the reservation table. In addition to inserting the row, you must obtain the reservation number and place the number in the model that will be displayed by a Velocity template. The reservation number isn't fancy; it's just the auto-incremented index value of the reservation table. The auto-increment column value is obtained by issuing a query against the database with the statement SELECT LAST_INSERT_ID(). You execute the query only if the INSERT to the table returns a value of 1 (indicating a row was changed or added to the database).

If the book reservation is successful, the Maverick system executes the goodBook.vm Velocity template, shown in Listing 18.9; the user sees the screen shown in Figure 18.8.

```
$request.setAttribute("title", "Good Book")

Your reservation number is: $model.id
```

Listing 18.9 The goodBook Velocity template.

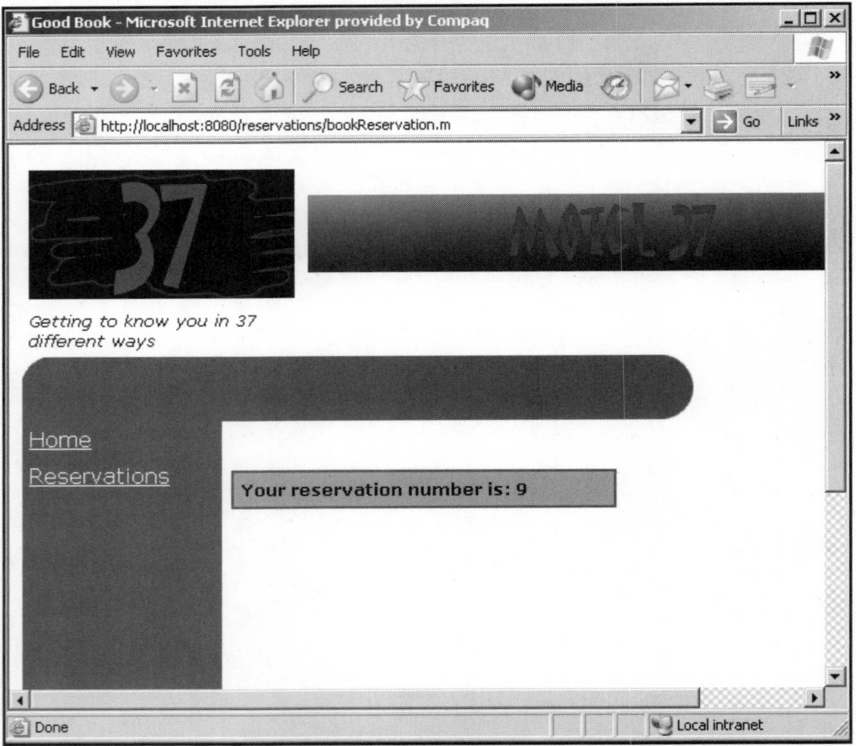

Figure 18.8 The successful reservation.

If the Web application encounters a problem inserting the new reservation into the table, an error occurs and the badBook.vm Velocity template (Listing 18.10) is displayed, as shown in Figure 18.9.

```
$request.setAttribute("title", "Bad Book")

We are sorry but something in the backend has occured when we attempted to
book your reservation.<BR><BR>  Please try again!
```

Listing 18.10 The badBook Velocity template.

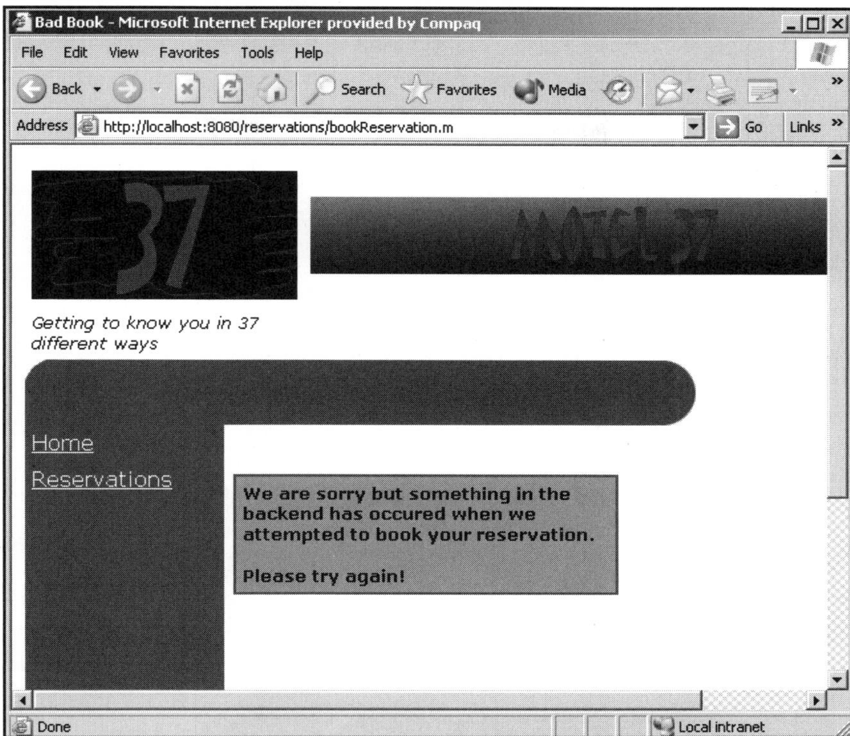

Figure 18.9 An unsuccessful reservation.

Looking up a Room

The last task that we cover is looking up a previously entered reservation. Listing 18.11 shows the code for the LookupReservation controller class, which is executed when the lookupReservation Maverick command is issued. This Maverick command is executed when users enter their reservation number in a form created by the template lookup.vm (Listing 18.12), as shown in Figure 18.10.

```
import java.sql.*;
import org.infohazard.maverick.ctl.Throwaway2;
import org.infohazard.maverick.flow.*;
import javax.servlet.http.*;
import java.util.*;

public class LookupReservation extends Throwaway2{
```

Listing 18.11 The LookupReservation class. (continues)

```
    public String go() throws Exception {
      String returnValue = "";
      Model m = new Model();
      ControllerContext cxt = this.getCtx();

      cxt.setModel(m);

      try {
        Class.forName("com.mysql.jdbc.Driver");

        Connection connection =
DriverManager.getConnection("jdbc:mysql://localhost/products");
        Statement statement = connection.createStatement();

        ResultSet rs = statement.executeQuery("SELECT * FROM
reservations WHERE id = " +
cxt.getRequest().getParameter("reservationnumber"));

        Vector v = new Vector();
        while (rs.next()) {
          v.add(new Result(rs.getString("id"),
                           "",
                           "",
                           "",
                           rs.getString("cost"),
rs.getString("adults"), rs.getString("children"),
                           rs.getString("indate"),
rs.getString("outdate")));
        }
        m.setResult(v);

        statement.close();
        connection.close();
        returnValue = SUCCESS;

      } catch(SQLException e) {
        System.out.println("SQLException: " + e.getMessage());
        returnValue = ERROR;
      }
      return returnValue;
    }


    public class Model {
      protected Vector v;

      public Vector getResult() {
        return this.v;
```

Listing 18.11 The LookupReservation class. (continues)

```
    }

    public void setResult(Vector v) {
      this.v = v;
    }
  }
}
```

Listing 18.11 The LookupReservation class. (continued)

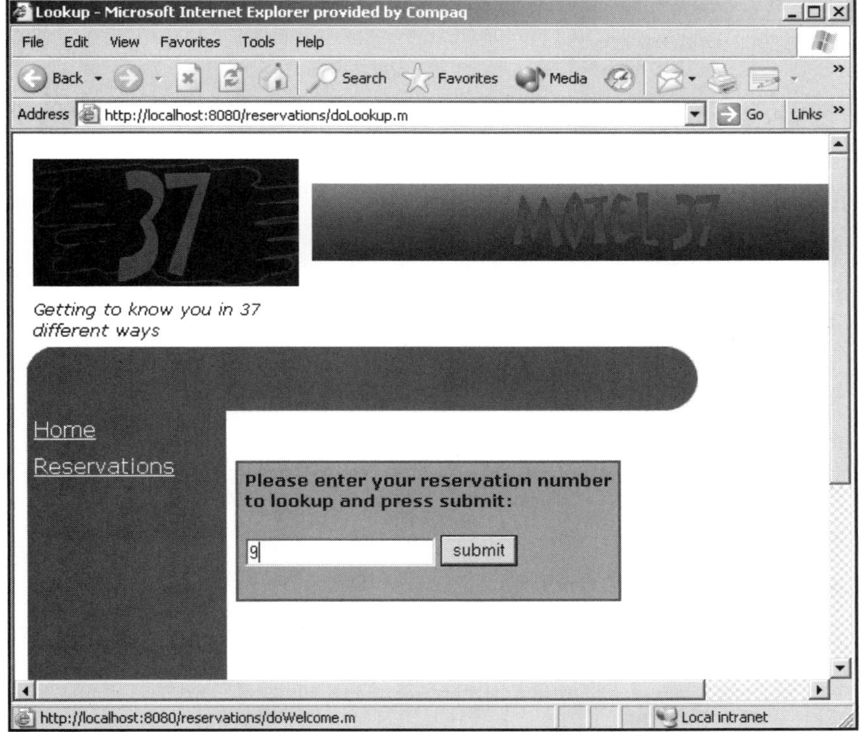

Figure 18.10 The lookup page.

```
$request.setAttribute("title", "Lookup")

Please enter your reservation number to lookup and press submit:
<form action="lookupReservation.m" method="post">
<input type="text" name="reservationnumber">
<input type="submit" name="Submit" value="submit">
</form>
```

Listing 18.12 The lookup Velocity template.

The controller class simply builds a vector based on the information returned in the ResultSet object after pulling all of the rows with the provided reservation number. The vector is placed in the model, and the displayReservation.vm Velocity template (Listing 18.13) displays information about the current reservation, as shown in Figure 18.11.

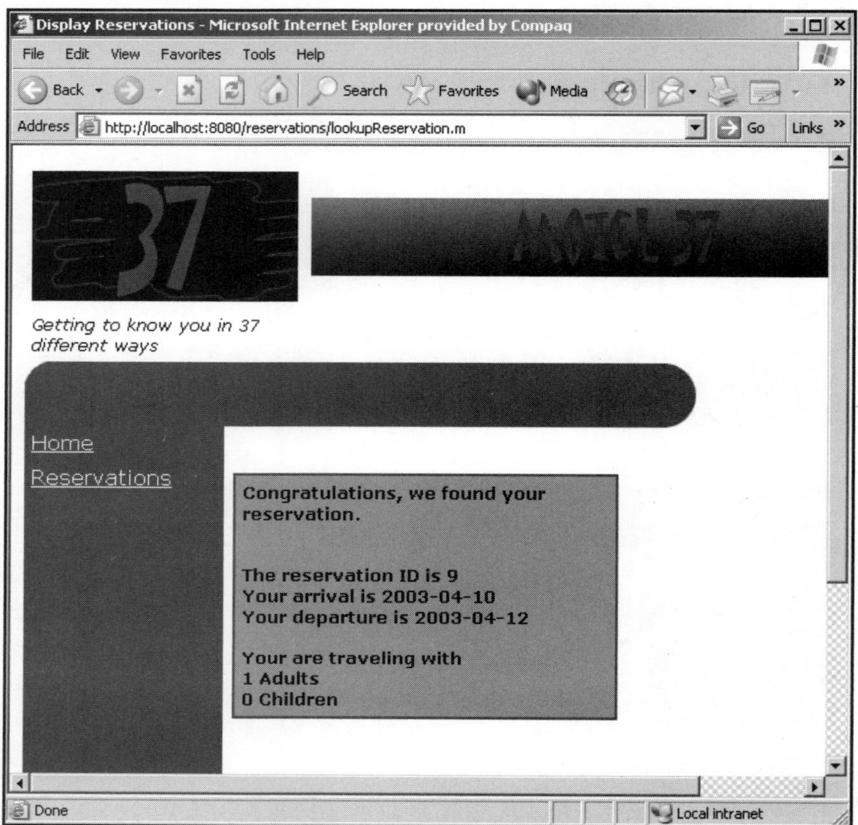

Figure 18.11 The results page.

```
public class Result {

  String id;
  String beds;
  String smoking;
  String refrigerator;
  String cost;
  String adults;
  String children;
  String indate;
  String outdate;
```

Listing 18.13 The displayReservation Velocity template. (continues)

```
  public Result(String id, String b, String s, String r, String
c, String adults, String children,
                String indate, String outdate) {
    this.id = id;
    beds = b;
    smoking = s;
    refrigerator = r;
    cost = c;
    this.adults = adults;
    this.children = children;
    this.indate = indate;
    this.outdate = outdate;
  }

    public String getId() {
      return id;
    }

    public String getBeds() {
      return beds;
    }

    public String getSmoking() {
      return smoking;
    }


    public String getRefrigerator() {
      return refrigerator;
    }

    public String getCost() {
      return cost;
    }

    public String getAdults() {
      return adults;
    }

    public String getChildren() {
      return children;
    }

    public String getIndate() {
      return indate;
    }

    public String getOutdate() {
      return outdate;
    }
}
```

Listing 18.13 The displayReservation Velocity template. (continued)

What's Next

In this chapter, we showed you a complete Web application that uses the Maverick MVC framework and about a dozen Velocity templates. You've seen how to move data between the context and the template, as well as how to use a common template for the look and feel. In the next chapter, we discuss using both JSP and the Velocity Templating Language in the same page.

CHAPTER 19

Using JSP and Velocity

The phrase “because I said so” can be so powerful--and yet so demoralizing. Now that you have a good appreciation for the simplicity of Velocity and its ability to bind seamlessly with the Java object model, it’s likely you don’t ever want to use another scripting/templating language. Of course, if you are working with legacy code or a manager who doesn’t understand new technology, the words “because I said so” will be familiar to you. However, all is not lost. Velocity provides the ability to use its directives and binding with legacy JSP. In this chapter, we explore how to accomplish this feat.

The Velocity Taglib

At this point, we are going to ignore the reasons why you would embed Velocity into a JSP page instead of refactoring. Consider the JSP page from the Maverick distribution shown in Listing 19.1

```
<%@ taglib uri="http://java.sun.com/jstl/core" prefix="c" %>
<c:set var="title" scope="request">Sign Up</c:set>

<p>To create an account, just fill out this form:</p>
<form action="signupSubmit.m" method="post">
  <table border="0">
    <tr>
      <td align="right"> Login Name: </td>
```

Listing 19.1 An example JSP file. (continues)

```
      <td> <input type="text" name="loginName"
       value="<c:out value="${model.loginName}"/>" /> </td>
      <td class="errorText"><c:out
       value="${model.errors['loginName']}"/></td>
    </tr>
    <tr>
      <td align="right"> Password: </td>
      <td> <input type="password" name="password" value="<c:out
       value="${model.password}"/>"/> </td>
      <td class="errorText"><c:out
       value="${model.errors['password']}"/></td>
    </tr>
    <tr>
      <td align="right"> Password Again: </td>
      <td> <input type="password" name="passwordAgain"
       value="<c:out value="${model.passwordAgain}"/>"/> </td>
      <td class="errorText"><c:out
       value="${model.errors['passwordAgain']}"/></td>
    </tr>
    <tr>
      <td></td>
      <td> <input type="submit" value="Signup"/> </td>
    </tr>
  </table>
</form>
```

Listing 19.1 An example JSP file. (continued)

Assume that a new feature must be added to the login JSP code in Listing 19.1, but instead of using JSP you want to take advantage of Velocity. You can do this by taking advantage of the Velocity tag library.

Installing the Velocity Taglib

The first step in using Velocity within the JSP page is to obtain the Velocity tag library code. When you downloaded the Velocity distribution in Chapter 4, “Installing Velocity,” you skipped over the directory /contrib/temporary/veltag. The Velocity taglib is currently considered contribution software and thus is not automatically compiled with the distribution. There are two ways to build the library: using JJAR and traditional compilation.

The release notes for the Velocity taglib state that the JJAR method might not always work; therefore, the release notes define both methods. The JJAR method allows the Ant application to gather the individual JARs needed for the tag library and place them in the appropriate location. To accomplish this step, change to the /contrib/temporary/veltag directory and execute the command

```
ant getjars
```

Issuing this command places all dependent libraries into the /contrib/temporary/veltag/lib directory. Now just compile the library with the command

```
ant jars
```

This creates a file called veltag-*xx*.jar (*xx* represents the version number of the current code). If any step in this process fails, do the following:

1. Place a servlet API JAR into the /contrib/temporary/veltag directory. You should be able to find such a JAR in the /lib directory of your application server. Under Tomcat, you can find it in the /bin directory.
2. Add the Velocity JAR to the same directory. Both of these JARs are expected to be in the /lib directory, but you could also change the Ant build file in the /contrib/temporary/veltag directory to reflect the location of the files.
3. Change to the /contrib/temporary/veltag directory and execute the *ant* command. This creates the veltag-*xx*.jar file for you.

Once you have a veltag JAR, you must install it in your application. Here are the steps you generally follow:

1. Copy the veltag-*xx*.jar file into the /lib directory of your application. The /lib directory is typically under the /WEB-INF directory.
2. Copy the taglib descriptor, veltag.tld, from the /examples directory of the Velocity distribution into the /WEB-INF directory of your application.
3. Update your web.xml file to include the following information about the new taglib:

```
<taglib>
  <taglib-uri>
    http://jakarta.apache.org/taglibs/veltag-1.0
  </taglib-uri>
  <taglib-location>/WEB-INF/veltag.tld</taglib-location>
</taglib>
```

Adding the Velocity Taglib to JSP

Let's now turn our attention to the JSP file shown in Listing 19.1. You want to be able to use Velocity directives and references in the same file as the JSP code without removing the JSP. The first thing you should do is add a taglib directive to the page, just like the page has for JSTL. Add this statement:

```
<%@ taglib uri="/WEB-INF/veltag.tld" prefix="vel" %>
```

This line tells the server that using tags from the Velocity tag library is possible, and also specifies the prefix used within the file for those tags. When you want to use Velocity within the JSP file, you must block the references, directives, and macros with these tags:

```
<vel:velocity>
</vel:velocity>
```

Within the block created by the tags, you can use the Velocity Templating Language and access objects in the context. You can access objects in the context using two methods: automatic and strict.

In automatic mode (the default), the system searches for an object when used in a reference in the order:

1. Page scope
2. Request scope
3. Session scope
4. Application scope

For most applications, automatic mode is appropriate; however, if there is a possibility that objects with the same names could be contained in the various scope levels, automatic mode could cause big problems. One application might place an object with the name of your object at a "lower" scope level; then, when you use a reference to the object, the methods and attributes won't be correct and an error occurs.

When that possibility exists, you should use strict-access mode. In strict-access mode, the Velocity context does not search for an object but instead relies on the developer to specify where to look. You turn on strict mode using an attribute to the <velocity> tag, as shown here:

```
<vel:velocity strictaccess='true'>
</vel:velocity>
```

You tell the context where to look for a reference by using the ScopeTool object. This object includes the following methods for specifying the scope:

- getRequestScope(string)
- getPageScope(string)
- getApplicationScope(string)
- getSessionScope(string)

For example, suppose you want to add the total number of people who have already signed up with your Web application using the login shown in Listing 19.1. Since you don't want to use JSP, use these tags:

```
<vel:velocity strictaccess="true">
A total number of $scopetool.getApplicationScope("signincount") users
have signed up with us.
</vel:velocity>
```

In this example, you told the system that you will be using Velocity language constructs in the section of code that follows and that the Velocity context should not try to find the objects on its own. Next, you specifically tell the context where to find a reference with the name of *signincount.* The ScopeTool object gains access to the Application scope and tries to find the object there.

Beans and Tags

When you're using the using the Velocity tags, you can access any JavaBean created in the JSP. For example, look at this code:

```
<jsp:useBean id="counts" class="CountBean" scope="session" />
<vel:velocity strictaccess="true">
         #set($ourbean = $scopetool.getRequestScope("counts"))
         $ourbean.total <br>

         #foreach($value in $ourbean.array)
            $item.showAccess <br>
         #end
</vel:velocity>
```

In this example, a bean of the type CountBean has been created and placed in the Session scope. You can use Velocity as well as JSP to access the methods of the bean. With Velocity, you can also place objects in a specific scope and allow other pages to access the objects.

What's Next

In this chapter, we looked at the process involved in incorporating both JSP and Velocity into a single page. Be sure to weigh the benefits of mixing different templating and scripting languages instead of refactoring the JSP code. In the next chapter, we cover DVSL and Velocity.

CHAPTER 20

DVSL and Velocity

The goal of the style language known as *Declarative Velocity Style Language (DVSL)* is to allow you to transform XML into another format. With the availability of XSLT, you may be wondering why you need DVSL. The biggest advantage of DVSL is Velocity's ability to access Java objects as well as the VTL functionality. At first glance, this might not seem like a big deal, but imagine being able to access a database based on information in the XML file. With DVSL, you are able to do this. If you know XSLT, you will be comfortable with DVSL because its syntax is similar, and control and selection of nodes within the XML structure is based on XPath. In this chapter, we examine DVSL and describe how to use it to make transformations.

Obtaining and Installing DVSL

The primary Web page for DVSL is http://jakarta.apache.org/velocity/dvsl/index.html. Here, you'll find a link to the nightly builds for DVSL. Click this link to obtain the DVSL source code based on the previous night's build or pull the source directly from CVS with this command:

```
cvs -d :pserver:anoncvs@cvs.apache.org:/home/cvspublic
  checkout jakarta-velocity-dvsl
```

Executing this command (or using the nightly build link) places a directory called jakarta-velocity-dvsl on your system. To compile the source code, you must have Jakarta Ant installed. (If you've gotten this far in the book, this shouldn't be an issue.) Change to the jakarta-velocity-dvsl directory and type

```
ant
```

This command executes and builds a JAR called velocity-dvsl-0.45.jar (or an equivalent) in the root directory.

Creating a Simple Transformation

DVSL as well as XSL are all about *matching*. The basic idea is to have an XML input file that contains information obtained from a database or another system. The input file is matched with a stylesheet containing DVSL commands. Probably the most important command is #match(string). This command watches for the "string" provided as a parameter within the XML file. If it finds this string, all of the statements between #match and #end are "executed." The commands might be HTML or output for XPath commands like applyTemplate().

Consider the XML in Listing 20.1 and the DVSL file in Listing 20.2.

```
<?xml version="1.0"?>

<cds>
    <cd artist="Rush" title="Exit...Stage Left">
        <track>The Spirit of Radio</track>
        <track>Red Barchetta</track>
        <track>YYZ</track>
        <track>A Passage to Bangkok</track>
    </cd>
    <cd artist="Rush" title="Grade Under Pressure">
        <track>Distant Early Warning</track>
        <track>Afterimage</track>
        <track>Red Sector A</track>
        <track>The Enemy Within</track>
    </cd>
</cds>
```

Listing 20.1 An example XML file.

```
#match("cds")
<html>
  <body>
    $context.applyTemplates()
  </body>
</html>
#end
```

Listing 20.2 An example DVSL file. (continues)

```
#match("cd")
  <hr>
  <b>CD Title:</b> $attrib.title<BR>
  <b>CD Artist:</b> $attrib.artist<BR>
  <b>Tracks</B><BR>
  $context.applyTemplates("track")
#end

#match("track")
    $node.value()<BR>
#end
```

Listing 20.2 An example DVSL file. (continued)

In Listing 20.1, you see an XML document used to describe two CDs in a CD collection. The root element, called <cds>, contains zero or more <cd> elements. Each <cd> element has two attributes: title and artist. In addition, the <cd> elements contain one or more <track> elements, which describe the tracks on the CD. It is assumed that the order of the <track> elements is the same as that on the CD itself.

Listing 20.2 contains DVSL statements designed to work specifically on the CD XML document and output a formatted HTML page. As you can see, the DVSL is basically a bunch of #match(string) statements. The statements are generally listed in the order the system will match them, but that isn't necessary. At the top of the list is the #match("cds") statement. This is your root element, and it handles output for the <HTML> tags and so forth. Notice the $context.apply Templates() statement. As it does in XSL, this statement tells the system to match other elements of the XML file. Because the method call includes no parameters, the system attempts to match the next XML element found. In this case, it is a <cd> element.

As you might expect, a #match("cd") method call is executed. The code within the <cd> match outputs more HTML and displays the information associated with the attributes of the <cd> element. All of this information is followed by another applyTemplate() method call, but now you are telling the system to match only <track> elements within the <cd> element.

Again, you have a #match("track") method that is called when <track> elements are found. When an appropriate match is found, the code outputs the value of the element.

Compiling the DVSL/XML

To invoke the DVSL against your XML file, you can either use command-line calling (as we discuss later in this chapter) or use an Ant task (as we did for Anakia in Chapter 11). Listing 20.3 shows an example of the Ant task.

```
<project name="dvsl-simple" default="doall" basedir=".">

<property name="local.repository"       value="../../lib" />
<property name="project.name"           value="velocity-dvsl" />
<property name="project.version"        value="0.43"/>
<property name="docs.src"               value="xdocs"/>
<property name="docs.dest"              value="docs"/>
<property name="compile.debug"          value="true" />

<path id="classpath">
  <fileset dir="${local.repository}">
    <include name="**/*.jar"/>
  </fileset>
</path>

<target name="compile">
  <javac  srcdir="${basedir}"
          destdir="${basedir}"
          includes="*.java"
          debug="${compile.debug}"
          classpathref="classpath" />

</target>

<target name="doall" depends="compile">
   <taskdef name="dvsl" classname="org.apache.tools.dvsl.DVSLTask">
      <classpath>
        <pathelement location=
          "../../${project.name}-${project.version}.jar"/>
        <path refid="classpath"/>
      </classpath>
   </taskdef>
   <dvsl
          basedir="${docs.src}"
          destdir="${docs.dest}/"
          extension=".html"
          style="${docs.src}/example1.dvsl"
          includes="example1.xml"
          classpath="."
        velocityConfigClass="ConfigVel"
      />
</target>
</project>
```

Listing 20.3 The Ant build file.

The vast majority of the information found in the Ant build file and task relates to configuration. The build file starts by defining properties. The most important ones are docs.src and docs.dest, which specify where the XML and DVSL files are to be found and where the output should be placed.

Under the <DVSL> tag, an attribute called style specifies the DVSL file that you want to apply to the XML file defined under the includes attribute. The files for this example appear in a structure like the following:

```
/sample/xdocs/example1.xml
/sample/xdocs/example1.dvsl
/sample/docs
/sample/build.xml
```

To execute the DVSL system, just change to the /sample directory and execute Ant with the command

```
ant
```

Executing this command creates new documents based on the input file and the DVSL template.

Using Nodes

As you can probably guess, the most important part of the DVSL is the *node*. Each element, attribute, and value in the XML file is a node. In our previous example, you saw a couple of the commands that you can use against a node, such as value() and $attrib. In this section, we look at the various features of a node.

Accessing the Node Hierarchy

In our first example, you moved through the XML input file using the applyTemplates() command. But what happens if you want to output a value at the current node based on a node farther down in the hierarchy but you don't want the system to traverse all nodes? The answer is to access the node hierarchy directory. For example, if you were in the matching code for #match("cds") and you wanted to access the information in the first track of the first CD, you could access the information with this command:

```
$node.cd.track.value()
```

The object $node represents a Node object based on the current position within the XML file.

Node API

The Node object contains a few methods that you can use to gather information about a node as well as provide the ability to traverse a node tree. Table 20.1 shows the available methods.

Table 20.1 Node Object Methods

METHOD	DESCRIPTION
$node	The current node.
$node.name()	The name of the node.
$node.value()	The content of the node.
$node.attrib("name")	The attribute of the node.
$node.selectNodes(xpathexpr)	A method that returns a list of nodes based on the provided XPath expression.
$node.selectSingleNode(xpathexpr)	A method that returns the first node based on the provided XPath expression.
$node.get(xpathexpr)	A method that returns the first node based on the provided XPath expression.
$node.children()	A method that returns a list of all children of the current node.
$node.copy()	A method that copies the current node's subtree to output.
$node.copy(List)	A method that copies the subtree of the specified node to output.
$node.valueOf(xpathexpr)	A method that returns an object based on the provided XPath expression.

The DVSL Toolbox

As we mentioned earlier, one of the features of DVSL is the ability to use the context and objects it contains. Consider the DVSL in Listing 20.4.

```
#match("cds")
<html>
<head><title>$toolbox.string.title</title></head>
  <body>
    $context.applyTemplates()
  </body>
</html>
#end

#match("cd")
```

Listing 20.4 DVSL with toolbox context. (continues)

```
  <hr>
  <b>CD Title:</b> $attrib.title<BR>
  <b>CD Artist:</b> $attrib.artist<BR>
  $context.toolbox.counter.reset()
  <b>Tracks</B><BR>
  $context.applyTemplates("track")
#end

#match("track")
    $context.toolbox.counter.getNext() $node.value()<br>
#end
```

Listing 20.4 DVSL with toolbox context. (continued)

The DVSL in Listing 20.4 looks like the first DVSL you created, but now you want to use a counter to keep track of the tracks in a CD so you can output a number for each of them. In the #match("cd") body, you have the call

```
$context.toolbox.counter.reset()
```

The *toolbox* is an object associated with the context where you place Java objects and access those objects within the DVSL code. You can also use the toolbox in the #match("track") code to output a number with $context.toolbox.counter.getNext().

You define a toolbox using a properties file, as shown in Listing 20.5. The properties file defines each of the objects the toolbox contains. As you can see in Listing 20.5, the toolbox contains a Counter object and a String called title. All user-defined objects are associated with the tool attribute of the toolbox. The title object is just an object is defined with the properties file itself. Listing 20.6 shows the Counter class.

```
toolbox.contextname = toolbox
toolbox.tool.counter = Counter
toolbox.string.title = CDs!
toolbox.string.sourcebase = ./xdocs/
```

Listing 20.5 A toolbox properties file.

```
public class Counter
{
  int counter = 0;
```

Listing 20.6 The Counter class. (continues)

```
    public void reset() {
      counter = 1;
    }

    public int getNext() {
      return counter++;
    }
  }
```

Listing 20.6 The Counter class. (continued)

The Counter class is very simple–it consists of a method that resets the counter and another that obtains the current value of the counter and increments it for the next call. The same build file can be used for the toolbox except you need to tell the system about the toolbox. Listing 20.7 shows the new <dvsl> task.

```
        <dvsl
             basedir="${docs.src}"
             destdir="${docs.dest}/"
             extension=".html"
             style="${docs.src}/cds.dvsl"
             excludes="**/project.xml"
             toolboxfile="toolbox.props"
             includes="**/*.xml"
        >
             <!-- Or, could specify this as an attribute -->
             <classpath>
               <pathelement location="." />
             </classpath>

             <!-- This overrides the same property in toolbox.props -->
             <tool name="toolbox.string.title" value="CD Collection" />

             <!-- Specify name and location of velocity log file -->
             <velconfig name="runtime.log"
value="${basedir}/dvsl.log" />

        </dvsl>
```

Listing 20.7 DVSL task changes.

Notice that you have two primary changes from the previous <dvsl> build task. The first is the addition of the toolboxfile attribute, which specifies which properties file you want to use. The second change is the overriding of the title string within the build XML file. Although you defined a title String in the properties file, the XML build file has the ability to override the value as needed.

The title of the HTML is "CD Collection"--which corresponds to the value given to the title property in the build XML file. Now each of the tracks in the output has a number corresponding to its play on the specified CD. Using what you've learned in this chapter, you can easily create an object that accesses a database and passes in the SQL values obtained from the XML file.

Using the Command Line

As we mentioned, you can execute DVSL from the command line. You simply combine your original XML and DVSL files with the command

```
java org.apache.tools.dvsl.DVSL -STYLE ./xdocs/example1.dvsl
  -IN ./xdocs/example1.xml -OUT ./docs/example1.html
```

This command uses the example1.dvsl file as the style and the example1.xml file as input. The result is placed in the /docs/example1.html file.

APPENDIX A

The Velocity Specification

The Velocity system consists of many classes, interfaces, and adapter classes. In this appendix, we provide a summary of those classes.

org.apache.velocity.Template

Extends: org.apache.velocity.runtime.resource.Resource

Description: This is a primary class that handles all template operations.

Class Summary

Constructors:

public Template( )

Methods:

public boolean process( )

public void initDocument( )

public void merge(Context context, Writer writer)

org.apache.velocity.VelocityContext

Extends: org.apache.velocity.context.AbstractContext

Implements: java.lang.Cloneable

Description: This class defines the application context used to transfer data from the application to the Velocity template. This class should not be shared because the HashMap it uses is not synchronized.

Class Summary

Constructors:

public VelocityContext( )

public VelocityContext(Map context)

public VelocityContext(Context innerContext)

public VelocityContext(Map context, Context innerContext)

Methods:

public java.lang.Object internalGet(String key)

public java.lang.Object internalPut(String key, Object value)

public boolean internalContainsKey(Object key)

public java.lang.Object[] internalGetKeys( )

public java.lang.Object internalRemove(Object key)

public java.lang.Object clone( )

org.apache.velocity.anakia.AnakiaElement

Extends: Element

Description: This is a JDOM element defined for Anakia.

Class Summary

Constructors:

public AnakiaElement(String name, Namespace namespace)

public AnakiaElement(String name)

public AnakiaElement(String name, String prefix, String uri)

Methods:

public org.apache.velocity.anakia.NodeList selectNodes(String xpathExpression)

public java.lang.String toString( )

public java.util.List getContent( )

public java.util.List getChildren( )

public java.util.List getChildren(String name)

public java.util.List getChildren(String name, Namespace ns)

public java.util.List getAttributes( )

org.apache.velocity.anakia.AnakiaJDOMFactory

Extends: DefaultJDOMFactory

Description: This is a JDOMFactory for Anakia.

Class Summary

Constructor:

public AnakiaJDOMFactory( )

Methods:

public Element element(String name, Namespace namespace)

public Element element(String name)

public Element element(String name, String prefix, String uri)

org.apache.velocity.anakia.AnakiaTask

Extends: MatchingTask

Description: This class allows Anakia to be used within an Ant task to facilitate XML transformations.

Class Summary

Constructor:

public AnakiaTask( )

Methods:

public void setBasedir(File dir)

public void setDestdir(File dir)

public void setExtension(String extension)

public void setStyle(String style)

public void setProjectFile(String projectAttribute)

public void setTemplatePath(File templatePath)

public void setVelocityPropertiesFile(File velocityPropertiesFile)

public void setLastModifiedCheck(String lastmod)

public void execute( )

org.apache.velocity.anakia.Escape

Description: This class allows for escaping CDATA sections.

Class Summary

Constructor:

public Escape( )

Method:

public static final java.lang.String getText(String st)

org.apache.velocity.anakia.NodeList

Implements: java.util.List, java.lang.Cloneable

Description: This class acts as a wrapper for JDOM objects so they can be used in templates.

Class Summary

Constructors:

public NodeList( )

public NodeList(Document document)

public NodeList(List nodes, boolean copy)

Methods:

public java.util.List getList( )

public java.lang.String toString( )

public java.lang.Object clone( )

public int hashCode( )

public boolean equals(Object o)

public org.apache.velocity.anakia.NodeList selectNodes(String xpathString)

public boolean add(Object o)

public void add(int index, Object o)

public boolean addAll(Collection c)

public boolean addAll(int index, Collection c)

public void clear( )

public boolean contains(Object o)

public boolean containsAll(Collection c)

public java.lang.Object get(int index)

public int indexOf(Object o)

public boolean isEmpty( )

public java.util.Iterator iterator( )

public int lastIndexOf(Object o)

public java.util.ListIterator listIterator( )

public java.util.ListIterator listIterator(int index)

public java.lang.Object remove(int index)

public boolean remove(Object o)

public boolean removeAll(Collection c)

public boolean retainAll(Collection c)

public java.lang.Object set(int index, Object o)

public int size( )

public java.util.List subList(int fromIndex, int toIndex)

public java.lang.Object[] toArray( )

public java.lang.Object[] toArray(Object[] a)

org.apache.velocity.anakia.OutputWrapper

Extends: XMLOutputter

Description: This class allows a tree to be effectively output to a String object.

Class Summary

Constructor:

public OutputWrapper( )

Method:

public java.lang.String outputString(Element element, boolean strip)

org.apache.velocity.anakia.TreeWalker

Description: This class allows a JDOM tree to be traversed.

Class Summary

Constructor:

public TreeWalker( )

Method:

public org.apache.velocity.anakia.NodeList allElements(Element e)

org.apache.velocity.app.FieldMethodizer

Description: This class allows an application to access static fields of a class. Velocity does not use introspection for the fields.

Class Summary

Constructors:

public FieldMethodizer( )

public FieldMethodizer(String s)

public FieldMethodizer(Object o)

Methods:

public void addObject(String s)

public void addObject(Object o)

public java.lang.Object get(String fieldName)

org.apache.velocity.app.Velocity

Implements: org.apache.velocity.runtime.RuntimeConstants

Description: This class provides overall Velocity services, like macros and initialization.

Class Summary

Constructor:

public Velocity( )

Methods:

public static void init( )

public static void init(String propsFilename)

public static void init(Properties p)

public static void setProperty(String key, Object value)

public static void addProperty(String key, Object value)

public static void clearProperty(String key)

public static void setConfiguration(Configuration configuration)

public static void setExtendedProperties(ExtendedProperties configuration)

public static java.lang.Object getProperty(String key)

public static boolean evaluate(Context context, Writer out, String logTag, String instring)

public static boolean evaluate(Context context, Writer writer, String logTag, InputStream instream)

public static boolean evaluate(Context context, Writer writer, String logTag, Reader reader) public static boolean invokeVelocimacro(String vmName, String logTag, String[] params, Context context, Writer writer)

public static boolean mergeTemplate(String templateName, Context context, Writer writer)

public static boolean mergeTemplate(String templateName, String encoding, Context context, Writer writer)

public static org.apache.velocity.Template getTemplate(String name)

public static org.apache.velocity.Template getTemplate(String name, String encoding)

public static boolean templateExists(String templateName)

public static void warn(Object message)

public static void info(Object message)

public static void error(Object message)

public static void debug(Object message)

public static void setApplicationAttribute(Object key, Object value)

org.apache.velocity.app.VelocityEngine

Implements: org.apache.velocity.runtime.RuntimeConstants

Description: This class allows an application to instantiate its own VelocityEngine object.

Class Summary

Constructor:

public VelocityEngine( )

Methods:

public void init( )

public void init(String propsFilename)

public void init(Properties p)

public void setProperty(String key, Object value)

public void addProperty(String key, Object value)

public void clearProperty(String key)

public void setConfiguration(Configuration configuration)

public void setExtendedProperties(ExtendedProperties configuration)

public java.lang.Object getProperty(String key)

public boolean evaluate(Context context, Writer out, String logTag, String instring)

public boolean evaluate(Context context, Writer writer, String logTag, InputStream instream)

public boolean evaluate(Context context, Writer writer, String logTag, Reader reader)

public boolean invokeVelocimacro(String vmName, String logTag, String[] params, Context context, Writer writer)

public boolean mergeTemplate(String templateName, Context context, Writer writer)

public boolean mergeTemplate(String templateName, String encoding, Context context, Writer writer)

public org.apache.velocity.Template getTemplate(String name)

public org.apache.velocity.Template getTemplate(String name, String encoding)

public boolean templateExists(String templateName)

public void warn(Object message)

public void info(Object message)

public void error(Object message)

public void debug(Object message)

public void setApplicationAttribute(Object key, Object value)

org.apache.velocity.app.event.EventCartridge

Implements: org.apache.velocity.app.event.ReferenceInsertionEventHandler, org.apache.velocity.app.event.NullSetEventHandler, org.apache.velocity.app.event.MethodExceptionEventHandler

Description: This class allows you to add event handlers to the system.

Class Summary

Constructor:

public EventCartridge( )

Methods:

public boolean addEventHandler(EventHandler ev)

public boolean removeEventHandler(EventHandler ev)

public java.lang.Object referenceInsert(String reference, Object value)

public boolean shouldLogOnNullSet(String lhs, String rhs)

public java.lang.Object methodException(Class claz, String method, Exception e)

public final boolean attachToContext(Context context)

org.apache.velocity.app.event.EventHandler

Description: This is the base interface for all event handlers.

org.apache.velocity.app.event.MethodException EventHandler

Implements: org.apache.velocity.app.event.EventHandler

Description: This class is called when an event method throws an exception.

Class Summary

Method:

public java.lang.Object methodException(Class claz, String method, Exception e)

org.apache.velocity.app.event.NullSetEvent Handler

Implements: org.apache.velocity.app.event.EventHandler

Description: This class implements a null event handler.

Class Summary

Method:

public boolean shouldLogOnNullSet(String lhs, String rhs)

org.apache.velocity.app.event.ReferenceInsertionEventHandler

Implements: org.apache.velocity.app.event.EventHandler

Description: This class implements a stream insertion event handler.

Class Summary

Method:

public java.lang.Object referenceInsert(String reference, Object value)

org.apache.velocity.app.tools.VelocityFormatter

Description: This class is a formatting tool for Context insertions.

Class Summary

Constructor:

public VelocityFormatter(Context context)

Methods:

public java.lang.String formatShortDate(Date date)

public java.lang.String formatLongDate(Date date)

public java.lang.String formatShortDateTime(Date date)

public java.lang.String formatLongDateTime(Date date)

public java.lang.String formatArray(Object array)

public java.lang.String formatArray(Object array, String delim)

public java.lang.String formatArray(Object array, String delim, String finaldelim)

public java.lang.String formatVector(Vector vector)

public java.lang.String formatVector(Vector vector, String delim)

public java.lang.String formatVector(Vector vector, String delim, String finaldelim)

public java.lang.String limitLen(int maxlen, String string)

public java.lang.String limitLen(int maxlen, String string, String suffix)

public java.lang.String makeAlternator(String name, String alt1, String alt2)

public java.lang.String makeAlternator(String name, String alt1, String alt2, String alt3)

public java.lang.String makeAlternator(String name, String alt1, String alt2, String alt3, String alt4)

public java.lang.String makeAutoAlternator(String name, String alt1, String alt2)

public java.lang.Object isNull(Object o, Object dflt)

org.apache.velocity.app.tools.VelocityFormatter. VelocityAlternator

Description: This class returns alternating values from a template.

Class Summary

Constructor:

public VelocityFormatter.VelocityAlternator(String[] alternates)

Methods:

public java.lang.String alternate( )

public java.lang.String toString( )

org.apache.velocity.app.tools.VelocityFormatter. VelocityAutoAlternator

Extends: org.apache.velocity.app.tools.VelocityFormatter.VelocityAlternator

Description: This class works with VelocityAlternator when rendering a template.

Class Summary

Constructor:

public VelocityFormatter.VelocityAutoAlternator( )

Method:

public final java.lang.String toString( )

org.apache.velocity.context.AbstractContext

Extends: org.apache.velocity.context.InternalContextBase

Implements: org.apache.velocity.context.Context, java.io.Serializable

Description: This class is an abstract base class for all Velocity Context implementations.

Class Summary

Constructors:

public AbstractContext( )

public AbstractContext(Context inner)

Methods:

public abstract java.lang.Object internalGet(String key)

public abstract java.lang.Object internalPut(String key, Object value)

public java.lang.Object put(String key, Object value)

public java.lang.Object get(String key)

public boolean containsKey(Object key)

public java.lang.Object[] getKeys( )

public java.lang.Object remove(Object key)

public org.apache.velocity.context.Context getChainedContext( )

org.apache.velocity.context.Context

Description: This is an interface class for the context.

Class Summary

Methods:

public java.lang.Object put(String key, Object value)

public java.lang.Object get(String key)

public boolean containsKey(Object key)

public java.lang.Object[] getKeys( )

public java.lang.Object remove(Object key)

org.apache.velocity.context.InternalContext AdapterImpl

Implements: org.apache.velocity.context.InternalContextAdapter

Description: This class is an adapter class for all context types.

Class Summary

Constructor:

public InternalContextAdapterImpl(Context c)

Methods:

public void pushCurrentTemplateName(String s)

public void popCurrentTemplateName( )

public java.lang.String getCurrentTemplateName( )

public java.lang.Object[] getTemplateNameStack( )

public org.apache.velocity.util.introspection.IntrospectionCacheData icacheGet(Object key)

public void icachePut(Object key, IntrospectionCacheData o)

public void setCurrentResource(Resource r)

public org.apache.velocity.runtime.resource.Resource getCurrentResource( )

public java.lang.Object put(String key, Object value)

public java.lang.Object get(String key)

public boolean containsKey(Object key)

public java.lang.Object[] getKeys( )

public java.lang.Object remove(Object key)

public org.apache.velocity.context.Context getInternalUserContext( )

public org.apache.velocity.context.InternalContextAdapter getBaseContext( )

public org.apache.velocity.app.event.EventCartridge attachEventCartridge(EventCartridge ec)

public org.apache.velocity.app.event.EventCartridge getEventCartridge( )

org.apache.velocity.context.InternalEventContext

Description: This interface supports events within the context.

Class Summary

Methods:

public org.apache.velocity.app.event.EventCartridge attachEventCartridge(EventCartridge ec)

public org.apache.velocity.app.event.EventCartridge getEventCartridge( )

org.apache.velocity.context.VMContext

Implements: org.apache.velocity.context.InternalContextAdapter

Description: This class is used internally for the implementation of Velocimacros.

Class Summary

Constructor:

public VMContext(InternalContextAdapter inner, RuntimeServices rsvc)

Methods:

public org.apache.velocity.context.Context getInternalUserContext( )

public org.apache.velocity.context.InternalContextAdapter getBaseContext( )

public void addVMProxyArg(VMProxyArg vmpa)

public java.lang.Object put(String key, Object value)

public java.lang.Object get(String key)

public boolean containsKey(Object key)

public java.lang.Object[] getKeys( )

public java.lang.Object remove(Object key)

public void pushCurrentTemplateName(String s)

public void popCurrentTemplateName( )

public java.lang.String getCurrentTemplateName( )

public java.lang.Object[] getTemplateNameStack( )

public org.apache.velocity.util.introspection.IntrospectionCacheData icacheGet(Object key)

public void icachePut(Object key, IntrospectionCacheData o)

public org.apache.velocity.app.event.EventCartridge attachEventCartridge(EventCartridge ec)

public org.apache.velocity.app.event.EventCartridge getEventCartridge( )

public void setCurrentResource(Resource r)

public org.apache.velocity.runtime.resource.Resource getCurrentResource( )

org.apache.velocity.convert.WebMacro

Description: This class is used to convert a WebMacro template to a Velocity template.

Class Summary

Constructor:

public WebMacro( )

Methods:

public void convert(String target)

public java.lang.String convertTemplate(String template)

public static void main(String[] args)

org.apache.velocity.exception.Method InvocationException

Extends: org.apache.velocity.exception.VelocityException

Description: This class is an exception thrown during reference invocation.

Class Summary

Constructor:

public MethodInvocationException(String message, Throwable e, String methodName)

Methods:

public java.lang.String getMethodName( )

public java.lang.Throwable getWrappedThrowable( )

public void setReferenceName(String ref)

public java.lang.String getReferenceName( )

org.apache.velocity.exception.ParseError Exception

Extends: org.apache.velocity.exception.VelocityException

Description: This is an application-level exception thrown during a template parsing.

Class Summary

Constructor:

public ParseErrorException(String exceptionMessage)

org.apache.velocity.exception.VelocityException

Extends: java.lang.Exception

Description: This is the base class for Velocity exceptions.

Class Summary

Constructor:

public VelocityException(String exceptionMessage)

org.apache.velocity.io.VelocityWriter

Extends: java.io.Writer

Description: This class implements a fast Writer class.

Class Summary

Constructors:

public VelocityWriter(Writer writer)

public VelocityWriter(Writer writer, int sz, boolean autoFlush)

Methods:

public int getBufferSize( )

public boolean isAutoFlush( )

public final void clear( )

public final void flush( )

public final void close( )

public final int getRemaining( )

public final void write(int c)

public final void write(char[] cbuf, int off, int len)

public final void write(char[] buf)

public final void write(String s, int off, int len)

public final void write(String s)

public final void recycle(Writer writer)

org.apache.velocity.servlet.VelocityServlet

Extends: HttpServlet

Description: This is a base class for using Velocity with servlets. You can extend this class, implement the handleRequest( ) method, add your data to the context, and then call getTemplate("myTemplate.wm").

Class Summary

Constructor:

public VelocityServlet( )

Methods:

public void init(ServletConfig config)

protected void initVelocity(ServletConfig config)

protected java.util.Properties loadConfiguration(ServletConfig config)

public void doGet(HttpServletRequest request, HttpServletResponse response)

public void doPost(HttpServletRequest request, HttpServletResponse response)

protected void doRequest(HttpServletRequest request, HttpServletResponse response)

protected void requestCleanup(HttpServletRequest request, HttpServletResponse response, Context context)

protected void mergeTemplate(Template template, Context context, HttpServletResponse response)

protected void setContentType(HttpServletRequest request, HttpServletResponse response)

protected org.apache.velocity.context.Context createContext(HttpServletRequest request, HttpServletResponse response)

public org.apache.velocity.Template getTemplate(String name)

public org.apache.velocity.Template getTemplate(String name, String encoding)

protected org.apache.velocity.Template handleRequest(HttpServletRequest request, HttpServletResponse response, Context ctx)

protected org.apache.velocity.Template handleRequest(Context ctx)

protected void error(HttpServletRequest request, HttpServletResponse response, Exception cause)

org.apache.velocity.texen.ant.Texen

Description: This is an Ant task for generating output by using Velocity.

Class Summary

Constructor:

public Texen( )

Methods:

public void setControlTemplate(String controlTemplate)

public java.lang.String getControlTemplate( )

public void setTemplatePath(String templatePath)

protected void processTemplatePath(String templatePath)

public java.lang.String getTemplatePath( )

public void setOutputDirectory(File outputDirectory)

public java.lang.String getOutputDirectory( )

public void setOutputFile(String outputFile)

public void setOutputEncoding(String outputEncoding)

public void setInputEncoding(String inputEncoding)

public java.lang.String getOutputFile( )

public void setContextProperties(String file)

protected void processContextProperties(String file)

public org.apache.commons.collections.ExtendedProperties getContext Properties( )

public void setUseClasspath(boolean useClasspath)

public void setProject(Project project)

public Project getProject( )

public org.apache.velocity.context.Context initControlContext( )

public void execute( )

protected void populateInitialContext(Context context)

protected void cleanup( )

org.apache.velocity.runtime.RuntimeInstance

Implements: org.apache.velocity.runtime.RuntimeConstants, org.apache.velocity.runtime.RuntimeServices

Description: The runtime system for Velocity, it is the single access point for all functionality in Velocity.

Class Summary

Constructor:

public RuntimeInstance( )

Methods:

public synchronized void init( )

public void setProperty(String key, Object value)

public void setConfiguration(ExtendedProperties configuration)

public void addProperty(String key, Object value)

public void clearProperty(String key)

public java.lang.Object getProperty(String key)

public void init(Properties p)

public void init(String configurationFile)

public org.apache.velocity.runtime.parser.Parser createNewParser( )

public org.apache.velocity.runtime.parser.node.SimpleNode parse(Reader reader, String templateName)

public org.apache.velocity.runtime.parser.node.SimpleNode parse(Reader reader, String templateName, boolean dumpNamespace)

public org.apache.velocity.Template getTemplate(String name) public org.apache.velocity.Template getTemplate(String name, String encoding)

public org.apache.velocity.runtime.resource.ContentResource getContent(String name)

public org.apache.velocity.runtime.resource.ContentResource getContent(String name, String encoding)

public java.lang.String getLoaderNameForResource(String resourceName)

public void warn(Object message)

public void info(Object message)

public void error(Object message)

public void debug(Object message)

public java.lang.String getString(String key, String defaultValue)

public org.apache.velocity.runtime.directive.Directive getVelocimacro(String vmName, String templateName)

public boolean addVelocimacro(String name, String macro, String[] argArray, String sourceTemplate)

public boolean isVelocimacro(String vmName, String templateName)

public boolean dumpVMNamespace(String namespace)

public java.lang.String getString(String key)

public int getInt(String key)

public int getInt(String key, int defaultValue)

public boolean getBoolean(String key, boolean def)

public org.apache.commons.collections.ExtendedProperties getConfiguration( )

public org.apache.velocity.util.introspection.Introspector getIntrospector( )

public java.lang.Object getApplicationAttribute(Object key)

public java.lang.Object setApplicationAttribute(Object key, Object o)

org.apache.velocity.runtime.RuntimeServices

Description: This is an interface class for internal runtime services.

Class Summary

Methods:

public void init( )

public void setProperty(String key, Object value)

public void setConfiguration(ExtendedProperties configuration)

public void addProperty(String key, Object value)

public void clearProperty(String key)

public java.lang.Object getProperty(String key)

public void init(Properties p)

public void init(String configurationFile)

public org.apache.velocity.runtime.parser.node.SimpleNode parse(Reader reader, String templateName)

public org.apache.velocity.runtime.parser.node.SimpleNode parse(Reader reader, String templateName, boolean dumpNamespace)

public org.apache.velocity.Template getTemplate(String name)

public org.apache.velocity.Template getTemplate(String name, String encoding)

public org.apache.velocity.runtime.resource.ContentResource getContent(String name)

public org.apache.velocity.runtime.resource.ContentResource getContent(String name, String encoding)

public java.lang.String getLoaderNameForResource(String resourceName)

public void warn(Object message)

public void info(Object message)

public void error(Object message)

public void debug(Object message)

public java.lang.String getString(String key, String defaultValue)

public org.apache.velocity.runtime.directive.Directive getVelocimacro (String vmName, String templateName)

public boolean addVelocimacro(String name, String macro, String[] argArray, String sourceTemplate) public boolean isVelocimacro(String vmName, String templateName)

public boolean dumpVMNamespace(String namespace)

public java.lang.String getString(String key)

public int getInt(String key)

public int getInt(String key, int defaultValue)

public boolean getBoolean(String key, boolean def)

public org.apache.commons.collections.ExtendedProperties get Configuration( )

public org.apache.velocity.util.introspection.Introspector getIntrospector( )

public java.lang.Object getApplicationAttribute(Object key)

org.apache.velocity.runtime.RuntimeSingleton

Implements: org.apache.velocity.runtime.RuntimeConstants

Description: The Runtime system for Velocity, it is the single access point for all functionality in Velocity but supports a singleton design pattern. [This is the same description for org.apache.velocity.runtime.RuntimeInstance]

Class Summary

Constructor:

public RuntimeSingleton( )

Methods:

public static synchronized void init( )

public static org.apache.velocity.runtime.RuntimeServices getRuntimeServices( )

public static void setProperty(String key, Object value)

public static void setConfiguration(ExtendedProperties configuration)

public static void addProperty(String key, Object value)

public static void clearProperty(String key)

public static java.lang.Object getProperty(String key)

public static void init(Properties p)

public static void init(String configurationFile)

public static org.apache.velocity.runtime.parser.node.SimpleNode parse(Reader reader, String templateName)

public static org.apache.velocity.runtime.parser.node.SimpleNode parse(Reader reader, String templateName, boolean dumpNamespace)

public static org.apache.velocity.Template getTemplate(String name)

public static org.apache.velocity.Template getTemplate(String name, String encoding)

public static org.apache.velocity.runtime.resource.ContentResource get Content(String name)

public static org.apache.velocity.runtime.resource.ContentResource get Content(String name, String encoding)

public static java.lang.String getLoaderNameForResource(String resource-Name)

public static void warn(Object message)

public static void info(Object message)

public static void error(Object message)

public static void debug(Object message)

public static java.lang.String getString(String key, String defaultValue)

public static org.apache.velocity.runtime.directive.Directive getVelocimacro(String vmName, String templateName)

public static boolean addVelocimacro(String name, String macro, String[] argArray, String sourceTemplate)

public static boolean isVelocimacro(String vmName, String templateName)

public static boolean dumpVMNamespace(String namespace)

public static java.lang.String getString(String key)

public static int getInt(String key)

public static int getInt(String key, int defaultValue)

public static boolean getBoolean(String key, boolean def)

public static org.apache.commons.collections.ExtendedProperties get Configuration( )

public static org.apache.velocity.util.introspection.Introspector getIntrospector( )

public static org.apache.velocity.runtime.RuntimeInstance getRuntimeInstance( )

org.apache.velocity.runtime.VelocimacroFactory

Description: This class factory manages the VMs for a Velocity engine.

Class Summary

Constructor:

public VelocimacroFactory(RuntimeServices rs)

Methods:

public void initVelocimacro( )

public boolean addVelocimacro(String name, String macroBody, String[] argArray, String sourceTemplate)

public boolean isVelocimacro(String vm, String sourceTemplate)

public org.apache.velocity.runtime.directive.Directive getVelocimacro(String vmName, String sourceTemplate)

public boolean dumpVMNamespace(String namespace)

org.apache.velocity.runtime.Velocimacro Manager

Description: This class manages VMs in all namespaces.

Class Summary

Methods:

public boolean addVM(String vmName, String macroBody, String[] argArray, String namespace)

public org.apache.velocity.runtime.directive.VelocimacroProxy get(String vmName, String namespace)

public boolean dumpNamespace(String namespace)

public void setNamespaceUsage(boolean b)

public void setRegisterFromLib(boolean b)

public void setTemplateLocalInlineVM(boolean b)

public java.lang.String getLibraryName(String vmName, String namespace)

org.apache.velocity.runtime.Velocimacro Manager.MacroEntry

Description: This is a wrapper class for VM information.

Class Summary

Methods:

public void setFromLibrary(boolean b)

public boolean getFromLibrary( )

public org.apache.velocity.runtime.parser.node.SimpleNode getNodeTree( )

public java.lang.String getSourceTemplate( )

APPENDIX B

Velocity Sites

In this appendix, we include some of the important Web sites available which discuss how to use Velocity in a real-world application or have other Velocity resources.

Jakarta Velocity Sites

The Jakarta Velocity Site

URL: http://jakarta.apache.org/velocity/

Description: This is the main Velocity site where you can find the most up-to-date information on Velocity.

Velocity Tools

URL: http://cvs.apache.org/viewcvs/jakarta-velocity-tools/

Description: Go here to download the Velocity tools. This code is the most up-to-date for Struts interfacing.

WebMacro

URL: www.webmacro.org/

Description: Velocity has its roots in WebMacro. This is the primary WebMacro site, where you can obtain design information.

DVSL

URL: http://jakarta.apache.org/velocity/dvsl/index.html

Description: This is the main location for information on DVSL and how to use it in Velocity.

Velocity Generator

URL: http://xml.apache.org/cocoon/userdocs/generators/velocity-generator.html

Description: This site shows how you to use a Velocity generator with Cocoon.

Velocity UI for Eclipse

URL: http://veloedit.sourceforge.net/

Description: This site teaches you how to interface Velocity syntax coding with Eclipse.

Tutorials

Template-Based Wizards in JBuilder

URL: http://community.borland.com/article/0,1410,28086,00.html

Start Up the Velocity Template Engine

URL: www.javaworld.com/javaworld/jw-12-2001/jw-1228-velocity.html

Getting Up to Speed with Velocity

URL: www.webtechniques.com/archives/2001/09/serv/

Take the Fast Track to Text Generation

URL: www.javaworld.com/javaworld/jw-07-2001/jw-0727-templates.html

What Is Velocity?

URL: www.freebok.net/help/velocity1.html

Template for Going Fast

URL: www.linux-mag.com/2002-12/java_02.html

Applications

Roller Web Logger

URL: www.rollerweblogger.org/page/project

Description: Roller is a server-based Web logging system that uses Velocity for its templates.

Maverick

URL: http://mav.sourceforge.net/

Description: This is the primary location for the Maverick MVC framework.

vDoclet

URL: http://vdoclet.sourceforge.net/

Description: This is the main location for the vDoclet system, which allows for automated Java code generation.

Turbine

URL: http://jakarta.apache.org/turbine/

Description: Turbine is an application server that uses Velocity as a view component.

WebWork

URL: http://sourceforge.net/projects/webwork/

Description: WebWork is an application development framework for J2EE that allows you to use Velocity.

JPublish

URL: www.jpublish.org/

Description: JPublish is a Web-publishing system that uses Velocity to produce output.

JeeWiz!

URL: www.jeewiz.co.uk/index.html

Description: JeeWiz! is an enterprise-level system builder.

Luxor

URL: http://luxor-xul.sourceforge.net/

Description: Luxor is an XML user interface language toolkit that uses Velocity for templating.

Melati

URL: www.melati.org/

Description: Melati is a tool for building Web sites that use databases for storage.

Velocity Support in OpenCms

URL: www.opencms.com/opencms/opencms/community/velocity.html

Description: This site describes how to interface Velocity with the OpenCms open source Web site content management system.

JetSpeed and Portlets

URL: www.collaborium.org/jetspeed/docs/portlet_config_Velocity.html

Description: This site shows you how to interface Velocity with JetSpeed.

JNLP to HTML Converter

URL: www.vamphq.com/hazelp.html

Description: This site illustrates using Velocity to convert JNLP to HTML.

Velocity and Web Album

URL: www.cs.adelaide.edu.au/users/esser/WebAlbum/

Description: This site examines how to use Velocity with Web Album to output information from the application.

Index

A

B

C

D

E

F

G

H

I

J

L

M

S

T